"This compendium of systematic theology has all the hallmarks of Jon Nielson's dynamic pastoral ministry: biblical fidelity, theological clarity, and a passion for the practical application of Christian doctrine. Ideal for classrooms and study groups, as well as for personal use, *Knowing God's Truth* includes frequent prompts for spiritual practices that will help readers know, love, and celebrate evangelical theology."

Philip Graham Ryken, President, Wheaton College

"There's a good reason why theology seems off-putting to many. Although it's the study of God, sometimes it's presented in a dry and dreary way. But in this book, Jon Nielson treats theology as a prayerful, joyful, sometimes challenging but always stimulating encounter with the self-revealing triune God. *Knowing God's Truth* not only informs but transforms."

Michael Horton, J. Gresham Machen Professor of Systematic Theology and Apologetics, Westminster Seminary California

"In *Knowing God's Truth*, Jon Nielson calls followers of Jesus to stop settling for lackluster, hand-me-down theological opinions. He calls us instead to dive deep into Scripture and to cultivate theological convictions by wrestling with God's truth. Each chapter guides readers to search the Bible for themselves and systematically apply biblical truths to real life. Our local congregations would benefit immensely from digesting this resource together."

Mary Willson Hannah, Director of Women in Ministry, Second Presbyterian Church, Memphis, Tennessee

"Jon Nielson has given us a gift—a clear, well-organized, and practical introduction to systematic theology. Through careful exposition, guided prayer, and practical application, *Knowing God's Truth* not only provides the content of each of the major headings of systematic theology, but also leads the reader to deepen his or her fellowship with, and worship of, the God in whom we believe. I praise God for this helpful resource!"

Brian Cosby, Senior Minister, Wayside Presbyterian Church, Signal Mountain, Tennessee; Adjunct Professor of Historical Theology, Reformed Theological Seminary, Atlanta

"With each page I turn, I find this book landing on another valuable point of doctrine. Jon Nielson says exactly what he needs to say—briefly, clearly, expertly, soundly—and then bounces on to the next equally helpful teaching. Young believers will eat this up and get a hearty meal. Youth leaders should keep a box of copies of this book nearby and hand them out to every student they know. This book is *that* readable, *that* theologically sturdy, and *that* dialed in to the truths our kids need to feed on."

Jack Klumpenhower, author, *Show Them Jesus: Teaching the Gospel to Kids*

Knowing God's Truth

KNOWING GOD'S TRUTH

An Introduction to Systematic Theology

JON NIELSON

CROSSWAY®

WHEATON, ILLINOIS

Cover design: Zach DeYoung

First printing, 2023

Printed in Colombia

Hardcover ISBN: 978-1-4335-8288-2
ePub ISBN: 978-1-4335-8291-2
PDF ISBN: 978-1-4335-8289-9
Mobipocket ISBN: 978-1-4335-8290-5

Library of Congress Cataloging-in-Publication Data

Names: Nielson, Jon, 1983- author.
Title: Knowing God's truth : an introduction to systematic theology / Jon Nielson.
Description: Wheaton, Illinois : Crossway, 2023. | Includes index.
Identifiers: LCCN 2022006185 (print) | LCCN 2022006186 (ebook) | ISBN 9781433582882 (hardcover) | ISBN 9781433582899 (pdf) | ISBN 9781433582905 (mobipocket) | ISBN 9781433582912 (epub)
Subjects: LCSH: Theology, Doctrinal. | Reformed Church—Doctrines.
Classification: LCC BT75.3 .N54 2023 (print) | LCC BT75.3 (ebook) | DDC 230—dc23/eng/20220805
LC record available at https://lccn.loc.gov/2022006185
LC ebook record available at https://lccn.loc.gov/2022006186

Crossway is a publishing ministry of Good News Publishers.

NP	31	30	29	28	27	26	25	24	23
14	13	12	11	10	9	8	7	6	5	4	3	2	1

To my wife, Jeanne.
Jeanne—may we help our daughters know
God's truth for their eternal joy in Christ!

CONTENTS

INTRODUCTION

This book is designed to help you think more deeply about the most important topic—the most important person—in the entire universe: God himself. There is no more important pursuit, no higher calling on your life, no greater purpose, than to know God your Creator rightly, be in a right relationship with him for eternity, and worship him the way you should. These aren't overstatements.

Given this reality, it's always been amazing to me that so many people who call themselves Christians think about *theology* as almost a dirty word! Or, if not that, they at least think about theology as *boring*. "That's something that scholars do," they sometimes think. "Theology is not for ordinary Christians like us." But is it?

In this book, you are going to get a simple, straightforward, and hopefully clear introduction to the Christian discipline of *systematic theology*. Because that term can sound intimidating, I've given the book a simpler title: *Knowing God's Truth*. That is, after all, what systematic theology actually *is*. It's talking about, thinking about, and considering God. It's trying to put together, in an organized way (always informed by the Bible), the truths about who God is, who we are, how God has created us and saved us, what God wants from us now, and what is ahead for us as God's people in eternity to come. The "systematic" part of systematic theology just means that we try to do this in an organized way; we go through topics one by one—*systematically.* What I really hope you'll see along the way is that this kind of theological thinking is *not* just for the scholars and the experts; it's for all Christians who want to better understand the God they love and serve—the God who has saved them through the work of his Son.

The other really important thing you should get as you read this book is this: systematic theology is not an exercise only for your brain; it's for your heart and your life. We are going to get into some difficult, mysterious, and complex truths about God in this book. But it's all meant to make a difference in the way you think, act, speak, and live for your gracious God. In other words, theology isn't just a mental exercise; it's practical. It's supposed to be *applied* in real life as you live for Jesus.

One of the ways I'll try to remind you of this is by encouraging you to take regular "breaks" in each chapter to "Pray!" This is a simple way for us to remember that we want to make sure we're actually talking *to* the God we're talking *about.* But theology is also supposed to be *personal* and *worshipful.* You should be praying to the God you're learning about even as you are coming to understand him more and more. Some theologians have explained that *theology* (talk about God) is always supposed to lead us to *doxology* (praising God). I really hope this is the case for you as you learn about God in this book and stop to talk to him often along the way.

Finally, a quick word about the organization of the chapters. Here's what you should be ready for:

- For each particular topic (or specific doctrine), you'll have a full chapter's worth of material.
- Each chapter is divided into about ten sections, each of which usually begins with a reading from the Bible. *Please* don't skip

those Bible readings. They are meant to be the foundation for the truths that we're discussing.

- As I've already mentioned, there will be frequent "breaks" in each chapter to "Pray!" I encourage you to take those breaks, pausing to talk to God for just thirty to sixty seconds as you're learning about him.
- Each chapter will have suggested verses for you to memorize—verses that are linked to that chapter's topic. Whether or not you memorize those verses is up to you, but this would be a great way to intentionally hide God's word in your heart as you learn more about him.
- At the end of many of the chapters in this book, we will have at least a brief discussion of the application of the doctrine that we are studying. We need to think through why a given subject matters to us—how it makes a difference in our lives as followers of God. At the end of each chapter, I'll pull together some key truths and themes for you to review. That's a tool for you to look back and remember some of the main points on a particular area of doctrine.

I hope you're ready to get started with "knowing God's truth." And I hope that what you learn in this book will give you a deeper love for your God—as you talk to him along the way and seek to live for this glorious and gracious one who has saved you through the work of his Son, Jesus Christ, by the power of the Holy Spirit.

WHAT IS THEOLOGY?

What comes to mind when you hear the word *theology*? Is it a picture of men with long beards in robes discussing biblical issues with somber faces? Is it an image of a pastor giving a long sermon filled with words that you do not understand?

In this book, we are going to begin to study theology. In this first chapter, our goal is simply to define this term and discuss how it relates to you right now. Then we'll take a brief look at the categories of theology that we will explore in the chapters ahead.

As you read this book, *you* are going to be learning and doing theology! This may excite you, frighten you, intimidate you, or even bore you. Yet this is precisely what you will be tackling in the chapters to come. We are going to learn theology together.

So what is the meaning of this word that we have been repeating over and over in the beginning of this chapter? *Theology* literally means "God talk." The root *theo* means "God," and the suffix, *-logy*, comes from the Greek word *logos*, which means "word." So when we do theology, we are talking together about God and things that relate to God. Theology, broadly, is the study of God. When you think about it this way, hopefully the term will seem less intimidating or alienating. After all, we already do this when we study God's word; we study God. All we will be doing now is a slightly different kind of theology (we will learn about the different kinds a bit later).

You need to understand an important point at the very beginning of this book on theology: *you* are a theologian. That is, if you have ever thought about God, made a statement about God, or explained something about God to someone else, you have done theology. Every person, really, is a theologian, provided that he or she has formed some opinion about God—who he is, what he does, and how we know about him. So theology is not only a discipline for seminary students and brilliant scholars; it is a practice that you should be actively engaged in as you seek to learn more about the God who created you.

In the coming chapters, we will seek to ground our theological work in the Bible—the source of God's revelation of himself. Christians believe that the Bible is the source of ultimate truth; it is the inspired word of God, and it is the best place to learn about him. Because of this, you will see, in our next chapter, that the first category of theology that we will discuss is the doctrine of Scripture. If we do not begin there, we will have no foundation from which to grow into a knowledge of God's truth.

You are going to learn much more about God in these chapters; hopefully that is exciting to you! Right now, you should begin to think of yourself as a young theologian—someone who is fully capable of reading and studying God's word and beginning to formulate beliefs about who he is, what he does, and how human beings are to relate to him.

Remember!

Your suggested memory verses for this first chapter come from the book of Exodus, when God revealed himself to Moses in a powerful way. God, in other words, gave Moses a theology of himself; he taught him about his character and his ways. As you pause to read these verses carefully, think about what God is saying about himself. Begin to form theology as you read.

The LORD, the LORD, a God merciful and gracious, slow to anger, and abounding in steadfast love and faithfulness, keeping steadfast love for thousands, forgiving iniquity and transgression and sin, but who will by no means clear the guilty, visiting the iniquity of the fathers on the children and the children's children, to the third and the fourth generation. (Ex. 34:6–7)

PRAY!

As you begin this introduction to theology, ask God to help you grasp what theology is—its meaning, value, and importance for your life even now. No matter your age, you can begin to practice theology as you learn more about the God who created you and saved you through his Son. Ask God to teach you about himself!

WHY DOES THEOLOGY MATTER?

Now we need to ask a very simple but incredibly important question: "Why does theology matter?" You see, it is one thing to define *theology*, and it is quite another to become convinced that this discipline actually has value for our everyday lives as followers of Jesus Christ. Does theology really matter? Does it make a difference in the way we live and think?

Probably the biggest critique of the discipline of theology, even by Christians, is that it is not *practical*. It is not surprising that people who do not know Jesus do not want to study theology. What is often quite disappointing is that many Christians look at theology as something that is not useful—something that does not really matter in everyday life. Perhaps you have not heard this yet, but you will! There is a very real sentiment from some Christians that careful theological thought and study is a waste of time; Christians, these people think, should be out helping people, preaching the gospel, and engaging in active obedience rather than learning about God and the Bible.

So why is theology important? Why give many chapters to its study? Here are just a few reasons:

Theology is about God. The most basic reason why theology is important is that it is about God; it is the study of our Creator, Savior, and King. In a very real sense, then, the study of theology is the best and most important study that we can ever engage in. It is not a waste of time to learn more about the God of the universe. It is, in fact, probably the most valuable thing we could be giving our time to do. The study of theology, of course, should not prevent us from helping people, sharing the gospel, and actively obeying Jesus; it should actually help us do these activities with even more knowledge of and love for God—and for human beings created by this God.

Theology affects the way we live. Many people do not realize that every decision we make is ultimately a theological decision. Everything we do is a reflection of our beliefs—especially our beliefs about God. What we say, how we think, the way we use our time—all of these ultimately reflect what we truly believe to be true about the universe and the meaning of life. In this sense, then, our theology really does affect the way we live. What we believe about God has an impact on the choices we make—even the small ones—every single day.

Theology helps us make sense of our world. Finally, a theological view of the world that is informed by the Bible helps us make sense of the world around us. God, in his word, reveals to us the deepest realities about our world: his role in creation, the sinfulness of humanity, his sovereign purpose and plan, and the salvation that is available only through Christ Jesus, his Son. Careful theological work, then, matters because it is a way for us to understand and make sense of the world. Theology is important because we come to see our purpose as we understand God's role in the world by listening to his word.

Hopefully you are beginning to understand the value of studying theology—speaking words about God that are informed by his word. Your thoughts about God are the most important thoughts that you have; they affect the way you live!

○ PRAY!

As you think about the importance of theology, ask God to make you more aware of how your beliefs about him actually make a difference in your everyday life. Pray that he would help you to take his word and his truth even more seriously as you see what an effect theology has on choices, thoughts, hopes, and actions.

BIBLICAL, HISTORICAL, AND SYSTEMATIC THEOLOGY

You have been learning about theology broadly as the study of God (or "God talk," to take the word very literally). I have urged you to begin understanding yourself as a theologian, so long as you are willing to begin learning about God, talking about God, and forming beliefs about God on the basis of his word. Hopefully this is exciting for you!

Next, we are going to consider the three major "subsets" of theology that are studied today and see which of these we will be engaging in over the coming chapters. Then, for the rest of this chapter, we will introduce the various "headings" of theology that we will be studying.

The three subsets of theology are:

Biblical theology. When we talk about biblical theology, we are referring to a label that has existed for only 150 years or so. Yet in another sense, this kind of theology dates back to the first work and sermons done by the apostles as they preached and explained the Old Testament, showing how it relates to the saving work of God through Jesus Christ. So biblical theology is theological study that follows the path of the Bible. It is the careful discipline of taking a theme or truth about God and tracing its development through the entire storyline of the Bible, seeing how it begins, grows in significance, and is ultimately fulfilled in the gospel of Jesus Christ. Biblical theology assumes, as we have been assuming in this book, that the Bible really is one big story of God's saving work in the world. It is God's inspired word, and therefore it "holds together" in a way that makes it legitimate and right for us to study its themes in this way.

Historical theology. Historical theology obviously involves history. It is related to systematic theology in that it is organized more around themes and less around tracing the Bible's development of those themes from Genesis to Revelation. But historical theology seeks to take into account the development of theological beliefs throughout history. So it involves studying the great theologians and thinkers of the past in order to see how, for example, the doctrine of grace or the doctrine of the Trinity has developed in people's opinions and articulations over time.

Systematic theology. This is the theological discipline that we will be engaging in over the coming chapters. Systematic theology has to do with just what it sounds like: theological study that is systematized or organized carefully around big themes of biblical truth. So, for example, we will study the doctrine of God as it is revealed in Scripture. We will focus on the doctrine of salvation and consider what the Bible teaches about this important subject. The goal of this discipline is not, like biblical theology, to constantly trace the development of the story of the Bible from beginning to end. It is to organize—systematize—our Christian beliefs around categories and themes. This should certainly not be done without any thought to biblical theology. Yet systematic theology is a valuable way to organize and carefully think through Christian core beliefs.

▲ PRAY!

Think about the different disciplines of theology that you have learned about. As you prepare to engage in systematic theology in the coming chapters, ask God to help you make this an exercise that is truly full of worship for him! Pray that this pursuit would not just be about acquiring "head knowledge," but that you would truly grow to love God more through all of this learning.

CATEGORIES OF SYSTEMATIC THEOLOGY

You now know a basic definition of theology. You have learned a bit about the importance of the study of theology. Also, you now know that the kind of theology we will be engaging in through the coming chapters is called systematic theology. Hopefully you now feel a bit more "situated" and ready to dive into theological study, conversation, and thought in the chapters to come.

The rest of this chapter will introduce you to the general categories of systematic theology that we will be using as we learn together. These categories are not the only ones there are—or ones on an official systematic theology list somewhere. They are, though, fairly basic categories that many theologians use as they organize their theological study. We will spend one chapter on each of these categories in this book. The goal is to help you become acquainted with these basic systematic theological categories, as well as with the questions that we will seek to answer in our study of each of them.

Scripture and God

The initial two categories of systematic theology that we will cover in the coming chapters are Scripture and God.

Scripture. We will begin our systematic theology study with the category of Scripture. We will do this not because the Bible somehow comes before God; God is obviously the eternal one, who has existed from eternity past—long before the Bible was ever inspired and written! We will begin with the doctrine of Scripture because it is so foundational to everything else that we will learn and discuss—especially truths about God himself. If we do not ground our study of systematic theology in the Bible, we will get off to a very shaky start. The Bible is God's revelation of himself, and it is therefore the very foundation of our study of theology.

We will try to answer these questions:

- What *is* the Bible really?
- What do we mean by "inspiration"?
- What role did God have in the writing of the Bible?
- What role did human beings have in the writing of the Bible?
- How should the Bible function in the lives of Christians today?
- What can the Bible really accomplish in the lives of believers?
- How do we know that the Bible is true and accurate?

God. In one sense, of course, the entire study of theology is the study of God. But the study of God himself is its own special category in systematic theology—known as "theology proper"—and this will be the second doctrine we will cover in our systematic theological study. Our goal is to carefully learn and express much of the basic truth that the Bible gives us about the God who is both Creator and Savior of the world.

We will seek to answer the following questions:

- What are God's attributes?
- What is God's character like?

- What does it mean to say that God is sovereign?
- How can we understand the Trinity?
- What role does God play in the world today?
- What *is* God?
- What does it mean to say that God is infinite and eternal?

This will be an exciting and challenging chapter because we will be learning about a being who is, ultimately, beyond our ability to fully comprehend!

◢ PRAY!

Pray that God would teach you much more about his word and his character when you dive into the chapters about Scripture and God. Talk to him about questions that you still have about these topics; pray honestly, as God already knows your heart and your struggles! Ask him to continue leading you to his truth as you seek to be led by his word, the Bible.

Man and Sin

The next two categories of systematic theology that we will learn about are man and sin. The more technical names for these systematic categories are *anthropology* (the study of man) and *hamartiology* (the study of sin). What will we cover in these categories, and what questions will we seek to answer?

Man. Obviously there is a broad academic discipline known as anthropology, which refers to a much wider study than we will be doing in this chapter! The kind of anthropology that we will be doing focuses explicitly and specifically on what we learn about human beings from the Bible. We will seek to gather all of the truth that the Bible gives us about human beings and use it to paint a careful and clear picture of who we are, why we are that way, and what this all means for our eternal purpose in the universe.

Some of the basic questions that will guide our conversation and study in the chapter on the study of man include:

- What are human beings, and how are they unique from the rest of the created order?
- What does it mean to be created in God's image?
- What does it mean to be created male and female?
- What are some implications of our creatureliness for the way we understand our purpose as human beings?
- How does eternity factor into our consideration of human beings' purpose and goals?

Sin. Obviously the topic of sin is all over the Bible; yet there are many different opinions and teachings about the reality of sin, its role and effect in the world, and God's interaction with it. We will seek to understand the doctrine of sin as biblically as possible. Hopefully this chapter also will help us come to a better understanding of the great salvation that God offers us in Jesus Christ.

In the chapter on sin, we will seek to answer the following basic questions:

- How did sin enter the world?
- What is God's relationship to sin if he is sovereign and completely in control?
- What is "total depravity," and what does that mean for the everyday experience of human beings?
- What are some of the implications of living in a sinful and fallen world?
- Is it possible for someone to live without sin?
- How does the holy and just God view sin?
- How does understanding the reality of sin help us see what salvation accomplishes for us?

● PRAY!

Ask God to help you learn much more about humanity and about sin in the chapters that focus on these topics. Pray that this time of learning will result in a great appreciation, in your heart, for the salvation that God has accomplished through his Son, Jesus.

Jesus and Salvation

The last two theological topics we considered—man and sin—lead well into the next two: Jesus and salvation. Even though we have already discussed the doctrine of God (theology proper), it is appropriate to devote an entire chapter to the study of Jesus (technical name: Christology) given the centrality and complexity of his work on earth and with God's people. We will talk more just below about what we will cover in that category of study.

The doctrine of salvation (soteriology) is also important enough to be set on its own as a distinct category. There are big questions to be addressed here, and the Bible has much to say about the method and meaning of salvation through the work of Jesus Christ.

The chapters on Jesus and salvation will be exciting ones, as they center on the substance, meaning, and understanding of the core elements of the Christian gospel. These chapters will give us opportunity to dig into the essence, meaning, and method of our salvation. Let's look at these categories and the questions we will seek to answer as we study them.

Jesus. The study of the person and work of Jesus could consume this entire book—and even more than that! It is impossible to get to the bottom of the mysteries of the God who became human, died for the sins of his people, rose from the dead, and now reigns supreme as the eternal King who will return to judge all the earth. Still, we will seek to answer the following big questions about Jesus:

- Who is Jesus, and how does he interact with the other persons within the Trinity?
- How did Jesus function before his incarnation?
- What is the incarnation, and how does it work?
- What does the incarnation of Jesus mean for us?
- How must we understand the life of Jesus on earth?
- How does Jesus exist now and what is he doing now?
- What will Jesus do and be, eternally, in relation to God's people?

As you can see, this will be a big chapter. There is a lot to cover.

Salvation. The study of salvation in this chapter will take us to the very heart of the Christian faith and of the core of the gospel. We are going to consider, quite simply, what the Bible says about how God accomplishes salvation for sinful people through the death and resurrection of his Son, Jesus Christ. We will examine what was achieved through Jesus's death and resurrection in order to gain a full and biblical picture of salvation to the best of our ability. We will seek to answer the following questions:

- What actually was accomplished through the death of Jesus Christ on the cross?
- How does Jesus's identity as both God and man factor into our understanding of salvation?
- What happens to our sin; how does God deal finally with rebellion and disobedience?
- What is the basic "order" of salvation?
- What is God's role in salvation, and what is the human role?
- How should we understand our experience of salvation now and our "final" experience of salvation in heaven?

There are, again, some big questions to answer here! We will need to ask for God's help for diligent work in his word and humble acceptance of his truth.

PRAY!

As you look forward to studying the categories of Jesus and salvation, ask God to prepare you for learning, growth, and humility as you study. Pray that he would protect you from feeling that you "know it all" already; ask him to make you humble and ready to see more and more about the wonderful salvation through his Son that is revealed to us through Scripture.

Heaven and Hell

Look back over the categories of systematic theology that we have already summarized and considered. Take a few moments to think about the questions and points of interest that you have with regard to each one:

- Scripture—What questions are especially interesting to you about this category?
- God—What more would you like to learn about the person of God?
- Man—What aspects of humanity would you like to discover more about?
- Sin—Why is it so important for Christians to have an accurate, biblical, and robust understanding of the doctrine of sin?
- Jesus—How could you grow in your understanding of the person and work of Christ?
- Salvation—What questions do you still have about the way your salvation "works"?

Now let's turn our focus toward another theological category that we will cover in this book. We'll spend a chapter on the doctrine of heaven and hell, seeking to discover what the Bible teaches about these important realities. It will be important for us—especially in this chapter—to be extremely committed to holding fast to what the Bible *does* and *does not* say about these topics. There is surely much confusion and false teaching about these categories in the church today! Let's take a brief look at what we hope to learn together.

Interestingly, while many people see Jesus as one who came with a message of good news, grace, and salvation (which, of course, is true), Jesus himself spoke often about the reality of hell. Heaven, too, is described in Scripture as a real place; the book of Revelation especially will inform our doctrine of heaven and hell. The chapter that covers these categories concerns eternal realities that are very clearly taught in the Bible. Our goal is to answer at least some of these big questions:

- What does the Bible teach about heaven?
- What does the Bible teach about what happens to human beings who die before the return and judgment of Jesus Christ?
- What does the Bible teach about the final resurrection?
- What does the Bible teach about the new heaven and new earth?
- What is hell? What will it consist of?
- How is God just in sending people to hell?
- What must Christians believe about heaven and hell, and what does the Bible remain unclear about?

These are big questions. As you can see, we will need God's help to search his word carefully for the answers that he has—and has not—provided for us there.

▲ PRAY!

Talk to God about your study of the fascinating topics of heaven and hell. Pray that he would help you make a commitment to say neither more nor less than what his word says about these topics. Ask him to give you a humble willingness to sit under the authority of the Bible and look for its direction to inform your views.

The Church

As you learn about the many different categories of systematic theology that we are going to cover in this book, hopefully you are not getting overwhelmed but excited!

The next category of systematic theology that we will cover is the church (ecclesiology), which will include a discussion of the sacraments (baptism and the Lord's Supper, or Communion). Because much debate and disagreement surrounds these subjects, it will be very important for you to make a commitment to carefully read and study God's word as you work through this category.

The doctrine of the church is a very important category for systematic theology because Christians live out their daily lives as followers of Jesus Christ today in the context of local churches around the world. This category, then, is incredibly practical for people, as it relates to their experience of worship, community, fellowship, Bible teaching, and spiritual disciplines week after week. The Bible, thankfully, has much to say about what the church is and how it is meant to function. In fact, much of the content of the Epistles of the New Testament is given to helping believers in Jesus Christ function well as his church. So in this chapter, we will have a lot of biblical material to work with.

As we consider the meaning of baptism and the Lord's Supper, we'll see that there can be much debate and tension about these sacraments (what they mean and how they are to be performed). For this reason, it will be good for you to dig carefully into Scripture and determine what you believe the Bible actually teaches about them.

In this chapter, then, we will seek to answer the following big questions about the church:

- What is the church, biblically defined?
- What did the church look like during its early years, and how should that determine the way we "do" church today?
- How is the church meant to function in the lives of believers in Jesus Christ?

- Biblically, how is a local church meant to be governed and led?
- What are the marks of a true local church, according to the Bible?
- What is the ultimate theological function of the church?
- What is the difference between the "universal" church and the "local" church?
- What is a "sacrament," and what makes it a sacrament?
- What are the roles of God the Father, God the Son, and God the Holy Spirit in the sacraments?
- Why are sacraments important at all?
- What are some of the different views on the Lord's Supper, and how have they emerged from biblical teaching?
- What are some of the different views on baptism, and how have they emerged from biblical teaching?
- What actually happens during the celebration of a sacrament?

There are some big questions here, as you can see!

🔺 PRAY!

Ask God again to give you a spirit of humility as you prepare to dive into systematic theological study through this book. Pray that he would help you learn much more from his word about both the church and the sacraments so that you will have a better understanding of how you, as a follower of Jesus, are called to worship God along with other believers.

Angels and Demons

Our next category of systematic theology has made way for many interesting, fanciful, and even downright imaginative teachings.

While the Bible does not teach many of the things about angels and demons that some people think it does, it certainly has much to say about the very real existence and function of a spiritual realm. There are angels—nonhuman spiritual beings created by God and in his service. There are also demons—nonhuman spiritual beings created by God but in the service of Satan. In this chapter, we will examine the Bible's teachings about this spiritual realm, which is both very real and often very misunderstood. We will seek to answer the following questions according to Scripture:

- What are angels, and how do they function?
- What is the relationship between angels and humans/the earth?
- What are demons, and how do they function?
- Who is Satan, and what is his role today?
- How have angelic beings tended to contribute to God's plans in the world in the past? How do they do so today?
- What will be the role and purpose of spiritual beings after the judgment and return of Jesus Christ?
- What is the nature of human interaction with angelic and demonic beings?

⬆ PRAY!

Take time to thank God for all his word has to say about the spiritual world. Thank him for his creation of angels and for the work they do in the world. Thank him also that he guards his people from the attacks of demons and their master, Satan. Pray that he will help you gain a biblical understanding of these real but unseen beings.

Last Things

You've now been introduced to several different categories of systematic theology. You have seen the way that systematic theology is distinct from biblical theology and historical theology, and hopefully you are excited about diving into study of the various systematic categories as you read this book! By God's grace, you will know much more about his word and his truth by the end.

Next we'll turn to the doctrine of last things, or the end times (eschatology). Much of this study will be grounded in the biblical book of Revelation. Yet there are pertinent truths and teachings that we can draw from the Gospels and some of the prophets as well.

There is much debate surrounding eschatology, so we need to walk a careful line as we approach this category. Many people have very strong opinions about the timing of certain events and the specific signs that will precede Christ's return. Our goal is to be led by God's word toward careful conclusions about the last things.

Let's look at the general tendencies in the study of eschatology, how we should approach it, and what questions we will seek to answer about this category.

First, many people, in their study of eschatology, fall into one of two "extreme" approaches. Some enter this study with a desire to debate other people; they want to make their case for a very specific interpretation of Revelation and the timing of Jesus's return, the meaning of the millennium, the identity of the antichrist in Revelation, or other key elements. Their focus is entirely on arguing for their specific eschatological position, and as a result, they can almost miss the big point of that debate!

The other extreme, though, can be equally dangerous. This is the attitude that says, "Jesus wins; who cares how it is all going to happen?" While it is true that Jesus will win in the end, the Bible still gives us a *lot* of information, prophecy, and teaching that we need to study and take seriously. While we should not be obsessed with debate and with our own opinions of how the end times will happen, we should study Scripture carefully and try to come to good conclusions. This is exactly what we will seek to do in this chapter on eschatology. We will seek to answer the following questions:

- What does Satan's influence on earth look like in the last days?
- What is the period of "tribulation" that the Bible describes?

- When will Jesus return to judge the world?
- What will happen at the final judgment?
- What does the Bible tell us about the final defeat of Satan and his followers?
- Can we know the identity of the antichrist?
- What can we know about the new heaven and new earth?

○ PRAY!

Say a prayer of thanks to God for the promises of his word about the last things. Thank him that Jesus will return. Thank him that all things will one day be set right. Praise him that his justice and love will reign forever. Ask him for strength and help to trust him, and also to study his word carefully to understand everything you can about the last things of this world.

The Holy Spirit

The final chapter in this book will focus on the third person of the Trinity: God the Holy Spirit.

While we will cover some aspects of the doctrine of the Holy Spirit (technical name: pneumatology) in the chapter on the doctrine of God, it will be good to spend an entire chapter on the Holy Spirit specifically. This is due, in part, to the great confusion and misunderstanding about the Spirit among Christians today. While we will never know God the Holy Spirit exhaustively, this chapter will seek to lay out clearly what the Bible says about him. We'll seek to answer these questions:

- What does the Holy Spirit do today?
- How was the Holy Spirit active in the creation of the world and during the days of the Old Testament?

- What are some mistakes people make when they think about the role and purposes of God the Holy Spirit?
- How is the Holy Spirit active in our salvation?
- In what ways is the Holy Spirit at work in our lives and hearts today as followers of Jesus Christ?

Our goal is to rightly honor, worship, and serve our great God in three persons: the Father, Son, and Holy Spirit.

⬆ PRAY!

Spend a few minutes in prayer, thanking God for the ministry of the Holy Spirit in the church and in your life. Pray that your study of this category of systematic theology will be fruitful in helping you understand what the word of God teaches about the Spirit and his crucial role in regeneration, sanctification, and worship.

REVIEW

Before you move on to the next chapter, consider spending some time reviewing the lessons and concepts that you have learned in this introductory chapter. Here are some key concepts to remember:

Theology

- Theology literally means "God talk"—it is the study of God.
- If you think thoughts about God and make statements about him, you are thinking and talking theologically.
- Theology is intensely practical because it affects the way we live, think, and make decisions.

Scripture and God

- We will begin with the doctrine of Scripture because, without God's revelation, we cannot know about God.

- While all of theology is about God, there is also the study of "theology proper," which seeks to answer questions about God's character, being, existence, and actions in the world.

Man and Sin

- The study of man is also called anthropology, and it seeks to identify all that the Bible teaches about humanity.
- The study of sin is also called hamartiology, and it seeks to summarize the Bible's teaching about sin, fallenness, and total depravity.

Jesus and Salvation

- While Jesus is fully God, it is appropriate to have a category of systematic theology fully devoted to his work in the world and in salvation because of his centrality and significance through his incarnation, death, resurrection, and eternal reign.
- Christology is the formal term for the study of Jesus.
- The study of salvation—soteriology—seeks to answer big questions about the way in which human beings are saved by God through Jesus.

Heaven and Hell

- Scripture describes both heaven and hell as real places.
- The Gospels show us that Jesus taught often about hell.

The Church

- The study of the church is also called ecclesiology.
- The study of the sacraments seeks to summarize all that the Bible teaches about baptism and the Lord's Supper.

Angels and Demons

- Both angels and demons are nonhuman spiritual beings created by God.

- While angels serve God, their Creator, demons are in the service of Satan.

Last Things

- The study of last things is also referred to as eschatology.
- Most people tend toward an obsession with debate about the end times or toward reluctance to engage carefully with the teachings of the Bible on this topic.

The Holy Spirit

- The study of the Holy Spirit (pneumatology) focuses on the third person of the Trinity: God the Holy Spirit, who is fully God and a distinct person of the Trinity, and has a unique role and purpose.
- It is important for us to understand the function and purpose of God the Holy Spirit, especially in light of the confusion about these things in the Christian world today.

Remember!

Consider the suggested memory verses for this chapter once more as we conclude this introduction. Think again about the God who reveals himself with these words to Moses. Consider his mercy and his grace—the fact that he is "slow to anger, and abounding in steadfast love." Consider his justice and holiness—the fact that he will "by no means clear the guilty." This is the God who poured out mercy and grace on sinful people by allowing his own Son to be treated as guilty for their sake. This is an amazing God!

The LORD, the LORD, a God merciful and gracious, slow to anger, and abounding in steadfast love and faithfulness, keeping steadfast love for thousands, forgiving iniquity and transgression and sin, but who will by no means clear the guilty, visiting the iniquity of the fathers on the children and the children's children, to the third and the fourth generation. (Ex. 34:6–7)

▲ PRAY!

Take a moment to pray about your ongoing study of all of these systematic theology categories. Ask God to expand your understanding of his character and his word, but also to help you connect this growing knowledge to your heartfelt worship of him.

Chapter 2

THE DOCTRINE OF SCRIPTURE

Welcome to your first category of systematic theology: Scripture. In this chapter, we are going to examine the nature of God's word and work through the concepts of inspiration, authority, clarity, infallibility, and power—as well as what all of those ideas mean for Christians as they interact with Scripture.

Why not begin systematic theology with the study of God? Why not start by examining God's existence, character, and actions, since God obviously has been around (infinitely) longer than the Bible?

Essentially, the reason why we are beginning our study of systematic theology with Scripture is that we are weak, finite creatures who cannot simply rely on reason and careful thought to lead us to the truth about the God of the universe. Certainly we could come up with some good ideas about God, but we cannot even start down this road in the right way until we have laid a solid foundation for study, discussion, and thinking about him. Scripture is this foundation; we will lay it down in this chapter and seek to build everything else on top of it in the coming chapters.

In order to further understand this starting point, read the following passage:

> *For the wrath of God is revealed from heaven against all ungodliness and unrighteousness of men, who by their unrighteousness suppress the truth. For what can be known about God is plain to them, because God has shown it to them. For his invisible attributes, namely, his eternal power and divine nature, have been clearly perceived, ever since the creation of the world, in the things that have been made. So they are without excuse.* (Rom. 1:18–20)

What are these verses teaching? They are teaching that—just from the world around us—we *can* see certain truths about God—namely, his "eternal power" and his "divine nature." In other words, without the Bible, and merely with the witness of the world we live in, we have enough to teach us that there is a God and that he is powerful. But what is the result of that knowledge? It is sufficient, according to Romans, to leave us "without excuse." What we can see about God from his world is enough to make us guilty for not accepting or seeking God, but *not* enough to actually lead us to salvation through God's Son, Jesus Christ.

Thankfully, and graciously, God did not stop with the "general revelation" of this world that he made, which points so clearly to his identity and power. God took a step further and gave us "special revelation"—the actual written word of the Bible, which he inspired through human authors who recorded it for us.

This is why we must start our study of systematic theology with a careful examination of Scripture. We can get to a certain point in our understanding of God without the Bible; we can see that he exists and that he is powerful. But we need his word to show us the rest of what we can know of him—the rest of the truths about his character, his actions, and his way of salvation through his Son. So we will seek to lay a foundation for all the rest of our study of systematic theology— God's word.

Remember!

Take some time to begin memorizing the following verses from Isaiah, which summarize the fundamental approach to God that he demands from his people and in which he delights.

Thus says the LORD:

"Heaven is my throne,
and the earth is my footstool;
what is the house that you would build for me,
and what is the place of my rest?
All these things my hand has made,
and so all these things came to be,
declares the LORD.
But this is the one to whom I will look:
he who is humble and contrite in spirit
and trembles at my word." (Isa. 66:1–2)

PRAY!

Before continuing to read this chapter, consider the way that you view Scripture. Do you seek to daily sit under its power, truth, and authority, so that you build your life on it? Do you listen to the Bible, knowing that you are listening to the very word of God? Talk to God about these things today. Ask him to remind you of the nature of his word. Pray that your study of theology would be grounded in a humble submission to all that he has spoken in the Bible!

WHAT SCRIPTURE TELLS US ABOUT GOD

We have seen that our learning about God has to start in God's special revelation—his word. Now we will look at what the existence of

Scripture itself tells us about the God who created this world. He is a God who *speaks*. This has important implications for the way that we approach Scripture. We come to it not as a "dead" book that we search for information, but as the living word of God that has significant things to say about every area of our lives.

READ!

Take a moment to read Psalm 33:4–9, noting what the psalm declares about the power of God's word. Why must we remember that we serve a God who speaks?

There is much that we can learn from the simple fact God—the God of the Bible—speaks to people. When we refer to the Bible as the "word" of God, we are saying that the one true God of the universe is a "speaking" God. He is not silent. He has not left human beings completely in the dark as to how they can know, love, worship, and serve him. He has spoken through his word.

So what do we learn from the very existence of the Bible?

First, we learn that the God of the universe wants to be *known*. This is a key point for us to consider. The God who created us has gone out of his way to communicate with human beings. He reveals himself to them through his word. He teaches them about his character, ways, and plan. He shows them how they can come into a right relationship with him. Our God speaks because he is committed to inviting people into relationship with him, so that they can actually know the God who created them!

Second, we learn that God wants to *relate* to his people through his word. This is not the same thing that we just said, although it is a related point. Throughout history, from God's first words to Adam and Eve, we see that God's primary way of relating to human beings is through his word to them. He spoke to Abraham. He gave the law to Moses. He spoke to his people through the prophets. His Son, Jesus, came as the "Word . . . made flesh," according to

John 1:14 (KJV). Now, Scripture—his word—guides Christians as they follow and relate to him. God's word is his primary way of relating to people. That's why his people have always been people of his word.

Third, then, we learn from the existence of Scripture that we must *listen* to God's word. Since it is the communication and revelation of our Creator—the only true God of the universe—the Bible is the most important word we can listen to! We should work hard to listen to the Bible because the God who made us has actually spoken in it. (This is exactly what we will try to do as we form beliefs and make statements about the various categories of theology that we will study in the coming chapters.)

⬆ PRAY!

Spend some time simply thanking God for communicating himself to us through his word. Thank him for being a God who speaks to us so that we can know about him and how to come into a relationship with him through faith in his Son. Thank him for not keeping silent but for making known to us the path of life!

ASPECTS OF THE DOCTRINE OF SCRIPTURE

We have discussed the reason for starting our systematic theology study with Scripture and some basic lessons about God (and our right response to him) that we learn from the very existence of the Bible. Now we will begin to look at some aspects of the doctrine of Scripture.

We will start with the truth of "inspiration" and seek to carefully define what we mean when we say that the Bible is "inspired" by God. This is a very important starting point for our understanding of the Bible—you need to have a good handle on this doctrine before moving on to other categories of theological study.

Because Scripture Is *Inspired*, It Really Is God's Word

What is inspiration?

READ!

Take a moment to read 2 Timothy 3:16–17, which will be explained below.

First, it is helpful to look at a couple of Bible passages that inform our understanding of this doctrine.

Here is what Paul writes about the word of God in the passage you just read: "All Scripture is breathed out by God and profitable for teaching, for reproof, for correction, and for training in righteousness, that the man of God may be complete, equipped for every good work" (2 Tim. 3:16–17).

Paul's phrase "breathed out" helps inform our understanding of inspiration. The Bible, according to Paul, is really "breathed out" by God. In other words, the Bible that we read and study is as closely tied to God as our words that we speak are tied to us!

How did God breathe out Scripture? He did it by the power of his Holy Spirit. This is what we mean when we speak of God inspiring human authors to write the books of the Bible. His Holy Spirit was actively and powerfully working in and through them as they wrote. Men such as Moses, Samuel, David, Paul, Peter, and John wrote with the inspiration of the Holy Spirit.

Now we need to make a distinction between inspiration and dictation. Inspiration does not mean that God dictated every word to the biblical authors or somehow magically grabbed their hands and forced them to write certain words without their minds being engaged at all! The very nature of the Bible tells us this is not the case; it was written with distinct human personalities, styles, and tones that are representative of the authors. Yet the truth of inspiration tells us that God's Holy Spirit was powerfully overseeing each part of the writing of Scripture, so that as Paul wrote (from his own experience and with his own style), he was writing words and truths that completely and truly lined up with what God wanted to say to human beings.

One other passage that we should consider here comes from the apostle Peter's second letter. Peter speaks of the prophets—who both wrote and spoke to God's people—as being "carried along" by the Holy Spirit (2 Pet. 1:21). This is just one other picture that the Bible gives us for inspiration. These men spoke and wrote by their own power, but they were "carried along" by the Spirit in a powerful way so that their words were perfectly united with his word to his people—in just the way that he intended.

So what does inspiration mean when we talk about the Bible? It means that God is directly behind the words of Scripture. He sovereignly oversaw its composition by the power of his Holy Spirit. He "carried along" the biblical authors and "breathed out" his word to us through their writing. Because of this, we can truly say that the Bible is God's word. We can say that when the Bible speaks, God speaks!

▲ PRAY!

Ask God to give you an ever-growing understanding of inspiration so that you value his word and commit to listening to it, studying it, and living by it. Thank him that he used human beings to compose the Bible, but powerfully oversaw all that he communicated to people he had created and would create.

Because Scripture Has *Authority*, We Must *Submit* to It

Because of the doctrine of inspiration, we can truly say that the Bible is God's word. We know that, in Scripture, we have a source of truth that comes directly from the sovereign God who powerfully inspired its words. God did this through human authors, who wrote out of their own situations—and with their own styles and personalities.

We can accurately say that the Bible is 100 percent human (written by human authors) and also 100 percent divine (inspired by God the Holy Spirit—every single word).

Now we will take a step forward from inspiration to discuss what this doctrine means for our understanding of the authority of the Bible. We will examine how the doctrine of inspiration implies the reality of Scripture's authority. We will explain what we mean by authority and how this truth impacts the lives of followers of Jesus Christ.

READ!

Read 1 Thessalonians 2:13, noting Paul's summary of the way the believers in Thessalonica received—and responded to—God's word. Think about this as a model for the way we listen to the Bible.

If there is one simple reality that we observe in every part of the Bible, it is this: *God rules his people by his word.* Consider how this truth emerges from just a few "stops" in the course of the story of the Bible:

- In Genesis, God *creates* the world by speaking his word, then rules Adam and Eve by giving them his word—his instructions—to tend the garden of Eden well and to not eat from one tree in it.
- In Exodus, God delivers a people from slavery in Egypt, then *rules* over them through his law—the word that he speaks to them through Moses.
- During the time of the kings in Israel, God *speaks* to his sinful people powerfully through the mouths of his prophets—men whom he inspires to speak true and convicting words to his people as they continue to turn to sin, idolatry, and rebellion.
- When Jesus comes to earth, he *explains* God's word to people with authority (see Matt. 7, the end of the Sermon on the Mount) and leads his disciples according to his word.

- As the church is formed and begins to grow during the days of Acts, it is the word of the gospel that Paul and the other apostles *preach* with power; people are converted because of this word.

At every phase of biblical history, we see God acting, ruling, and leading his people according to his *word*. To put it in a slightly different way, God's word is always attached to God's *authority*—his rule over his people with power, protection, and strong instructions and commands. Whenever God speaks, he speaks with authority.

Hopefully you can see, then, how the doctrine of inspiration must necessarily lead into the doctrine of the authority of Scripture. If the Bible really is inspired by God—if it is "God speaking" by the power of his Holy Spirit—then the Bible is a book with great authority. It is the actual word of God.

This means, quite simply, that there is no greater authoritative word in the entire world than the Bible. Because it is truly God's word, it is a word of authority and power; we must listen to it, respond in faith and obedience, and position ourselves under its authority.

We will talk more about the practical applications and implications of the authority of the Bible later. For now, we will simply mention that the authority of the Bible should have an impact on:

- the formation of systematic theology, and every belief and statement about what is true
- the daily lives of Christians as they seek to follow God
- the way Christians conduct church life and worship
- the way Christians understand Jesus and the path to salvation
- the view of Christians about the world around them

God's word, throughout history, has carried power and authority. This is true, then, of the Bible. The God of the universe has spoken; this is his authoritative word, and we do well to listen to it and obey it.

▲ PRAY!

Ask yourself whether the Bible truly has the place of authority in your life. Are you living under the authority of God's word or living as your own authority? Talk to God about this honestly. Confess the ways that you fail to allow his word to rule in your life. Ask him to give you humility and faith to place your life and heart under the authority of his good and perfect word.

Because Scripture Is *Clear*, We Can *Understand* It

Have you ever become discouraged as you read and studied the Bible? Have you ever thought, "This is a confusing and mysterious book, and I just do not understand parts of it"? We all have felt that way at one time or another. There are certainly confusing, deep, and difficult parts of the Bible that are hard to understand. In fact, there are some passages that Bible scholars and brilliant professors will probably be studying and debating until the day that Jesus returns! We all have a lot of room to keep growing in our understanding of the Bible.

Think for a moment about all that you *do* know about the Bible. Consider the huge and basic truths that *are* clear from the teachings of Scripture. Remind yourself of the "big-picture" things that are evident—the creation of the world by God, the sinfulness of human beings, the identity of Jesus Christ, and the way to salvation through his death for sins on the cross and his resurrection from the dead. Those are all hugely important truths, and they are evident from the clear teaching of Scripture!

This is the concept of the "perspicuity," or clarity, of Scripture. What does this concept teach us?

◗ READ!

Take a moment to read Romans 3:23–25. Notice the clarity and straightforwardness of this passage, especially in what it declares about sin, the death of Jesus, and the need for faith. The message is clear, even if many do not accept it!

The concept of perspicuity essentially explains that while there are certainly difficult and complex teachings in the Bible, the basic truths of God, humans, and salvation are understandable to all those of ordinary intelligence who read it carefully.

In other words, the Bible is not intentionally confusing or mysterious. He is not trying to be vague in the way that he presents himself to human beings. He has not given his word to the world in a kind of secret code—something that has to be "cracked" by experts, who can then interpret it to other people. No, the Bible is clear, and any person can pick it up, read it, and understand it. This is actually a great kindness from God to human beings; he has made himself very clear through his word.

As we think about the doctrine of perspicuity, there are two important implications that we should consider—one about God and one about human beings and our interactions with them:

First, God (as we have said before) truly desires to be known by human beings. He has not hidden himself and has not chosen to make his word too difficult to understand! He has spoken not only powerfully, but also *clearly*. He is a gracious God, who has enabled all people who desire knowledge of him to have it through his word.

Second, the best way to show and teach others about God is to direct them to his word—the Bible. They may not understand every part of it right away, but the basic truths about salvation are there—clear and evident.

PRAY!

Ask God to remind you—especially during times of frustration and confusion in Bible study—that his word is clear with regard to the "big" truths of salvation, forgiveness, eternal life, and Christian obedience. Ask him to help you grow daily in your understanding of his word and pray that he would protect you from frustration as you work through difficult passages and teachings.

Because Scripture Is *Infallible*, It Will Not *Mislead* Us

We have now discussed and learned about the inspiration, authority, and perspicuity of Scripture. Hopefully you are coming to a fuller understanding of the beauty and power of the book that you are able to hold, read, study, and believe! This is a book that comes to us inspired by the Creator of the universe, with his authority and clarity, so that we can come to a saving belief in his Son.

Another important truth about the Bible is that it is infallible. By the end of this section, you should be able to see that Scripture is true—something that we can trust. This is true, ultimately, because of the God who stands behind the Bible. He is perfectly true and trustworthy, so we can trust that his word is the same!

READ!

Read 2 Peter 1:19–21, noting what Peter says about the truthfulness and reliability of the "prophetic word." How does this remind us that God's word is trustworthy and true?

The doctrine of the infallibility of the Bible determines Christians' approach to Scripture. It deals with the all-important question, "Can the Bible be trusted?" and answers with a resounding yes! Christians believe that the Bible is the inspired word of God, and it is therefore infallible.

So what do we mean when we say that the Bible is infallible? We mean:

- that everything the Bible affirms and teaches is *true*
- that the Bible is not *intentionally misleading* or *deceptive*
- that the Bible is absolutely *trustworthy*

First, the doctrine of infallibility means that everything the Bible affirms is true. The Bible asserts nothing that is false. We can trust that the stories it tells are true, the things that it says happened really happened, and the realities of the world that it presents to us are accurate.

Second, the doctrine of infallibility means that the Bible does not, at any point, intentionally or actively mislead or deceive anyone. This is not to say that people cannot twist the Bible or misunderstand it in very serious and harmful ways. But the Bible itself is not deceptive; when understood correctly, it always leads people to the truth about God, human beings, and reality itself.

Third, the doctrine of infallibility means that the Bible is trustworthy. In other words, we can "bank" on the Bible. It is reliable and worthy of our complete trust and confidence. By affirming this about the Bible, we are ultimately affirming our trust in God himself. He who spoke the words of Scripture is reliable and trustworthy.

One thing that we do *not* mean when we talk about the infallibility of Scripture is that the Bible teaches everything there is to know about everything in the world! The Bible is not designed to teach us math or to instruct us in how to play the sport of baseball. There are many other worthy academic pursuits that can teach us wonderful things about God's world. The Bible tells us things that are true; it does not inform us of every truth. It does, however, teach us the most important truths. It tells us that God created this world. It tells us that human beings are sinful and in need of a Savior. It tells us that this Savior is Jesus. It instructs us as to how we can meet this Savior and live life completely for him and for the eternal life that he brings.

The infallibility of the Bible is a doctrine that, like authority, flows necessarily out of the Bible's inspiration by God. Since God, through his inspiration of the Bible, is ultimately its divine author, it makes sense to take the next step toward infallibility. He is God, and God does not lie! To affirm the infallibility of the Bible is to declare that the God of the universe does not speak falsely. He communicates the truth in his word, and we can completely trust that his word is true.

⬤ PRAY!

Thank God today for his infallible word. Thank him that he is a God who speaks truth to this world and all the people in it. Ask him to help you hold on, in faith, to the truths of the Bible so that you will know how to rightly believe and rightly speak the truth of the gospel to the world around you.

Because Scripture Is *Powerful,* It Can *Change* Us

As you look back on the truths about Scripture that you have already read about, you can hopefully see the picture of the Bible that is coming together. This is no ordinary book! It reveals God's character and salvation to sinful human beings. It is authoritative, clear, and infallible—the true and ruling word of the very God of the universe!

Our words are not powerful in the way that God's word is powerful. Human beings can, of course, speak words that have powerful effects—either for good or for evil. A hateful insult, for example, can have a powerfully damaging effect on someone (you may have had experience with the pain that such words can cause). Conversely, an inspiring locker room speech from a coach can get a team "pumped up" and motivated to play. But when we talk about the power of God's word, we are not talking about the powerful effects that his word can have. We are talking about the intrinsic power that his word actually has. God's word, in and of itself, is powerful. This is unlike any human word!

📘 READ!

Read Psalm 148:5–6. Notice the song, sung by spiritual beings in heaven, in praise to the Creator God. How do they point to his glorious creation by his word?

Think back to the very beginning of the Bible, when God created the heavens and the earth just by speaking words (see Gen. 1). God's word conveys his creative power. The God of the universe is able to "speak" things into existence! Jesus, God's Son, demonstrated this same kind of power with his words when he spoke to the storm in the Sea of Galilee and, in an instant, calmed the waves and the wind.

God's word also has power to actually convict people of truth and bring them to repentance for sin. In other words, God's word has saving power! As human beings hear God's word read, taught, or preached, it works by the power of God's Holy Spirit to change their hearts and convince their minds of the truth of the gospel, so that they turn in faith to Jesus Christ. No other "word" in the world can change someone's heart and life in this eternal way.

Finally, consider again the key passage from 2 Timothy that we have discussed before: "All Scripture is breathed out by God and profitable for teaching, for reproof, for correction, and for training in righteousness, that the man of God may be complete, equipped for every good work" (2 Tim. 3:16–17). Do you see what these verses promise about the powerful work of God's word in a person's life? The Bible is able to teach, reprove, and even train people for righteous living. Just one verse earlier, Paul reminded Timothy that the Scriptures are able to make people "wise for salvation" (v. 15). God's word is the powerful tool by which the Spirit brings faith to human beings. It is also God's powerful way to grow and equip Christians to do his work in the world. It has "growing" power in our lives, in other words. This should be an important reminder for us to be reading the Bible every day!

To summarize, God's word has power. It is, and always has been, God's powerful way of doing his work in this world and in the lives of his people. God created the world by his word, he formed a people by his word, and he now grows and matures that people as they read, study, and are powerfully affected by his word. This is no ordinary human word; this is God's powerful and effective word!

🔺 PRAY!

Ask God to allow his word to do its powerful work in your life as you read it, study it, and hear it taught to you. God is able to accomplish his powerful work in you as you expose yourself to the raw power of his word. The question is, are you doing this? Are you exposing yourself—daily—to the Bible? Talk to God about this right now!

RESPONDING TO THE DOCTRINE OF SCRIPTURE

Now that we have discussed some of the main theological points about the doctrine of Scripture, we are going to move to application—first to ourselves and then more broadly to the study of systematic theology. As you know, we have intentionally started with Scripture so that we might move into the rest of our theological study with that solid foundation in place. Now we need to discuss the relationship between Scripture and systematic theology, and how we will apply this relationship in our study.

The Doctrine of Scripture in Our Lives

What is the right human response to God's word, the Bible? What should be our attitude toward God's word given every truth that we have learned about it so far (its inspiration, its authority, its perspicuity, its infallibility, and its power)?

READ!

Read Isaiah 66:1–2 again, noting the response God desires from his people. How are we supposed to respond to God's word, according to these verses?

As we look around our world today, we see many responses to God's word. Some people dismiss it completely and pay no attention to it. Some people have a certain level of respect for the Bible as a kind of "holy book," yet they do not read or study it. Many Christians claim to love and respect the Bible, but they, too, do not work hard to understand it and to build their lives on it. What is the right response to the Bible for people who truly understand what it is? How should followers of Jesus interact with God's word?

You'll be encouraged to memorize Isaiah 66:1–2 for this chapter; this passage gives us a good start in answering this question. God, in these verses, identifies the kind of people to whom he will "look" in favor and love—those who are "humble and contrite in spirit" and who "tremble" at his word. This is the starting point, with regard to attitude, as we consider the right response to God's word. We are to humbly "tremble" at it as we come under its authority and rule in our lives.

What does this look like? How do we, as Christians, respond with humility to the word of God that has been entrusted to us?

First, we commit to *study* it. Many people claim to love and value the Bible as God's word, and yet they do not put forth any energy to actually study it and know it well! This is a bit like receiving a letter from someone you claim to love but never reading it. The first way that we show humility toward God and love for his word is to actually put forth effort to grow in our knowledge of it.

Second, we live under its *authority*. A humble and contrite spirit, in response to God's powerful and inspired word, means that the Bible becomes our ultimate authority for truth, life, and instruction. Another way to put this would be to say that we do not seek to simply use the Bible for our purposes; instead, our goal is to sit under the rule of Scripture, seeking to live as it instructs us to live.

Third, we build our *lives* on its truth. As we have said before, since the God of the universe has truly spoken to us through Scripture, there is no more important word for us to know and on which to establish our lives. The Bible should be our ultimate guide for truth and for right living as we follow Jesus in this world.

PRAY!

Talk to God honestly and openly about your response to his word. Consider your attitude toward it and the ways that you might need to change your response. Confess that you do not thank him enough for his clear revelation of himself to us. Ask him for help to study the Bible with more joy and enthusiasm. Pray that he would give you a humble and contrite spirit that trembles at his word, so that you want to obey it.

The Doctrine of Scripture in Systematic Theology

Because the Bible is so central and essential to what we are doing in this book, we also need to ask this question: How should all that we have learned about Scripture impact our study of systematic theology in the coming chapters?

READ!

Read Revelation 22:1–5. From what you know of the story of Genesis (and the garden of Eden), what familiar themes and images also show up here at the end of the Bible? What does this tell you about the Bible's unity as one big story?

As you recall, systematic theology is set apart from the discipline of biblical theology. While biblical theology seeks to trace themes as they develop throughout the Bible story (from Genesis to Revelation), systematic theology is organized around specific categories and topics, such as God, man, sin, and the church. These systematic theological categories drive the study, unlike in biblical theology, where the text of the Bible itself is the driving factor. This does not mean that biblical theology is better or somehow more "biblical" than systematic theology. Systematic theology is incredibly important because it is a discipline that helps us give an overall "shape" to a Christian view of a certain doctrine. Christians have been doing this for centuries, and it has been very helpful to the church!

Yet there can be certain dangers in the study of systematic theology since it is less directly driven by the text of Scripture than biblical theology. Here is the biggest danger: *systematic theology can sometimes become more philosophical than biblical if theologians do not intention-*

ally ground their discussion and study in the truth and witness of God's word. In other words, we need to be very careful to always return to the Bible as we do systematic theology. While we organize our study of systematic theology with our own categories, the only foundation for finding truth in those categories is God's inspired word.

Consider, for example, the study of the person of God, which we will begin in the next chapter. We have chosen that category ourselves; there is no book in the Bible called "The God Book" that lays out in systematic sentences all that Scripture has to say about God! This is good; it is appropriate for us to create a category like this. Danger can come, though, if we begin to speculate about what God must be like, how he relates to this world, or what aspects of his character must be most central without grounding each part of our discussion and study in the actual witness and authority of the Bible.

Sadly, some systematic theologians seem to attempt to do systematic theology without making Scripture their ultimate reference point—their foundation. If their foundation for study is not the Bible, then of course it will be something else—their own logic, human reason, or another source of authority. But in our study of systematic theology, we will seek to come back to the Bible at every point possible. While we will not have Bible verses that specifically address every question that we ask, we will constantly be seeking to ground our thoughts and discussions in biblical truth. After all, we have established in this chapter that it is the Bible—not our own reason—that is inspired by God, authoritative, clear, infallible, and powerful.

▲ PRAY!

Talk to God about the categories of systematic theology that are ahead of you. Ask him to help you to have the proper foundation—his word—for all of the study that you will be doing. Pray that, in every area of your life, you will look to his word, Scripture, as the ultimate authority and source of truth.

REVIEW

In this chapter, you have taken your first step into the discipline of systematic theology as you have examined the doctrine of Scripture. You have learned that we have started our study of systematic theology with this doctrine very intentionally, as Scripture must be our foundation for the study of every other category of theology. If we are not guided by the Bible in our study of theology, then we will necessarily be guided by something that is much less reliable! Here are some key concepts to remember:

Inspiration

- "Inspiration" refers to the way in which God "breathed out" his word—by powerfully working through human authors who were under the direction of the Holy Spirit.
- Peter describes the prophets as being "carried along" by the Holy Spirit.
- The doctrine of inspiration is what allows us to call the Bible "God's word."
- The Bible is a completely divine book (inspired by God) and a completely human book (written by human authors).
- The doctrine of inspiration means that where the Bible speaks, God speaks.

Authority

- Whenever God interacts with his people through the Bible, he is ruling over them by the power of his word.
- God's word is—and has always been—authoritative for his people.
- Christians are called today to live under the authority of Scripture.

Perspicuity

- The doctrine of perspicuity teaches that God's word is clear about the necessary and central truths of God, sin, and salvation.
- This doctrine does not mean that there are no parts of the Bible that are difficult to understand.

- This doctrine shows us that God seeks to be known; he wants to clearly communicate himself to human beings.

Infallibility

- The doctrine of infallibility means that God's word is completely true, reliable, and trustworthy; it does not teach or affirm anything that is false.
- Infallibility does not mean that the Bible teaches us everything that can be known about everything in the world.
- The doctrine of infallibility is grounded in the truth of the character of God, who is completely true, reliable, and trustworthy.

Power

- God's word has intrinsic power (power unto itself), while human words can only (sometimes) have powerful effects.
- God can create and save through the power of his word.
- God's word is powerful to bring people to the knowledge of the truth, and also to equip Christians for life and ministry.

Scripture and Systematic Theology

- Many people make the mistake of attempting to engage in systematic theology without grounding every part of their study in Scripture.
- In our study, our goal is to make the Bible the foundation of truth, guiding every part of our discussion about each category of systematic theology.

Remember!

Review your memory verses for this chapter (Isa. 66:1–2) one final time as you conclude your study of the doctrine of Scripture. How are you responding to God's word today?

◉ PRAY!

Ask God to make you even more convinced of the truth of his word, the Bible. Thank him for the amazing and powerful gift of his revelation, which makes clear to us who he is and how we can come into a right relationship with him. Then ask him to help you return again and again to Scripture as the ultimate authority of truth for all that you learn!

Chapter 3

THE DOCTRINE OF GOD

A. W. Tozer once said, "What comes into our minds when we think about God is the most important thing about us" (*The Knowledge of the Holy*). If this is true, then what we are about to study in this chapter should not be taken lightly. We are, on the basis of Scripture, going to begin forming right thoughts about the only true God of the universe. This is the God who created us and made himself known in Scripture. What we think and believe about this eternal being is the most important thing about us!

We are going to work—and think—hard in this chapter. It is very important to recognize and admit, though, that this theological work has limits. We, as humans, are finite beings who are seeking to learn about one who is infinite. God is ultimately beyond total human comprehension; no one can understand him fully or grasp everything about his character, identity, ways, and purpose. When human beings attempt to study God, they are wading into waters that quickly go over their heads. So do not expect that you will be able to "box him up" and someday know everything that there is to know about him!

This is an important starting point for the study of God. We must begin with a humble acknowledgment that God, in his essence, is *other*. He is different. He is separated from us. He is not a human being; he is the infinitely powerful, infinitely wise, and eternally existent God of the universe. We can only hope— through our very best efforts—to gain a small understanding of this amazing God.

Yet we will try! As we do, we know that we have God's revealed word to guide us toward true knowledge of him. This is why we began with the study of Scripture in the last chapter; it will be our foundation—or our roadmap—as we engage in study about God. Our goal, in other words, will not be *complete* knowledge of God but *accurate* knowledge of him through the good gift of his inspired word.

You may be thinking, "Isn't *all* of theology the study of God?" It is, ultimately! As you have learned, theology literally means "God talk," or the study of God. This is the broad and general term for everything we are doing in this book.

But "theology proper," which we are focusing on in this chapter, is different. It refers to the specific study of the being, attributes, and works of God. While all of theology is ultimately the study of God, theology proper is more focused on these aspects of God's identity and his work.

As we saw earlier, there is no one book of the Bible that is called "The God Book." The Bible, rather, teaches about God along the way as it records accounts of his words, actions, and plan in this world and in the lives of his people. So we will seek, in this chapter, to gather from Scripture many truths about our wonderful God that he has made known to us by his grace. Hopefully, by the end of this chapter, your thoughts about God will be even more lined up with the truths of his word and you will have a better grasp of his identity, character, and works, according to the way that he has revealed himself through the Bible.

Remember!

Your suggested memory verses for this chapter come from the book of Revelation—a scene from the "throne room" of heaven, where the angelic beings cry out constantly in worship to God. These verses record two of the statements of praise that they make as they sing in worship to God. Take a moment to simply read these verses carefully, considering all that they teach us about our amazing God:

And the four living creatures, each of them with six wings, are full of eyes all around and within, and day and night they never cease to say, "Holy, holy, holy, is the Lord God Almighty, who was and is and is to come!" . . . [And the twenty-four elders say,] "Worthy are you, our Lord and God, to receive glory and honor and power, for you created all things, and by your will they existed and were created." (Rev. 4:8, 11)

PRAY!

As you begin this chapter, ask God to give you wisdom and humility as you learn about him. Pray that he would give you understanding to grasp more truth about who he is, but also humility to know that you can never box him up and understand everything about his power and his ways.

WHAT IS GOD?

We want to begin by asking one simple question: "What *is* God?" As you can imagine, this is not a simple question to answer, as it is not easy to describe a being who is wondrously and gloriously other than us! Bible scholars and professors will be discussing this question until

Jesus returns. We will probably even be working to fully answer this question long after eternity in heaven has begun, because there will be more to learn about the eternal and infinite God every day. Yet we will do our best, with our finite human minds, to discuss what Scripture shows us about our God.

📖 READ!

Read John 1:18. What does this verse tell us about God the Father?

As we dig into the concept of theology proper, we will seek to gather up four key ideas from the Bible that will help us put together a faithful (if not fully complete) picture of what, exactly, our God is.

First, there is the constant witness of the Old Testament that for sinful people, getting even a glimpse of God means instant death. His glory, in other words, is overwhelming! God's holiness is unlike anything we can even imagine; to see him up close would mean instant death for you and me. God, then, is *a being so infinitely holy (perfect and set apart from his creation) and glorious that human beings cannot hope to survive even a glimpse of him.*

Second, there is the witness of the Old Testament that God does not somehow "dwell" in the temples or other places that people build to worship him. In 1 Samuel 4, for example, we find an account of the Israelites carrying the ark of the covenant into battle with them, thinking that it somehow "contained" God's presence and would therefore help them defeat their enemies. They were wrong, and God allowed the Philistines to capture the ark. However, the Philistines also misunderstood God, because they assumed they had somehow conquered the God of Israel. God struck them with a plague, showing that he had not been captured or defeated (1 Sam. 5). So the witness of the Bible is that God is *a being who cannot be contained by any structure or space, but who is omnipresent (present everywhere at all times).*

Third, there is the witness of John 1:18 that "no one has ever seen God." This verse is in the context of God making himself known through the person of Jesus Christ, his Son (we will talk more about the Trinity soon). But John makes it clear in this verse that God is *a being who is invisible—who keeps himself unseen by human eyes.*

Fourth, there is the explicit statement of Jesus in John 4:24 that "God is Spirit." In other words, God does not have a body (although Jesus *does* have a resurrected human body; he exists forever as perfectly human and perfectly God). So the witness of Jesus himself is that God is *a being who is not flesh and blood, but a spirit.*

The Westminster Shorter Catechism—a wonderful summary of Christian faith and belief that many Reformed churches use today— asks and answers the question we are considering:

Q4. What is God?

A. God is a Spirit, infinite, eternal, and unchangeable, in his being, wisdom, power, holiness, justice, goodness, and truth.

Given what we have seen from the witness of Scripture so far, that seems to be a very good summary.

So what is God? He is a spirit; he is not like human beings in that he does not inhabit just one place, as we do with our bodies. God, as spirit, is omnipresent (everywhere). He is eternal, unchangeable, and infinitely holy and glorious. This God is beyond our comprehension. He is completely other than us, even though we reflect him as beings made in his image. How great is this God! We praise him that we can know him *accurately* by his word, but we should never assume that we can know him *exhaustively.* Even throughout eternity to come, we will be discovering new and wonderful things about our God.

● PRAY!

Consider what you've just learned about God. Pray to him as you try to be very conscious of his amazing holiness, glory, and omnipresence. Remember to pray with humility, knowing that he is a God who is other than you. But pray with confidence, knowing that he has promised to hear you through the grace of his Son, Jesus Christ!

THE ATTRIBUTES OF GOD

We saw above that the Westminster Shorter Catechism says that God is "a Spirit, infinite, eternal, and unchangeable, in his being, wisdom, power, holiness, justice, goodness, and truth." The qualities mentioned here are known as "attributes" of God. We will now turn to a consideration of several important attributes of our God, beginning with his triune nature.

The Three-Person God (the Trinity)

One of the most difficult and complex doctrines in all of systematic theology is the doctrine of the Trinity—that there is one God in three persons. This doctrine is clearly taught in Scripture, yet it is mysterious and hard for us to completely grasp. In a way, the very mystery of this doctrine reminds us that we are seeking to learn about a God beyond our comprehension. So it makes sense that aspects of his identity and existence are difficult for us to completely understand!

READ!

Read Genesis 1:26. What is surprising to you about the pronouns God uses for himself as he articulates his intention to create?

The goal of this section is not to summarize all of the teaching and truths about the doctrine of the Trinity; we could easily spend this entire book discussing this doctrine and still not get to the bottom of it. Our goal is to see a few examples of the way that the Bible points to the truth of the Trinity and summarize the basic Christian beliefs about this important doctrine about God.

The term. *Trinity* is a term that is never used in the Bible. However, it is helpful to carefully summarize a truth that all evangelical biblical scholars agree is carefully taught and developed throughout the Bible: the truth that the God of the Bible has existed—and will always exist—as one God in three distinct persons.

The Trinity at creation. Something very interesting happens in the record of God's creation of the world. In Genesis 1:26, God speaks these words: "Let us make man in our image, after our likeness." In that verse, God speaks in the plural; he says "us" when referring to the creation of human beings. This is just one place that theologians point to as they see God existing eternally as three persons—with each person active in the creation of our world.

The Trinity in the Gospel of John. The Gospel of John is one of the most helpful books for putting together our doctrine of the Trinity. John begins with theology, explaining that Jesus is the "Word," who is "God"—and who then becomes "flesh" to dwell with human beings on the earth (1:1, 14). Jesus, then, is presented to us as the second person of the Trinity, completely equal to God the Father in divinity. Then we see Jesus teaching about the sending of the Spirit, the third person of the Trinity, to be with his disciples after he returns to heaven (see John 16:5–15). So throughout the Gospel of John, we have a very clear witness to the work of God in the world being done through God the Father, God the Son, and God the Holy Spirit.

The Trinity in other Scripture passages. Many other passages in Scripture bear witness that the one God has existed eternally in three persons. Many of Paul's letters in the New Testament begin and/or end with a "Trinitarian" greeting or blessing that mentions the Father, the Son, and the Holy Spirit. The apostle Peter speaks of the reality of the Trinity, as well (see 1 Pet. 1:1–2). So while the term *Trinity* is never used, the doctrine of the Trinity is certainly evident throughout the Bible.

Summary of the doctrine of the Trinity. We could go on to many other passages of Scripture, but we will simply summarize what the Bible seems to teach about the trinitarian God we worship. Here is what orthodox (right belief based on Scripture) Christianity affirms about this doctrine:

- God has always existed as one God in three persons, and he will exist eternally in this way.
- The three persons of the Trinity exist without confusion; that is, they are distinct persons of one God.
- God remains perfectly one—unified in who he is.
- No human analogy can perfectly describe how the Trinity exists and functions, though many people have tried to use analogies (an egg, water, etc.). There is mystery here, and we simply need to affirm what the Bible says.
- In general, Scripture presents God the Father as the person who initiates the sovereign plan of salvation and judgment; God the Son as the person who carries out God's plan by taking on human flesh to die and rise again; and God the Spirit as the person who works in human hearts to bring belief, speak through the word, and point people to Jesus Christ, the Savior.

To say much more than this, at this point, would only be confusing. There is much more depth to the doctrine of the Trinity, but this should serve as a good introduction to the biblical foundation for this important doctrine.

▲ PRAY!

As you pause to pray now, probably the best thing to do is to admit to God that he is beyond your full comprehension. The Trinity is a doctrine that is taught in Scripture, but it is hard for us to fully grasp; how can God be one and also three? Yet this is what God's word teaches. Ask him to give you faith and trust to keep following him and believing exactly what his word says about his being and existence. We cannot claim to understand the doctrine of the Trinity without any remaining mystery—but we can work to summarize accurately what the Bible does clearly teach us about our God, who is three in one.

The Eternality and Aseity of God

How are you doing so far? Are you overwhelmed by the greatness and mystery of God? Are you feeling a bit unprepared and unfit to even begin to comprehend him? If so, that is probably because you are rightly seeing how immensely great and overwhelmingly glorious the Creator God really is. Our response, as we do theology, should be to see our limits as human beings more and more clearly as God becomes even greater and more glorious to our minds and hearts.

Now we will move into two more aspects of God, both of which relate to the doctrine of the Trinity, which we've just been learning about. We will discuss God's "eternality" and "aseity."

READ!

Read Revelation 1:4. What does this verse teach us about God's eternal existence?

In our definition of the Trinity, we mentioned that God has existed eternally as one God in three persons; we will now dig deeper into his eternal existence. We will also see how the Trinity—and God's eternal existence—point to God's aseity. This doctrine will be very important for our understanding of God—and of our salvation through Christ!

God's eternality. Eternity. Think about this idea for a moment. It is impossible to grasp, is it not? Our human minds are simply not capable of totally understanding a God who has no beginning and no end. Yet this is exactly what the Bible teaches about God. Listen to the way God is described as the book of Revelation begins: "Grace to you and peace from him who is and who was and who is to come" (1:4).

Our God is described as absolutely *eternal*. There has never been a time when God has not existed, and there will never be a time when God will not exist. Thinking back to our discussion on the Trinity, this means that God has always existed as one God in three persons. Long before there was a creation, God existed as the Father, the Son, and the Holy Spirit—in perfect unity and relationship.

God's aseity. This eternal existence of God leads us to another very important characteristic about God: his *aseity*. To talk about God's aseity is to talk about the fact that he does not need anything or anyone. God is completely sufficient and satisfied in himself. He does not need to be served by "human hands" (Acts 17:25); God does not need anything or anyone.

What does this mean for the creation of the world and of human beings? God did not create human beings because he was lonely or needed company; God was satisfied in himself for all eternity! So why did a perfect God, with total aseity, choose to create the world and to save some human beings through sending his own Son into that world?

Your memory verses for this chapter tell you that God created all things by his "will." Another possible translation of that word is "pleasure." Think about that for a moment. God chose to create all things for his own pleasure. In other words, he created the world out of a joyful overflow of his own goodness and character. Also, God—who needs nothing—chose to create *you* for his pleasure! This points us to the amazing grace of the eternal God of the universe. He who needs nothing chose to create this world and to give his own Son so that you might have eternal life.

PRAY!

As you consider the eternality and aseity of God, thank him that although he has existed eternally in complete and perfect joy and satisfaction, he chose to create human beings and to save some through his Son, Jesus Christ. Praise him for this today! Put your hope and trust in him! Ask him to give you a heart to thank him and praise him more!

The Justice of God

We turn next to God's *justice*. God is perfectly just; we know that from Scripture. Our goal in this section is to say what the Bible says about the justice of God, and then to see how knowledge of this attribute contributes to our understanding of both God and the salvation that he offers through Jesus, his Son.

READ!

Read Exodus 34:6–7, noting God's attributes that he reveals to Moses. How is God gracious? How is he just?

What do we mean when we speak of the justice of God?

A just God. God is perfectly, wonderfully, and consistently just. Unlike any other being in the universe, he maintains absolute and perfect justice all the time; he has done this for all eternity past and will do it for all eternity to come.

But what do we mean by the justice of God? It is his absolute, perfect righteousness. God is perfectly fair, good, and right in every way possible. The word *righteous* is actually quite connected to *justice* when it comes to God's character (and these terms are often used side by side in Scripture when God is described as "righteous and just"). When we say that God is just, we mean that he is not unfair or wrong in any of his ways, decrees, decisions, or words.

God mentioned his justice when he presented himself to Moses in the passage from Exodus 34 that we looked at in chapter 1. He told Moses, as he passed before him, that he was a God who would "by no means clear the guilty" (v. 7) (or "not leave the guilty unpunished," NIV). In other words, God is so perfectly righteous and just that he cannot let sin simply continue; his justice demands that he punish it righteously and fully.

This concept—God's "need" to punish sin—can sometimes throw us off a bit. We can sometimes think that if God is gracious, he should be able to just "wave his hand" and make sin go away. But we have to understand that if God were to ignore sin, it would be a complete denial of his just and righteous character. The universe would literally unravel were God to do this. God—in his perfect righteousness—must punish sin and make all things right through his just judgment.

Just punishment. This brings us to sinful human beings. Ever since the fall of Adam and Eve, every human being has been born with a sinful nature (prone to sin) and has sinned in reality. This sin leaves us guilty and condemned before God, who is perfectly just and who therefore must punish sin. This is a serious dilemma for sinners!

So how did God find a way to remain perfectly just and righteous while saving sinners who deserve only wrath and punishment? Take a moment to read Romans 3:21–26 slowly, carefully, and intentionally.

God did this through the cross of Jesus Christ! By pouring out his just wrath and punishment (which sinners deserve) on Jesus, God satisfied the righteous demands of his justice toward sin and thus is able to save sinners eternally. In fact, when Paul says that Jesus is the "propitiation" by his blood (Rom. 3:25), he is using a word that specifically refers to the removal of wrath. This is why Paul can conclude his discussion of our salvation by saying that, in Christ, God is both "just" (righteous to punish sin) and the "justifier" (declaring sinners righteous) (v. 26).

Is it not amazing how our perfectly just God saves sinners in a way that is perfectly just?

● PRAY!

Talk to God as you think deeply about his perfect justice. Consider the justice that we all deserve because of our sin: just wrath and punishment.

Then thank God that he provided a way for sinners to be forgiven while still maintaining perfect justice in the universe. The cross was the answer; thank God for this today!

The Grace of God

God's *grace* is, like his justice, an attribute that he revealed to Moses in Exodus 34. As God presented himself to Moses, he said that he is "merciful and gracious," and he told Moses that he is "slow to anger, and abounding in steadfast love and faithfulness" (v. 6). In other words, God pointed Moses to his grace as an essential part of who he is.

READ!

Take a moment to read Ephesians 2:1–10. Focus on what this passage teaches us about God's grace. How does God demonstrate his grace in our salvation and forgiveness? What jumps out at you from this passage?

As we proceed, we will see how God's grace dominates and shapes his actions toward sinful human beings at every phase of the story of the Bible and of the world he created.

God's grace in creation. A few pages back, you learned about the "aseity" of God. This doctrine teaches us that God created the world not because of any need or deficiency in him (because he is eternally satisfied in himself), but purely out of the overflow of his goodness, grace, and love. This means that creation itself is a wonderful act of God's grace! He did not need to create human beings or to deliver them from sin and death, but he graciously chose to do all this for his pleasure and for the eternal good of his people. We see the grace of God in his very creation of this world.

God's grace in salvation. Of course, as you learned from the Ephesians passage that you just read, we see God's grace wonderfully and amazingly through the salvation that he brings to sinners through Jesus Christ. Ephesians 2 makes it clear that, apart from Christ, human beings are "dead" in sin and following the "prince" of this world (vv. 1–2); in other words, they are slaves of Satan himself! Verse 4 speaks of the God who is "rich in mercy"—he chooses to save sinful human beings because of his grace toward them. In this passage, Paul goes out of his way to repeat this phrase: "by grace you have been saved" (vv. 5, 8). Through God's saving action toward human beings through the death and resurrection of his Son, we see his amazingly gracious character.

God's grace in patience. The apostle Peter teaches us another interesting and encouraging aspect of God's grace as it relates to the timing of the final judgment and the end of the world. Why, according to Peter, has Jesus not returned to judge the world? It is because God is gracious and "patient," giving people time to repent (see 2 Pet. 3:9). So we can even see God's grace as every day of life on this earth goes by. The very fact that God has not yet ended history is a sign of his amazing grace. He is holding back his final judgment, giving more people time to repent of their sins and turn in faith to Jesus Christ. God is graciously showing patience—even now—toward this rebellious world.

God's grace in eternity. Finally, God's people will experience his full and amazing grace through all of eternity to come. God will justly punish and judge Satan and all who reject Jesus; we know that from the Bible. Yet for those who do repent and believe in Jesus, there is grace not only for forgiveness but also for an amazing eternal future with him in the new heaven and new earth. The Bible is not shy about pointing us to the amazing glories that God has prepared for his people in the life to come. Those who follow Jesus as Savior and Lord will have an eternity full of the experience of his amazing grace and love as they dwell forever in his perfect presence!

PRAY!

Thank God that he is full of grace! Thank him that, for as long as this world has existed, he has acted toward the human beings he has created with grace, mercy, and love, which they surely do not deserve. Ask him to help you understand his grace more clearly so that you live with more joy, thankfulness, and love toward both him and the people around you.

The Sovereignty of God

Think back over all that we have learned so far in our study of "theology proper." We have learned about God's existence as the Trinity—one God in three persons. We have studied his eternality and aseity. And we have learned about his perfect justice and grace.

READ!

Now read Ephesians 1:1–10. Go slowly and carefully; there is a lot of truth packed into these verses. As you read, think about what this passage teaches about God's sovereignty in his salvation. What is God's role in saving people?

Now we turn to the subject of God's *sovereignty*. What is this unusual word teaching us about God?

A sovereign God. This is not an easy doctrine to fully grasp or explain. When we talk about God's sovereignty, we are dealing with his complete power, control, and might, which determines everything in this world and in the entire universe he created. We are talking about a God who not only knows the future, but who actually (according to the Bible) orchestrates all events, actions, and occurrences according to his perfect plan. We are talking about him as the all-powerful ruler of all—the one who executes his plan and his will perfectly.

We will examine the sovereignty of God in four distinct categories.

God's sovereignty in creation. In the passage from Revelation 4 that you're encouraged to memorize as you read this chapter, we see God's sovereignty in his creation of the world. No one helped God create the world; he made it according to his own will and for his own pleasure. This is an important starting point in discussions about the sovereignty of God! It reminds us that God, as the only Creator of this world, has the right to control and work out all things according to his perfect purpose and plan. He created this world for his own glory, and he has a perfect plan for it. This leads to our next point.

God's sovereignty in his plan. The story of the Bible, again and again, points us to God's sovereignty—his perfect power and control—in working out his plan in this world and in the lives of his people. In Exodus, for example, we read about God raising up Pharaoh so that God would be able to demonstrate his glory and power in Egypt through the deliverance of his people from slavery there (see Ex. 9:16). Pharaoh opposes God and his people—and is completely responsible for his actions. Yet God is presented as the one who sovereignly orchestrates all of these events to bring glory to himself and good to his people.

As the story of the world moves forward, Scripture points to God's sovereign hand in everything—even controlling the actions of kings such as Cyrus of Persia, whose heart God "stirred up" to send the Lord's people back to the promised land after their Babylonian exile (2 Chron. 36:22–23). God is sovereignly working out his plan; he is controlling the course of history. This aspect of God's sovereign rule is sometimes referred to as his *providence*, by which he orders every event in the universe at every moment!

God's sovereignty in salvation. In Ephesians 1:1–10, the passage you read just above, the Bible teaches about God's sovereignty in human salvation. According to this passage, even before his creation of the world, God chose some to be his people and receive salvation (v. 4). This is a hard truth for many people to grasp or accept; it is sometimes referred to as "predestination" (see v. 5). The Bible does teach that God chooses to save some people, and even chooses them as his children before the foundation of the world. This is his sovereignty in salvation. It is important to remember that throughout Scripture, human beings are presented as responsible creatures who make real choices to accept or reject God; we are not robots who are guided by remote control. Yet the Bible really describes salvation as sovereignly controlled, orchestrated, and planned by a perfect and all-powerful God.

God's sovereignty in judgment. Finally, the Bible shows that one day God will be clearly seen as sovereign, glorious, and all-powerful in his final judgment of the world and his eternal reign. In Philippians 2:10–11, Paul speaks of a day to come when every knee will bow and every tongue will confess that Jesus Christ is Lord. There will come a time, in other words, when no doubt will remain in people's minds about the sovereignty of God—believers and unbelievers alike. God will conquer evil forever, judge the world through Jesus Christ, and reign forever over his people. This is the future of the perfect plan of the sovereign God!

PRAY!

Spend a few minutes in silence, considering the perfect sovereignty of the almighty God of the universe. Think about his power, control, and perfect plan in everything he does. After spending a few minutes in deep thought, pray a prayer of simple worship and humility toward God. Declare that you know he is sovereign and powerful. Thank him for choosing to show grace to you through his Son. Ask him to help you humbly and faithfully follow him by the power of the Holy Spirit.

The Glory of God

Glory is not an unfamiliar term for us, but we often use it without really thinking carefully about what it actually means. Our goal now is to see how God's glory is an essential part of his character and his pursuits, and also how this relates to our eternal good.

READ!

Take a minute to read Ephesians 1:11–14. Read it carefully at least two times. Notice the phrase that is attached to the end of both sections of this passage, at the end of verses 12 and 14: "to the praise of his glory." What is the significance of that phrase? How might it begin to help you think about God's glory in relation to our salvation?

What do we mean when we talk about the "glory" of God? By glory, we mean God's well-deserved praise, honor, and *fame*. This is different than human fame, of course, which is often cheap, fake, and short-lived. The glory and fame of God is his splendor and greatness that is displayed in human lives, the earth he has created, and the entire universe.

By this definition, then, there are two ways to talk about the glory of God. He has glory all by himself; God was glorious long before there were any beings who were able to "glorify" him by singing his praises and shouting the truth about him. Yet through God's creation of angels, other heavenly beings, and humans, God can now be praised and glorified by the creatures he has made. So while God is glorious (praiseworthy and honorable) all on his own, it is possible for his creatures to glorify him (bring him praise, declare his fame, and so on).

God's pursuit of his own glory. God is ultimately after his own glory. He wants to be lifted up and glorified in the right way. Furthermore, he is not willing to share his glory with anyone else. In Isaiah 48:11, God says very explicitly, "My glory I will not give to another."

As we first think about this, it can seem almost selfish or arrogant. Is it not wrong for God to be so focused on his own glory? Well, if God were a human being, it *would* be wrong! It would not be appropriate for any sinful human creature to want to be glorified—declared worthy, just, true, and perfect. God, though, is worthy of being declared

THE DOCTRINE OF GOD

to be all of those things. He is the only one who *should rightly receive all glory, praise, honor, and fame.* So for God to pursue his own glory is actually the most right thing in all the universe.

In everything that God does, he aims to glorify himself and to lift up his name. His creation is about his glory. The salvation he provides is about his glory. For all eternity, his people will declare his praises and glorify his name, because that is right, good, and perfectly fitting, given who God is.

There is some very good news about God's pursuit of his glory.

God's glory and our good. Here is the good news: God's glory is not disconnected from the greatest good of human beings. In fact, our greatest good is very tied up with God getting the most glory! God is glorified—made famous and declared loving and merciful—when sinners are redeemed through the blood of his Son, Jesus.

Think back to the passage that you read from Ephesians 1 just above. It talks about the amazing "inheritance" that we have in Christ through faith in him (v. 11). This is the eternal inheritance of heaven for all who believe, and it is guaranteed to us through God's gift of his Holy Spirit to us (v. 13)! As we noted above, each section of this passage ends with the phrase "to the praise of his glory." That is the end—the goal—of our salvation. When God saves us, it is for the praise of his glory; it is so he looks great, wonderful, gracious, and glorious. His glory is bound up with our good—with providing an eternal inheritance for us in Christ Jesus.

So remember, God is after his own glory. Yet his word reminds us that his glory is bound up with the *good* of human beings as he offers salvation and eternal life to them through his Son. Our salvation is for God's glory, and he has designed that he will be greatly glorified as he pours out rich blessings on us through Jesus.

▲ PRAY!

Pause to pray, asking God to help you be more and more focused on his glory. Remember, that is his great purpose, and your greatest good is wrapped up in his greatest glory! Ask God to show you how you can study, work, play, and speak for his glory, not your own. Pray that you would want to see God glorified in the world around you.

HOW SHOULD WE RESPOND TO GOD?

Think back over all that we have considered about God in this chapter thus far. You have learned about his triune nature and his eternality. You have explored his aseity and justice. You have studied his grace, his sovereignty, and his glory. There is much more that we could learn about the God of the universe! This chapter has been simply one step toward what could be a lifelong study of the God who created you, as he is revealed to us in the Bible. Hopefully this has not been just an academic study about God, but you have begun thinking about what all these truths about him mean for the way that humans should respond to him—and you have been moved toward personal worship of him yourself.

It is the right response to God that we will focus on now. The goal is to make sure that our theology (our "God talk") does not simply remain as talk, but forms lives that are fully devoted to following, loving, and serving this amazing God.

Take a moment to read Isaiah 66:1–2 at least two times (this was your memory verse in the last chapter), focusing on the kind of person to whom God promises to "look" (v. 2). How can you adopt this kind of attitude?

READ!

Read Job 40:3–5. How does Job model a humble and reverent response to the God who has just spoken to him?

We have seen how the Scriptures reveal a triune, eternal, just, gracious, sovereign, and glorious God; how, then, should we respond as sinful human beings to this amazing Creator and Savior? Let's think together about four attitudes and actions with which human beings should respond to him.

Humility. First, we should respond to God with humility. We should begin all theology—and all of life—by humbly recognizing that the great God who created us is gloriously other than us. He is holy, but we are sinful. He is powerful, but we are weak. He is righteous, but we are foolish, proud, and fallen. The truth about God that we find in his word should lead us to a great sense of humility. Isaiah 66:1–2 points us to this; it speaks of God accepting those who are "humble and contrite in spirit" (v. 2).

Worship. Second, it is absolutely right and necessary for us to respond to this great God in praise and worship. This means singing his praises with other believers at church, but also living lives that are given in worship to him. Since God is truly after his own glory, as we have considered together, then our lives should be completely devoted to glorifying him and spreading his fame around the world. God is worthy to be praised; we should take our cue from the heavenly beings in Revelation 4 and sing his praises all the time!

Obedience. Third, God is the God of the Bible, and his word demands that we obey him. The Isaiah 66 passage that you read and considered above points us to this as well; it says that God wants people who "tremble" at his word (v. 2), which implies their obedience to it. Our response to our great God must be to give our lives to follow him, obey him, and tremble at his word as we submit to its rule in our lives and hearts.

Gratitude. Finally, because God has provided salvation, forgiveness, and eternal life for us through his Son, our response should be immense and eternal gratitude! We should be characterized every day by thankfulness to him for the grace that he has shown us in Jesus Christ. This is amazing grace; he did not have to save us, but he chose to do it freely through the death and resurrection of his Son!

What is your response to the glorious God of the universe? Are you humble before him? Do you seek to worship him every day? Are you obeying his word? Are you grateful to him for his gracious salvation?

▲ PRAY!

Thank God for giving you the revelation of who he is in his word so that you can know how to respond to him in humility, worship, obedience, and gratitude. Pray that he would protect you from purely academic learning about him so that you truly are able to respond in worship to God as you learn truths from his word.

REVIEW

You have learned about several aspects, attributes, and actions of God in this chapter, although there is much more still to learn about the amazing Creator and Savior of humanity. Here are a few key points for you to remember:

What Is God?

- God is spirit, so he is omnipresent but invisible to human eyes.
- God is absolutely and perfectly glorious, holy, and "other," so that an encounter with him would be absolutely overwhelming to sinful human beings.
- While God does not have a physical body, Jesus does have one, and always will.

Trinity

- God has existed eternally as one God in three persons—the Father, the Son, and the Holy Spirit.

- The persons of the Trinity exist in perfect unity and without any confusion.
- The doctrine of the Trinity is clearly taught in the Bible, although the term *Trinity* is not actually used.

Eternality and Aseity

- God is absolutely eternal; he has no beginning and no end.
- God has existed eternally—long before his creation of the world and human beings—and has always been perfectly and completely God, not depending on anything else for existence.
- The doctrine of aseity refers to the fact that God has no need of anyone or anything; he is completely satisfied in himself. Therefore, he must have created the world and saved his people out of the overflow of his joy, love, and grace.

Justice

- God is perfectly and completely just, right, and true.
- God's justice demands that he punish sin perfectly and completely, or he would cease to be God.
- God's justice is perfectly satisfied at the cross, where Jesus took the full penalty of sin in the place of God's people.

Grace

- God revealed himself to Moses in Exodus 34 as the God who is "merciful" and "slow to anger."
- God is perfectly gracious, even providing salvation to sinners through the death of his Son on the cross.
- God, even now, is gracious and patient, delaying the return of Christ so that more people have time to repent and be saved.

Sovereignty

- The Bible clearly teaches that God is completely sovereign—in powerful control of the universe he has made.
- God is constantly working out his sovereign plan in his intended way.

- God's sovereignty extends to our salvation, although the Bible clearly presents human beings as responsible creatures who make real choices.

Glory

- God, ultimately, is pursuing his own glory.
- Glory refers to God's worthiness, honor, praise, and fame in all the universe.
- God's glory, ultimately, matches up with our greatest good; this is good news, because God is glorified in saving sinners and giving them an inheritance.

Remember!

Review your memory verses one final time: Revelation 4:8, 11. Remember what these verses teach you about your great, eternal, glorious God.

PRAY!

As you end this chapter in prayer, spend a few moments in silence thinking about all the truths about God that you have studied in this chapter. Consider his justice, his grace, his sovereignty, and his glory. Think about the way that he has revealed himself to us through his word. Then pray in these three ways:

- *Ask God to remind you of who he is daily as you read and study his word.*
- *Ask God to help you respond to him personally as you continue to learn more truths about him.*
- *Ask God to strengthen you to make him known in powerful ways to the people around you who need to meet Jesus as Savior and Lord.*

Chapter 4

THE DOCTRINE OF MAN

In the last two chapters, we examined the doctrines of Scripture and God, and you worked hard to see the basic truths that the Bible teaches about these subjects. There is much more to learn about both of these areas, but hopefully you have begun to think biblically about the word of God and about the God who created you to worship him. If so, you are on a path to a deeper understanding of him.

In this chapter, you are going to examine the doctrine of man (we will be using the word *man* in this chapter to describe humanity in general—men and women). The technical term for the category of systematic theology that we are exploring now is *anthropology*—the study of man—but it should really be called *biblical anthropology*. There is an entire field called anthropology that studies human beings in a purely *scientific* way. We are now focused on studying human beings in a *theological* way.

Our goal is to discover key points that the Bible teaches about humanity in order to better understand who we are, what we are, and why we have been created by God. To reach this goal, you will focus on four key aspects of who we are as human beings:

- Our *origins*. Where do we come from?
- Our *essence*. What are we, really, as human beings?
- Our *purpose*. Why were we made?
- Our *end*. Where are we headed, and how do we make sure that we are ready?

As we address these questions, we will ground ourselves in a very focused way in the doctrine of creation. For the study of man, the truth of God's intentional and unique creation of man and woman is a very important starting point. You need to know that the doctrine of God's unique creation of Adam and Eve is hotly debated in our world today. The basic question for you is whether you will accept the clear teaching of God's word about this doctrine.

From the doctrine of creation (and all that it implies and entails), we will move to the issues of the purpose and end of man. We will look at various relevant Scripture passages that will guide us in this aspect of our study. By the end of this chapter, you should have a clearer grasp of who you are, why you are here, and the purpose for which God has made you.

Remember!

Your suggested memory verses for this chapter come from the very beginning of the Bible story—from the book of Genesis, which records God's creation of the world (including human beings). These verses are absolutely foundational for our study in the doctrine of man because they put forward an idea that has almost countless implications for why we exist and our eternal value to God. What is that idea? It is the idea that human beings are made in "the image of God," or the *imago Dei*. Scripture is absolutely clear about this, although there is much debate about the precise meaning of this phrase. No matter what, though, it means that human beings have eternal value and deep meaning to God. As we will see in our discussion, they are unique in all of God's creation!

As you begin this chapter, simply read through these verses several times and begin thinking deeply about them.

Then God said, "Let us make man in our image, after our likeness. And let them have dominion over the fish of the sea and over the birds of the heavens and over the livestock and over all the earth and over every creeping thing that creeps on the earth." So God created man in his own image, in the image of God he created him; male and female he created them. (Gen. 1:26–27)

PRAY!

We want to continue to link our "God talk" (theology) with talk to God (prayer). We want this study to be worshipful—not just academic! So thank God right now for giving you his word so that you can better understand his purpose for you and the meaning of your life and existence. Ask him to guide you in this chapter as you learn more about the crowning point of his creative work: the creation of human beings.

THE *ORIGINS* OF MAN

We are now ready to start at the very beginning of the story of the Bible (a place where we will stay for a while, in fact) in order to see the uniqueness of human beings within the rest of God's creation. As you will see, the simple truth of the separation that God makes between man and the rest of the world is eternally important for understanding who we are and why God created us.

📖 READ!

Take a few moments to read Psalm 8. Read it at least twice, paying special attention to verses 3–8. Think about the way in which David, the psalmist, talks about the unique role of human beings in God's world. How does he describe this role? What is his response to this reality?

Many movements today seek to deny the exact truth that we are learning in this chapter—that human beings are absolutely unique in the created order and have been set aside in a special and distinct way by the Creator God. Many people, denying biblical truth, seek to describe human beings as only another animal species—mere creatures that have no ultimate or eternal distinction from the rest of the plants and animals on this earth. This is not the witness of Scripture.

Now it is true that we *are* creatures. In fact, the most basic starting point as we begin to approach God, listen to his word, and discover our purpose for existence through his revelation is to admit that we are creatures and he is the Creator. However, while we are creatures, we are not "just like" every other creature that God has made. Human begins are distinct, unique, and set aside for God's special and eternal purpose. We see this clearly in the following passages:

Genesis 1:26–27. In this passage, which you are encouraged to memorize as you work through this chapter, we find that human beings are set apart—right at the beginning—by God for a special role in creation. They are not listed along with every other species on earth; they are actually given "dominion" (v. 26) to rule well over every other creature God has made! This, then, is an indication, from the very creation of the world, that God has made human beings absolutely unique—distinct from the rest of his creation. This, of course, does not mean that we have the right to abuse or harm other species in cruel ways. Yet God has given dominion and rule to human beings—and no other species.

Genesis 1:31. Look carefully, also, at the way God concludes his various creative works. Each day concludes with God looking at what he has created and seeing that it is "good" (vv. 4, 10, 12, 18, 21, 25). But what happens at the conclusion of the sixth day, in verse 31? What does God see after he has created man and woman? He sees that his creation, which now includes man, is "very good." This is one more small indication that human beings, from the very beginning, have been unique to God and distinct from the rest of his creation.

Psalm 8. Finally, consider the psalm that you read above. David praises God because he sees the exalted and honored position that God has given to human begins in all of creation. They are made "a little lower than the heavenly beings" and are given dominion and rule over all the animals and all the world (vv. 5–8). David sees this clearly, and his response is humility and praise to this wonderful God who has chosen to give such an exalted place in creation to human beings.

We will talk more about where the uniqueness of human beings ultimately comes from. For now, simply understand that human beings have been intentionally set apart by God, from the beginning, from all the rest of creation. They have been given dominion and called to rule over this world. God has a special and eternal purpose for human beings that he does not have for any other part of his creation.

● PRAY!

Thank God that he has made you distinct and unique from all the rest of his creation. Give him praise for setting you apart for his grace and his eternal purposes in your life. Ask him to help you see how much he loves and values you so that you can respond in the right way to his word and his love to you in Jesus Christ.

CHAPTER 4

THE *ESSENCE* OF MAN

But how are human beings absolutely unique and distinct from the rest of creation? How are we set apart, and what makes us different from every other creature in the world? What is it about human beings that makes them fit to have God-given dominion and rule in the world?

The *Imago Dei*

These questions bring us to the question of man's essence and to the doctrine of the *imago Dei*. This phrase simply means "image of God." The Bible clearly affirms the fact that all human beings are made in God's image, so we will seek to understand this doctrine and then think through some implications of it.

READ!

Take a moment to read through your memory verses for this chapter: Genesis 1:26–27. They are the first verses that clearly articulate the truth of the imago Dei *of humanity. Think about what these verses mean and the way that they give eternal significance to the creation, existence, and purpose of all human beings.*

The image of God is a concept that is so clearly taught in Scripture that no one who takes the Bible seriously can deny it. Yet, the precise meaning of it is hotly debated, and people have many different understandings of exactly how we are made in God's image.

Genesis 1 makes the simple truth very clear: humans, and only humans, are created in God's image. Nothing in creation besides men and women has the label "made in God's image" attached to it.

What this means, at the very least, is that human beings *reflect* God in a significant and real way. There is something—or many things—about us that shines out the identity of our Creator and points to what he is like. Another way to look at this is to note that while human beings are not like him in *every* way—we are sinful, fallen, and weak, whereas he is eternally good, righteous, and powerful—we are like him in *some* significant ways. Consider a few ways that we reflect God and are like him:

- Relationships. God, as we learned in the previous chapter, has existed eternally as one God in three persons—in an eternally perfect "relationship" with himself (see Gen. 1:26, "Let *us*"). We, too, relate to God and to other people.
- Communication. God, as we know from the Bible, is a speaking God. Likewise, we communicate with one another—and with God—in a way that no other species on earth can.
- Eternal sense. Human beings have a sense of eternity—higher purpose, meaning, beauty, and truth—that no other animal on earth has. If you do not believe this, try interacting with a monkey about the meaning of life. It will not be a very rewarding conversation! We reflect God in our uniquely human capacity for transcendent thoughts, desires, and worship. Our God is eternal, and he has created us with a desire for eternally significant relationships and meaning.
- Love. Human beings are capable of deep and incredible love, devotion, and sacrifice. This ability to love and feel things deeply is certainly part of the *imago Dei*.
- Intellect. Think about the capacity of human beings to reason, argue, and even invent and create things. All of these abilities surely reflect the all-wise Creator of human beings.

There are many more aspects of humanity that we could add to this list! Probably, the *imago Dei* refers to *all* of these aspects and capacities of human beings. Human beings have been created to reflect and be like their Creator in many ways.

▲ PRAY!

As you consider the big themes and truths you are studying, give thanks to the God who has placed his image in all of us. Thank him that, as a human being, you actually are like him in some ways. Begin thinking through some of the implications of this. Ask him to give you more understanding as you seek to respond to him in the right way.

Implications of the *Imago Dei*

The biblical truth that all human beings are created in God's image has many important implications. Now we need to think through some of the major ones. What does the doctrine of the *imago Dei* mean for the way we think about ourselves? What does it mean, practically, for the way we view and treat the people around us?

READ!

Take a minute to read James 3:1–12—a wonderful passage about the importance of "taming the tongue." Pay attention especially to verse 9, and consider the way that James briefly applies the doctrine of the imago Dei *to the importance of speaking lovingly and carefully to other human beings. How can you see this principle being applied to other areas of life?*

We need to think through two major implications of the truth that every human being is created in the image of God:

Our eternal value. First, the doctrine of the *imago Dei* should affect the way that we think about ourselves. As we come to believe that, as the Bible teaches, we have been created in God's image, we begin to see that we therefore have eternal value. We have been made by God and for God; he has an eternal purpose for the people in whom he has placed his image. This has incredible importance for the way that we understand our value and purpose. We are not worthless or without meaning in life. We are intentionally and carefully designed creatures of God, who reflect the glorious, gracious, and all-wise Creator. We are very dear and valuable to him. When we add to this the fact that God has sent his own Son into the world to redeem the people he created, our eternal value in God's sight becomes even more evident!

Our treatment of other people. Second, in the passage you read from James just above, you saw the way that he briefly used the doctrine of the image of God to ground his rebuke to his readers for using their mouths to curse one another. With these curses, James reminded them, they were cursing people who had been made in the "likeness," or image, of God (3:9). In this passage, James points us to a very important implication of the doctrine of the *imago Dei*—it means that we should treat other human beings with the respect demanded by the image of God that they carry and reflect. This is an important point for Christians to grasp: since all people are made in the image of God, all people have dignity and are worthy of respect, honor, love, and care. This does not mean, of course, that we agree with everything that every human being says or does; many people who are made in the image of God make terrible choices about life and belief. Yet it does mean that we value every human being as a creature made with the *imago Dei*. We value human life and respect the people whom the Creator God has carefully formed in his own image.

● PRAY!

As you think over these important implications of the doctrine of the imago Dei *in human beings, talk to God honestly. Ask him to help you understand and believe this truth more deeply about yourself, so that you are reminded of the way that God loves and values you. Then pray that he would help you remember this truth as you interact with other people, so that you are even more motivated to love them, respect them, and share with them the gospel of Jesus Christ.*

The Human Being

There is yet another step forward we can take in our examination of the essence of man. We will discuss the complexity of human beings, who are both physical and spiritual creatures. This is just one more way that we are set apart from every other creature in the world (a dog, for example, is only physical, not spiritual). It is a sign that God has made us for eternity and wants to have a relationship with the people he has created.

READ!

Pause and read Psalm 16. Read it carefully and thoughtfully, taking note of the way that David talks about his "heart" and his "soul." David was obviously a physical person—like you and me—but he had a very real sense of the deeply spiritual aspect of who he was.

Humans are incredibly complex! Think for a moment about the different ways that you react to situations throughout a regular day. You have a physical response to things; you might feel pain, for example, if you stub your toe. You have an emotional interaction with life; you might feel love, anger, compassion, or sadness because something happens. You have a capacity for spiritual thought and depth; you might worship God through listening to his word or singing a song to him. You are a complex being created in the image of God.

Because of this complexity, Christian thinkers and scholars through the centuries have tried to identify the main "parts" or "aspects" of human beings. Some people have said that human beings are made up of two parts: body and soul. Other people have said that human beings are made up of three parts: body, mind, and spirit. We will not argue for the validity of one of these viewpoints; rather, we will simply highlight the amazing complexity of God's creation.

Physical beings. You are a physical being. You know that because you walk around, eat food, experience pain, grow tired or sick, and engage in this world in other physical ways. While we are not like irrational animals (we are distinct and unique in all of creation), we have appetites, weaknesses, and instincts just like other creatures God has made.

Spiritual beings. The Bible (and our experience) shows us that we are spiritual beings as well as physical beings. We are not merely irrational, unthinking animals; we are deeply spiritual and we were made to worship, so we long to find transcendent meaning in and through our lives in this world. Solomon puts it this way: "He [God] has put eternity into man's heart" (Eccles. 3:11). To be human is to be spiritual, even if that spirituality is rejected completely or directed toward a false god or set of beliefs.

The Bible talks about the reality of the eternal soul, which all human beings have. This is, of course, not a physical organ, but is the Bible's way of talking about the part of human beings that is eternal and spiritual—the essence of who they are. Even though you cannot see it, you have an eternal soul that is given to you by God. He has made you to worship him, and you will not be spiritually satisfied until you do!

What does this complexity mean for us? First, we need to consider our complexity as we seek to care for our hearts and follow God well in this world. We need food and sleep, but we also need the influence of God's word, prayer, and other believing people. Many people care for their bodies only and neglect the care of their souls. Second, this doctrine has implications for the resurrection, which will mean eternal life for God's people—body and soul. This is an important point: God will restore us to life—eternal life—in full! Jesus, who was the first to die and rise again, rose with a resurrected physical body, and so will we. There will come a day when Christians will dwell forever in the very physical, very real, new heaven and new earth, to enjoy an eternity worshiping Jesus Christ, the Savior and Lord.

▲ PRAY!

Thank God for making you a complex being; you are physical and spiritual, and you have the capacity for an eternal relationship with the Creator God. Praise him for this and ask him to help you take your spiritual and physical health seriously as you follow the Lord Jesus Christ.

The Physical Nature of the Body

Sometimes we can fall into a dangerous overemphasis on one of the two elements of human identity and experience—physical and spiritual. That is what we will tackle and warn against next as we look ultimately at the incarnation and resurrection of Jesus Christ to explain the hope that Christians have for both physical and spiritual existence—and the value that God himself attaches to these parts of who we are as human beings. By the end of this section of the chapter, you should have a clearer picture of the way that your salvation—if you have trusted Jesus Christ as Lord and Savior—is wrapped up with both your physical and spiritual life. Our salvation is perhaps even bigger and better than we have imagined!

◣ READ!

Read Job 19:25–27. This passage is just three verses long, so read it at least two times through. Think about what this passage is teaching about Job's hope in the resurrection. Reflect about how this can inform your thoughts about your spiritual and physical existence.

If we are not careful, we can fall prey to a very dangerous idea about the interaction of our physical and spiritual existence as human beings. We can begin to think that our physical bodies do not matter because we need to focus on caring about our souls. There is some truth to this! Our physical bodies will grow weak and die, so it is vital that we care for our hearts and souls by trusting Jesus as Savior, reading his word, and worshiping with his people. That *is* more important than physical exercise and health! But sometimes people can begin to think that our physical bodies—our physical existence—are somehow opposed to our spiritual existence. They can begin to think that these aspects of who we are as human beings have no effect on each other at all.

This idea is actually very close to the teaching of an ancient group (from the days of the apostles) known as the "gnostics." People from this group taught that everything physical was evil and doomed to destruction. Their goal was to reach a higher, more transcendent "spiritual" knowledge, which would mean salvation for them. They rejected all physical matter as essentially evil. Sadly, many of these gnostics made no effort to use their bodies in holy and pure ways. Their way of thinking became an excuse for all kinds of physical sin because they believed that what they did with their physical bodies did not matter! This idea is alive and well today, but the Bible's teaching about Jesus helps to combat this dangerous way of thinking.

What does the incarnation of Jesus (and his resurrection to a glorified human body) teach us?

- The physical is not evil! The very fact that Jesus took on a human body tells us that physical matter—flesh—in itself is not sinful. It is true that we live in a fallen, sinful world, but to be human is not in itself a problem. Jesus assumed real human flesh; he really lived in this physical world. He did this without sin, of course, proving to us that there is hope for physical existence.
- Salvation is for our souls *and* our bodies! Jesus not only took on flesh, but he also died and rose again with a resurrected physical *body*. The same will be true of us—our bodies will be saved as surely as our souls. Paul tells us that Jesus is the "firstfruits" of all who will be saved and resurrected (1 Cor. 15:23). This means that his resurrected body is the pattern and the model for all

who will be raised to eternal life at the end of the world. Those who trust Jesus as Lord and Savior have hope for spiritual *and* physical salvation.

- Eternal life will be physical! Since we will experience physical resurrection, that means that eternal life with Jesus will be a physical existence. The Bible tells us, in Revelation 21, that there will be a new heaven and a new *earth* (Rev. 21:1). God is going to make a new place—a very physical place—that is finally free from sin, death, sickness, and pain. Christians have hope of a very physical, very wonderful eternal life with the resurrected and reigning Lord Jesus Christ.

All of this has implications for how we live now. Unlike the gnostics, we value and watch what we do with our bodies. Our goal is to honor Jesus Christ in all that we do—physically and spiritually—because we know that our bodies, too, will one day be redeemed by him.

⬛ **PRAY!**

Take a few minutes to think quietly about Jesus's embrace of human flesh. Think about what the incarnation means for our physical existence. Consider the humility that Jesus demonstrated by coming down to the earth he created and taking on a real human body. Then thank him for this, giving him praise and glory! Thank him that, one day, all who follow him will have resurrected physical bodies in which they will enjoy life with him forever.

God's Communicable and Incommunicable Attributes

As we continue to think about the essence of man, we will turn next to a consideration of God's "communicable" and "incommunicable" attributes, and how they relate to our understanding of human beings. This will be one more step toward our understanding of the *imago Dei* in human beings, which is so central to the way they were created by God.

READ!

Read Galatians 5:22–26, the well-known passage about the "fruit of the Spirit." Think about the ways that this "fruit" is described in this passage. All of these characteristics point us to the perfect character of God. When we have his Holy Spirit within us through faith in Jesus Christ, these characteristics (which correspond to God's "communicable attributes") really can "grow" from our lives.

In the chapter on theology proper (the study of God himself), you learned much about the attributes of God. We waited for this chapter, though, to make a distinction between two kinds of divine attributes: communicable and incommunicable. Here is what we mean by those terms:

- God's *incommunicable* attributes are those that *cannot* be "communicated" to human beings. In other words, they are unique to God, and we cannot practice them. These attributes include his eternality, his omnipotence (power), his omnipresence, his omniscience (all-knowing nature), and his absolute perfection.
- God's *communicable* attributes are those that *can* be communicated to human beings, at least to some level. The "fruit of the Spirit" passage that we just read speaks to some of these. Human beings can reflect the character of God in, for example, their love, kindness, patience, justice, humility, wisdom, and peace. None of us will do this perfectly, of course. Yet God allows his people to reflect his attributes in these ways as they follow and serve him.

So what does the reality of the communicable attributes of God teach us about human beings?

First, this is one more aspect that we should add to our understanding of the concept of the *imago Dei* in human beings. Not only do we bear the likeness of God in our essence (as we have been created), but we also can begin to reflect God's attributes and characteristics as we follow him and love him, and as his Holy Spirit works powerfully in us.

Second, the communicable attributes of God help us understand the concept of the "fruit of the Spirit," which we read about earlier in the chapter. As human beings turn in faith to God, they bear "fruit" as a result of being connected to him in faith. They begin to resemble their Creator and their Savior in their thoughts, words, and actions. This is an amazing work of God in human lives!

Third, the communicable attributes of God point us again to his special purpose and grace toward human beings. He has set them apart for his eternal purpose in this world and has proved this by allowing them to "communicate" something of himself—his attributes—to this world.

PRAY!

Talk to God about the divine attributes that you would like to see more powerfully displayed in your life. Ask him to help you make him known more fully and clearly to the people around you. Pray that he would help you grow in love, truth, wisdom, kindness, grace, and other traits as you interact with others near you in Jesus's name.

THE *PURPOSE* OF MAN

While we have touched on the topic of salvation several times already, we have not yet really dug into what it means for human beings to be saved. There will be entire chapters devoted to the topics of sin and salvation later in the book. For now, our goal is to show how salvation relates to the purpose of human beings, according to Scripture.

Think about these questions, which we'll try to answer in the following pages:

- How does the doctrine of the *imago Dei* relate to human salvation? In light of this doctrine, why might God work in special saving ways in the lives of human beings as opposed to animals?
- From what you know of the teachings of Scripture, why do human beings need salvation? What do they need to be saved from?
- What does it tell you about God that he offers salvation to human beings? What must that mean about their value to him?

READ!

Read Ephesians 2:1–10—one of the clearest and fullest articulations of the gospel of our salvation in all of the Bible. Focus especially on the original situation of human begins, the grace and salvation that God shows to them in Christ Jesus, and the good purpose that God has for human beings who are saved by Jesus. Also, simply enjoy the good news that this passage gives to sinful human beings who need to be saved!

In many ways, the entire Bible is really the story of God's salvation of human beings. So it would be wrong to spend an entire chapter learning about human beings without mentioning the great salvation that God has planned for them in and through his Son, Jesus Christ!

What is this salvation, and what does it teach us about humans, according to God's word?

First, the Ephesians passage that you just read reminds us about the situation of all human beings born into this world. While we all have God's image (the *imago Dei*), we are also all born into sin. Because of sin, we are spiritually "dead" to God, according to Ephesians 2:1. We follow Satan and are deserving of eternal punishment and God's just wrath (v. 3). This is true of every human being who has ever lived.

Second, Ephesians 2 tells us that God, in his mercy and grace, has offered eternal salvation to sinful human beings through the redemption and forgiveness that have come through the death and resurrection of Jesus Christ (vv. 4–5). This is the only way by which sinful human beings can be saved—through the perfect sacrifice of the perfect Son of God. This is a sacrifice that is accepted only through faith (v. 8); Paul intentionally reminds us twice in this passage that we are saved by God's grace alone, not by our works (vv. 5, 8).

Third, Ephesians 2 reminds us that our salvation is part of God's eternal plan; we are his "workmanship" and we were created by him to do good works that he has long prepared for us (v. 10). So our salvation has a purpose to it. We are made by God, saved by God, and now live to serve God as he intended.

What are some implications of this great salvation that God offers to sinful human beings? What do we learn about the nature of man from this rich doctrine? First, we clearly see the eternal *value* that God has placed on human beings. They are sinful, yes, but God cares so much about their salvation that he is willing to send his only Son into the world to die for them. You are valuable in your Creator's eyes! Second, we learn here that human beings have an eternal *purpose* in God's plan. His salvation is not random; it is part of his plan for his people to walk in the way that he intends and to work for him to his great glory and praise.

God does not work in this saving way for any creatures in the world other than human beings. His saving work, through his Son, is made available to the human beings whom he has created. This salvation should point us to the value and purpose of every human being that we meet, and we should do our best to point them to the only Savior who can help them live out that purpose.

⬤ PRAY!

Talk to God with thankfulness for the rich salvation that he offers through Jesus Christ. Ask him to help you be realistic about your sin and your need for him, and pray that you would better understand his great purpose for you as his child. You are his workmanship—his masterpiece!

THE *END* OF MAN

We have learned much about the biblical perspective on human beings so far in this chapter. Hopefully you have gained a new perspective on our eternal value, our uniqueness, the *imago Dei* in us, and our capacity for relationships with the eternal Creator God who made us.

Our goal now is to think a bit more about the eternal end of human beings, according to God's word. What is the big picture of our existence here on earth? To what end has God created us? How does this make a difference right now in the way we live, as well as in the way that we think about our eternal futures?

READ!

Scan over Psalm 16—a beautiful prayer of David to his God—once more. As you read this psalm, consider what implications it has for your ultimate end as a follower of God through Jesus Christ. Think about David's source of true joy and his ultimate hope for eternal delight and pleasure.

As we consider man's eternal destiny, here are three basic truths that emerge from Scripture:

Created for God's glory. Based on the witness of the Bible and a careful examination of the character of God, we see that human beings have ultimately been created for the glory of the great God of the universe. We exist to bring him praise and honor. God creates for his own glory, and the universe itself speaks to his power and glory (see Ps. 19). God also saves sinners for his own glory; the glorious and gracious salvation that he offers through Jesus is all about the praise of his glory (see Eph. 1:6). The entire eternal experience of human beings who are saved through Jesus Christ will be one of giving glory and praise to the only true God and Savior. We are created primarily for the glory of God—both now, and in the eternal ages to come!

Our eternal destiny is the delight of living for God's glory without the stain of sin or the sting of death.

Eternal destinies. Scripture also shows clearly that human beings have eternal destinies—eternal life or eternal punishment. We are too uniquely made by God to simply die and cease to exist! Solomon talks about the "eternity" that God has placed into our hearts (see Eccles. 3:11). The reality of the *imago Dei* shows that God's image and likeness is reflected in every human being he has created (see your memory verses for this chapter). All of these truths point to the fact that humans are not simply animals; they are eternal creatures that have souls. We are made for eternity—either eternity with God in the praise of his name or eternity apart from God in punishment for rejecting his Son, Jesus Christ.

Enjoying God forever. Finally, as we consider the end of mankind, we see that the only good choice for eternal, image-bearing humans is to enjoy God through faith in Jesus and praise his name in an eternity spent with him. It is to embrace the attitude of King David, when he declares to God, "You are my Lord; I have no good apart from you" (Ps. 16:1). David goes on to speak of the "pleasures" that are at God's right hand forever (v. 11)—eternal pleasures that will be shared by all who truly love him and follow his Son. The right choice—the good end—for human beings, is to follow God, believe his word, repent of sin, trust Christ, and enjoy life in God's presence forever and ever. God has provided a way for this through the death and resurrection of his own Son!

The Westminster Shorter Catechism puts it this way:

Q1.   What is the chief end of man?
A.   To glorify God and enjoy him forever.

Is that your destiny? Is this the end for which you are living?

PRAY!

Spend just a minute thanking God for his role in the creation of human beings and asking him to help you pursue an eternal destiny with him through faith in Jesus Christ. Pray that God would help you fulfill your greatest purpose so that you really do seek to glorify him and enjoy him forever.

REVIEW

In this chapter, you have taken a careful look at the nature of human beings according to the Bible and have seen the amazing design of God for the people he has created. You have examined many different aspects of humans—their origin, their essence, their purpose, and their eternal end. Hopefully you now have a better understanding of why you are here and how you can fulfill your eternal purpose by following and loving the Lord Jesus Christ. Here are a few key points for you to remember:

Distinct and Unique

- Human beings are both distinct and unique from all the rest of God's creation.
- Unlike any other creature, God has given human beings rule and dominion over the world he created.
- Unlike any other part of creation, human beings are made with the capacity for eternal relationships with the Creator God.

The *Imago Dei*

- *Imago Dei* simply means "the image of God."
- God created human beings—only human beings—in his own image and likeness.
- This doctrine means that all human beings reflect God in some ways—and probably in many ways.

Complex Beings

- Humans beings are complex in that they are both physical and spiritual.
- The Bible teaches very clearly about the existence of the human soul—the eternal heart of human beings that has the capacity for loving God and worshiping him.
- Our physical aspect is not inherently evil; matter itself is not the problem, but sin is!

Jesus and Humanity

- Jesus's incarnation shows us that God values humanity and that there is hope for physical existence in the life to come.
- Jesus's resurrection reminds us that the new heaven and new earth will be a physical place where redeemed human beings will live and worship God.

Divine Attributes

- God has some incommunicable attributes, which cannot be transferred to human beings (such as his omnipresence, omnipotence, and omniscience).
- God also has communicable attributes, which human beings can reflect in some ways (love, patience, justice, etc.).

Salvation

- The need for salvation comes as a result of the "situation" of every human being on earth; we are all sinful and fallen, and therefore guilty before the holy God.
- God secures salvation for his people through the death and resurrection of his own Son; his salvation is totally an act of his grace.
- God's salvation comes with a purpose for human beings; he saves them for good works, which he prepared for them long ago (Eph. 2).

Purpose and End

- The ultimate purpose of human beings, according to the witness of the Bible, is to bring glory to God.
- David, in Psalm 16, points us to the enjoyment of God forever as the final end of God's people.

Remember!

Review your memory verses from the beginning of this chapter one final time, considering their implications for your understanding of yourself as a human being created in the image of the almighty God.

PRAY!

As you end this chapter in prayer now, think back on all you have learned about God's creation of human beings. Consider his eternal purpose for the people he has created and the way that he has provided for the salvation of all who will trust in his Son, Jesus Christ. Give him praise! Thank him for making you and for inviting you to be his child. Ask him to help you follow Jesus every day and to make your life about bringing glory to his name.

Chapter 5

THE DOCTRINE OF SIN

You probably already have a decent understanding of what sin is. But you probably have not studied this doctrine in detail—at least in a systematic and organized way. In this chapter, we will seek to learn and apply what the Bible has to teach us about sin—this infection that has spread into the entire world and demands a final solution.

So what is sin? It is, essentially, *any lack of conformity to the perfect will and character of God.* This is a very broad definition—probably much broader than the way that you often think about sin! When we hear the word *sin*, we often think of seriously wrong actions, such as violence, theft, or extreme lies. But sin is more basic and widespread than these actions. Sin is *any* deviation from God's perfect will and character. It is anything that is out of step with who God is. Notice, then, a few aspects of this definition of sin that relate to the way that we will study this doctrine in this chapter:

- Sin is the opposite of God. It is very important that we ground our definition of sin in its relationship to the perfect character of God. He is the Creator of the universe; his character is the standard for what is good, right, true, and honorable. Therefore, sin has to be—by definition—all that is opposed to the character and will of the perfectly good God of the universe.

- Sin comes in various categories. We noted above that sin is not only bad actions. Sin can be evil thoughts, wrong tendencies, cruel words, and even, according to the book of James, the failure to do something good that could have been done (4:17). Sin is *any* failure to be completely like God and obey his word.

- Sin is widespread. As we can see, then, by both our definition of sin and our experience in this world, sin is very widespread. It is like an infection that has gone everywhere. From the earliest days following the fall of Adam and Eve (which we will learn about just below), sin has spread throughout God's world and made its ugly way into every part of creation.

As we study the doctrine of sin in the coming pages, we will examine its *origin* (how it entered the world), its *effects* (what it means for human beings and for this world, and how God has dealt—and is dealing—with it), and its *ultimate defeat* (how God will finally do away with the sin that has infected his creation). Hopefully, by the end of this chapter, you will understand sin more clearly, but also appreciate the great grace and salvation of our God with more joy as well.

Remember!

Your suggested memory verses for this chapter come from the prophet Isaiah, who describes human sin very clearly, but also looks forward to the amazing salvation that God would offer his people through the "suffering servant"—Jesus Christ. Read these verses carefully and thoughtfully, thinking about all that they teach about sin and the sacrifice that sin demands.

> But he was pierced for our transgressions;
>> he was crushed for our iniquities;
> upon him was the chastisement that brought us peace,
>> and with his wounds we are healed.
> All we like sheep have gone astray;
>> we have turned—every one—to his own way;
> and the LORD has laid on him
>> the iniquity of us all. (Isa. 53:5–6)

⬆ PRAY!

Spend a few moments thinking quietly about the effects of sin that you see in the world around you. Think about all the relationships and situations that are infected by sin. Then think about the effects of sin in your own life and heart. Consider the ways that you struggle to conform to the image of God, who is holy, pure, righteous, loving, and good. Now pray to God along these lines as you begin this chapter:

- Ask him to help you understand sin more clearly for what it really is.
- Pray that he would help you repent of sin fully and turn to Jesus as Savior.
- Ask him to help you have hope of his great salvation and his final victory over the sin that has infected and damaged his creation.

THE *ORIGIN* OF SIN

We began by defining sin as any lack of conformity to the perfect will and character of God. This definition is grounded in the character of God; it is a broad definition because God is the ultimate source, foundation, and basis for all that is good and true. Sin is anything, then, that is opposed to God. Hopefully this definition helps you understand the widespread nature of sin in the world today.

Now we are going to go back to the very beginning to examine the fall of mankind—the moment when sin first entered the world God had created. You are going to read about the story of Adam and Eve, and their decision to disobey God and rebel against his word. This is a real story, and the actions of the man and the woman had an immediate effect on the life of every human being who has ever lived—or will live—on this earth.

READ!

Take a few minutes to read Genesis 3—the entire chapter. This is the account of the fall of Adam and Eve, and the entry of sin into the world. You are probably very familiar with this passage, but try to read it with fresh eyes. Pay attention to the steps that the man and the woman take toward sin. See how they actively choose to reject God's word and his rule over them. Look at God's response and the effect that it has on the world.

As we consider Genesis 3, the basic question about sin that we are trying to answer is, "Where did sin come from?" It is important to start here so that we understand the origin of sin and its first roots in the world in which we live.

Sin was *not* always present in the world. As we saw in the previous chapter, as God created things, he looked around and described them as "good" (Gen. 1:4, 10, 12, 18, 21, 25). But when humans were added to creation, God labeled it all "very good" (v. 31). This tells us that in the beginning, there was no sin. Because of that, Adam and Eve lived in perfect communion with God and with the world he had created. They listened to his word and enjoyed a sweet relationship with him.

In the passage you just read, though, you saw the very active and intentional choice that Adam and Eve made. God had given them a very clear command: they were not to eat of just one tree in the garden of Eden. But the man and woman actively and intentionally disobeyed that command. This, of course, was sin—by any definition! Adam and Eve did not allow God to rule over them. In fact, they tried to essentially *be* God by making their own decisions and acting as their own rulers. This was pride, which is at the root of every sin that we commit. Ultimately, all sin is saying to God, "I want to be god, and not you!"

But think for a moment about the sinful steps that led Adam and Eve to the actual eating of the fruit:

1. Eve listened to the lies of Satan (the serpent), who began by questioning God's word (Gen. 3:1).
2. Eve responded to Satan by adding to God's word, saying that she and Adam were not allowed to even "touch" the tree (v. 3). God had never said that.
3. Adam was "with" Eve the whole time, but he never defended God's word or called her to obey (v. 6).

So you can see that there were sinful steps along the way that resulted in the sin of Adam and Eve. Ultimately, they disobeyed and ate the fruit of the tree that God had forbidden them to eat.

The immediate effects of sin are evident in this passage. Adam and Eve felt shame because they were naked; they felt the urge to cover themselves because they sensed their sin and their separation from the holy God. God cursed the ground because of them, and also told Eve that bearing children would be very painful. Sin affected Adam and Eve, but it also immediately affected the entire world that God had made!

So this was the beginning of sin; this was how this disease entered our world. From that point, there has never been a day when sin has not been present in human lives, hearts, and experience. From this first choice of Adam and Eve to rebel against God's word and disobey his commands, sin has always had a presence in this world. While many people seek to label sin with other words (mistakes, weaknesses, bad choices), the Bible is very clear that every one of us is a sinner—and has sinned against our holy and perfect Creator. That is the fundamental problem with each one of us.

Next we will explore a bit more about the effects of sin, which we feel even in our world today. Sin, as we will see, always brings *death*; the first sin resulted in our world falling under God's curse. Thankfully, it is a curse that can be broken through the saving work of God.

▲ PRAY!

Ask God to help you see yourself in the sinful actions of Adam and Eve. We have all done what they did; we have rejected God's rule in our lives through our sinful actions and choices! Sin entered the world on that day in the garden of Eden, and it plagues our world today. Confess your sins to God and be honest with him about your need for forgiveness, mercy, and grace.

THE *EFFECTS* OF SIN

Now that we have looked into the origins of sin, we are going to dig more deeply into its real effects. As you saw at the end of the passage from Genesis 3, God cursed the ground because of Adam and Eve's sin, and told them of the difficult lives that now lay ahead of them. The biggest and saddest consequence of sin, as we will see, is *death*.

If Adam and Eve had not sinned, they would have continued living forever in perfect happiness and relationship with God in the garden of Eden. If there had been no sin, there could have been eternal life in this state! But with sin came death. This death did not come immediately (Adam lived more than nine hundred years), but eventually, Adam and Eve both died. Their sin had brought the reality of death into human existence.

READ!

Read Romans 5:12–21. Read it carefully and thoughtfully, considering the contrast that the apostle Paul is making between the death that comes through sin and the life that comes through Jesus Christ.

The passage from Romans 5 that you read presents this truth about death. Think back to the phrases that Paul uses to describe the death that is connected to human sin:

- "Sin came into the world through one man, and death through sin" (v. 12).
- "Death spread to all men because all sinned" (v. 12).
- "Many died through one man's trespass" (v. 15).
- "Because of one man's trespass, death reigned through that one man" (v. 17).
- "One trespass led to condemnation for all men" (v. 18).
- "By the one man's disobedience the many were made sinners" (v. 19).

Do you see what Paul is saying here? He is showing us that, through Adam, sin and death entered the world in a powerful and effective way. Everyone is born into a world full of sin. They all have sinful natures (we will talk more about this soon). Human sin leads to death because death "reigns" in sin.

Paul puts this in a slightly different way just one chapter later in the book of Romans when he says that "the wages of sin is death" (6:23). In other words, death is the right "payment" for sin—the wages that all sinners deserve to be paid. Why is this?

Do you remember our definition of sin from the beginning of the chapter? We said that sin is any lack of conformity to the perfect will and character of God. God, in his very being, is life. He is eternal life—abundant, overflowing life! To rebel against him and turn to sin, then, is to oppose God and everything about him: it is actually to reject life and choose death! Sin *must* lead to death because it is rejection of God and opposition to God, who is the only true giver of life.

Ultimately, the Bible teaches that while sin caused mortal death (the death of our physical bodies) to enter the world, it also leads to spiritual death—eternal punishment in hell, away from God's love, joy, and pleasure. God is just, and hell is the just punishment for sinners who reject him. This is how awful human sin against the holy God really is.

Thankfully, the passage you read from Romans reminds us that while sin does lead to death—and even eternal death—there is good news through Jesus Christ. Adam brought death into this world through his sin. Jesus brings life into this world through his death and resurrection. We will talk much more about this in pages to come.

▲ PRAY!

Ask God to help you think seriously and realistically about the sin in your heart and life. Pray that he would remind you how deathly and dangerous sin is and how seriously you must seek to fight it and put it away. Remember to thank him, though, that he sent his only Son to pay the final penalty for sin—through death on a cross—and has freed you to live for him with joy and eternal life.

Guilt and Wrath

In addition to God's curse and physical and eternal death, sin creates guilt before God and sparks God's wrath. These are weighty concepts to consider, and they are not easy to discuss. Yet this is what the Bible teaches, and we must take seriously all that Scripture tells us about the attitudes and actions of the holy and righteous God toward the sin that is rebellion against his perfect character and word.

◆ READ!

Take a moment to read Romans 1:18–32. This is a very sad passage; in it, Paul lays out the vast picture of human sin. As you read, think about the very real guilt of human beings, who sin against God in word, thought, and deed. Then consider God's wrath, which Paul says is "revealed from heaven" (v. 18) against every sin in this world.

Guilt and wrath. Most people do not like to talk about these two ideas. Many people in the world today cannot stomach the fact that human beings could actually be held guilty before the holy God and condemned to eternal punishment because of their sin. Other people struggle with the idea of the wrath of God. They do not like to talk about a God who is so angry against sin that he is determined to punish it.

It is true that the Bible paints a picture of a God who is merciful, gracious, slow to anger, and abounding in steadfast love (Ex 34:6). The God of the Bible came in human flesh to lay down his life for the sins of his people! But the God of the Bible is also holy. He hates sin and holds sinners guilty. He is a God who will pour out his wrath against sin fully, violently, and completely.

Why is this? Why does God hold sinners guilty and pour out his wrath against sin? It comes back to our definition of what sin is. Sin is the exact opposite of God's perfect and holy character. It is anything that does not conform to—reflect—his perfect love, righteousness, truth, and justice. Therefore, God's wrath against sin and his punishment of sinners is totally justified; it is right because it is completely aligned with his character. If God were *not* to punish sin, he would cease to be God!

So we must say, as we look at the witness of Scripture, that sin really does create guilt before God. Human beings—all of them—stand completely guilty in the presence of the holy God because of their sin. Paul says, in the passage you read just above, that even the wonder of creation itself makes all men "without excuse" for rejecting God, because his power and glory are revealed in this world (Rom. 1:20). Every human being, even from birth (we will talk about this soon), is guilty before God because of sin. We all have real guilt and deserve real death and punishment because we have not perfectly conformed to the character of our holy Creator God.

Paul makes another frightening statement in the passage that you just read. He says that God's wrath is poured out from heaven against "all ungodliness" and sin of human beings (Rom. 1:18). Did you look down the list of sins that Paul mentions in verses 28–32 of this passage? Murder makes this list, but also lying, disobedience to parents, boastfulness, and foolishness. In other words, this list includes sins that are true of all of us! What does this mean? It means that all of us—according to the Bible—are under God's wrath because of our sin. His righteous anger burns against sin, and we need to find a way to escape it.

This is not a happy thought, is it? You and I both stand guilty before God because of sin, and we are, along with every other human being in the world, under his wrath. But even if this isn't a happy thought, it is good for us to understand this truth, because we cannot see the beauty of God's solution to this problem until we really grasp the depth of the problem itself. Sin is the disease that will kill us and bring God's wrath down on us if it is not killed first.

⬤ PRAY!

Spend some time right now talking to God honestly about your sin. Confess sinful thoughts, attitudes, and actions. Admit to him that, apart from Jesus Christ, you would be completely guilty before him and would deserve only his wrath. Then spend a few minutes simply thanking him for the grace that is found in Jesus Christ. Thank him that his own Son bore his wrath, which should have been justly poured out on you because of your sin.

Sinful Natures

Now we need to go a bit deeper into a discussion of the nature of sin and the way it affects every human being in this world. We saw from Romans that death entered the world through Adam's sin, but we have not yet really discussed how this sin in the world affects us as individuals. How does sin touch us? What is our role in sin? Is it possible to live a sinless life? These are some of the questions we will seek to answer now.

READ!

Read just a few verses from a familiar psalm—Psalm 51:1–5. Read these verses slowly and thoughtfully, paying special attention to what David says in verse 5. How do David's words here relate to an understanding of the sinful nature with which human beings are born? Consider these verses deeply.

Do you remember the first time you sinned? Think back to something bad that you did when you were very young. Perhaps you told a lie or stole something that did not belong to you. Maybe you hurt your brother or sister, or disobeyed your parents in an obvious way. Did anyone have to teach you to do those things? Did someone sit you down and say, "Today I am going to teach you how to tell a lie"? Of course not. We all sin very *naturally*.

This simple example from real life points to a biblical truth that we are examining now as part of our study of the doctrine of sin. Here is that truth: because of the sin of Adam and Eve, all human beings born into this world after them have *sinful natures*. In other words, every human being born into this world is prone to sin; people sin naturally because such behavior is in accord with who they actually are.

In the story of the Bible, it does not take long to see this reality demonstrated; the story of Cain and Abel shows us the world's first murder, as Adam and Eve's son Cain killed his brother out of hatred and envy (Gen. 4:1–16). Sin spread very quickly in this fallen world.

David, too, points to this truth, as you saw in Psalm 51. He says that he was "brought forth in iniquity" and that his mother conceived him "in sin." David takes an honest look at his birth and knows that he came into the world with a sinful nature, and therefore guilty before God.

So having a sinful nature simply means that everyone in the world is born with a natural bent toward sin. This is something that none of us can avoid; it is the way we are because of the fall. Is it possible for a human being to somehow live an entire life without sinning—to resist his or her sinful nature and perfectly obey God? Sadly, it is not. Even if a human being resists the big and obvious sins, the reality of the sinful nature means that this person would still fall far short of God's perfect glory, goodness, and holiness— in actions, thoughts, and words. Because of the sinful nature, it is impossible for any of us—by our own strength—to please God and earn his favor.

This reality of the sinful nature is what makes the cross of Jesus Christ so necessary—and so beautiful. Jesus paid for the sins of God's people; he died for those who could never be saved were it not for his grace. Also, by faith in him, he gives the gift of God's Holy Spirit to dwell inside believers (we will learn more about this in future chapters). That is the only way that a sinful nature can be overcome; God must conquer it by his strength and presence!

▲ PRAY!

Spend a minute in prayer, thinking about ways that your sinful nature is evident in your life and thanking God for offering you forgiveness through his Son, Jesus Christ. Thank him that, in Christ, you can actually receive a new nature; you can have the Holy Spirit dwelling in you and helping you say "no" to sin.

Total Depravity

We've seen that sin has plagued this world since the days of Adam and Eve. It has infected every inch of creation and has brought the curse of death into what was once a completely good place. Because of it, all human beings are born with sinful natures; we are prone to sin and actually do sin. It is impossible for any human being to live a life that is completely pleasing to God and deserving of his salvation.

But there is more to say about how sin affects the human condition. We are going to examine a doctrine called "total depravity," which relates to the extent of sin's effects in people. By the end of this discussion, you will hopefully have a more realistic picture of your own sin, but also of the amazing grace and salvation that God offers to sinners through Jesus Christ.

READ!

Read Genesis 6:5–6. These two short verses show God looking down on the earth during the days of Noah and observing the sad extent of sin in every part of the world he had created. Think deeply about this description of human sin and get ready to think more about these verses in the next section.

Most people in the world today would probably say that human beings are "basically good." They would look at societies, cultures, and people doing nice things for each other, and try to make the point that, in general, humans are good. The problem with this opinion is that the standard for what is good is almost always defined in human terms rather than in God's terms.

The doctrine that you are learning about now tells us that human beings are *not* basically good; in fact, they are quite the opposite. We find our way to this doctrine by starting with God—his holiness, perfection, goodness, and righteousness—rather than with a human opinion or idea about what is good. When we do this, we see that, in God's eyes, we are all "totally depraved."

Definition. What do we mean when we use the term "total depravity" to describe the human condition? We mean that human beings are completely sinful and fallen in every way. *Depravity* refers to fallenness, sin, and ungodliness. *Total depravity*, then, implies that we are completely fallen and therefore totally separated from God.

Clarification. It is important to clarify what total depravity does *not* mean. When we say that we are totally depraved, we do not mean that we are all as bad as we could possibly be. Not everyone in the world is a murderer, and you have probably not actually done all the evil things that you have been tempted to do. This reality—that the world, including human beings, is not as bad as it could be—is a sign of God's grace. He gives grace so that sin does not cause even more damage than it already does to the world he has made.

What we mean by total depravity is that every part of us—our hearts, minds, and actions—is affected by sin. Sin has touched and infected every part of who we are as human beings. By using this term, we are speaking to the "total" and complete effects of sin in our lives.

Implications. The doctrine of total depravity has significant implications. We have no hope of earning our way into favor with God and thereby saving ourselves because we are infected by sin in every way, and we know that the holy God cannot dwell in the presence of sin. Because of our sin, any good works we might try to do to please God are really no good at all. Think, then, about how great the salvation that is in Jesus Christ must be. Think about how much sin he had to pay for through his death on the cross. We have only one hope as totally depraved and fallen sinners: we must trust the finished saving work of Jesus Christ, who died in our place to save us from our sins.

PRAY!

You will not fully understand the wonder and grace of your salvation in Christ unless you first understand the depths of sin and guilt that plague your heart and life apart from him. Ask God to help you better understand his perfect holiness and your sin and total depravity. Then ask him to help you see more clearly the wonder of the salvation and forgiveness that he has offered to sinners through the death of his only Son, Jesus.

Propitiation

Having examined our sinful nature and the total depravity that plagues every human being, we now will move toward a fuller examination of what happened on the cross, where Jesus died for the sins of God's people. First we will seek to define the concept of "propitiation" (which we briefly considered when we looked at God's justice in chap. 3) and grasp all that it means for our understanding of the weight and seriousness of human sin against an eternal and infinitely holy God.

📖 READ!

Take a minute to read just one verse: 1 John 4:10. Read it several times, both silently and out loud. Think about the word propitiation, *which is used in this verse. Consider how John links this word to God's love for us, not our love for him! Talk with one of your parents or teachers about what this word means. It is a word that Paul also uses (Rom. 3:25), as we saw in chapter 3.*

Let's remind ourselves of the steps that, according to the Bible, lead us to a right understanding of the concept of propitiation. Here is what we have learned from Scripture so far:

1. God is holy. He is infinitely perfect, righteous, loving, and just in every way. He is "other" than human beings and completely upright and true in all he does. In fact, God himself is the standard for what is good and right; we define sin as what is opposite or opposed to all that God is.
2. Humans are sinful. This is what this entire chapter has been about. We are born into a world that is plagued by sin, and we have sinful natures that make it impossible for us to live without sin.
3. Sin brings curse and death. The natural result of sin, as we have seen from Scripture, is curse and death. Sin cannot just disappear; it leads to death because it is opposed to the one God, who gives life.

4. God must punish sin. If God did not punish sin rightly, he would cease to be God. He is completely just and righteous, so he must punish what is evil and bring judgment on all that truly requires it.

5. Total depravity means that humans can never save themselves. As we learned earlier, human beings are infected by sin in every way. Our sin is eternal and unbearable, because we have sinned against an eternal and infinitely holy God. We are therefore doomed to eternal punishment.

Our situation is bleak and hopeless. But the Bible shows us how Jesus Christ entered the scene. How did his work on the cross provide an answer to human sin and rebellion? Here are two reasons that help us understand the nature of sin more clearly:

- Jesus is the perfect sacrifice. No human being—because of sin and total depravity—could ever fully bear the weight of God's wrath and punishment against sin. This point is extremely important for understanding our need for the work of Christ on the cross. Because sin against an eternal and infinitely holy God is an eternal and infinite offense, sinful human beings would have to endure the punishment for their sin for all eternity. There is only one who could actually bear this full, eternal, infinite punishment for sin: God himself. This is why Jesus Christ is the only perfect sacrifice for sin. He is truly human, identifying himself with God's people. But he is also fully God—able to bear the eternal and infinite punishment for sin all at once!

- Jesus is the propitiation for sin. This is the amazing reality of what happened at the cross. The word *propitiation* actually refers to the removal of wrath. Jesus became, through his death on the cross for sin, the propitiation for us; he took God's full wrath against sin in the place of sinners who deserve to bear God's wrath for all eternity. But because Jesus is God's Son, he was able to bear that wrath all at once; his death was enough to pay the complete price for sin. His resurrection proved this; because Jesus did not stay dead, we know that he fully "drained" the cup of God's wrath against the sins of his people. Jesus is truly the propitiation for sins!

As we close this discussion, think about what *propitiation* means for our understanding of sin. How awful must sin be if God's own Son had to die in order to rid God's people of its curse and punishment? How much grace has God given to us by sending his own Son to pay the full penalty for sin and bear all of God's wrath!

PRAY!

Ask God to remind you of the propitiation that happened at the cross. Jesus's death was not just symbolic or some kind of an example; it really was the act of God pouring out his wrath against sin on his own Son, who was the only perfect one who could actually pay the full price for sin. Think silently about the cross for a few minutes. Then talk to God humbly about all that Jesus means to you.

Christians and Sin

As we conclude our study of the effects of sin, we will consider the interaction and attitude that a Christian should have with and toward sin. According to the Bible, Christians (those who have repented of sin and trusted Jesus Christ as Savior and Lord) were once dead in their sins and enslaved to death. But in Christ, they are no longer forced to interact with sin in that way. The reality of changed lives points to the power of God's salvation through Jesus!

READ!

Read Romans 6:1–14—a passionate part of Paul's letter to the Romans. Read this passage carefully, thinking deeply about Paul's reaction to people who were suggesting that the gospel is an excuse for Christians to sin since it is a message about God's overwhelming grace through Christ. Look at how passionately Paul responds to this suggestion!

The good news of the gospel is that followers of Jesus can actually change—in their relationship to and with sin in their lives. Here are just a few things about sin that change for a person who begins following Jesus:

The penalty for sin is paid. Earlier, you learned about propitiation— the truth that Jesus Christ really drained the cup of the wrath of God, which was poured out against sin. Christians have confidence that Jesus really has paid the full penalty for their sin, so they will face no punishment. This simple fact should be a great motivation for forgiven sinners to live lives of obedience to their gracious Savior.

The power of sin is broken. As Paul points out in Romans 6 (the passage that you read just above), the good news for Christians is not just that the penalty for sin has been paid, but also that the power of sin in their lives is gone. Apart from Christ, every person in the world is not just a sinner, but a slave to sin. Unbelievers have no choice but to sin; they are enslaved to it. But the Holy Spirit actually dwells within Christians and gives them power to say no to sin. In Christ, by the power of the Spirit, Christians can come out from under the controlling power of sin in their lives and begin to live in obedience to God and his word. This is why Paul can say, "For sin will have no dominion over you, since you are not under law but under grace" (Rom. 6:14).

The pleasure of sin disappears. Not only is the power of sin broken in Christians' lives, but the pleasure of sin begins to disappear as well. Our desires for sin are replaced with new desires—the desires of the God who lives within us by his Holy Spirit. For followers of Christ, sin (whether of thought, word, or deed) begins to lose its "taste." It is less appealing and less satisfying.

All of these changes in the lives of Christians point to the amazing grace of Jesus Christ. His grace saves us and also helps us live for God as those freed from slavery to sin.

⬤ PRAY!

Thank God that if you have put your faith in Jesus Christ as Lord and Savior, his Spirit really does dwell inside of you. Ask the Spirit to help you fight sin with all of your strength, trusting that his presence with you really can give you the strength to say no to sin. Pray that your desire to fight sin would come from deep thankfulness for what Jesus did on the cross for you.

THE *ULTIMATE DEFEAT* OF SIN

In this chapter, you have gained a deep and expansive view of the reality of human sin and rebellion against God. Is it deeper than you thought? Is your sinfulness worse than you had imagined? Is your guilt bigger than you had hoped?

As we come to the end of this chapter, we are going to look forward to the very end of the Bible story (and the story of the world) to see what will ultimately become of sin—this infection that plagues our world and our lives and hearts. How will God finally deal with this terrible disease? What is the final hope for Christians who still struggle to fight sin in their lives?

📖 READ!

Take a few minutes to read Revelation 21—the entire chapter. Focus especially on verses 5–8 and 22–27 with regard to the end of sin in the great eternal city of God. Think deeply about this amazing picture of all that is to come. Consider all that is ahead for God's people, when sin and evil have finally been destroyed by Jesus.

Even though the power of sin has been broken, many Christians still struggle with sinful thoughts and actions. Do you? Also, even though followers of Jesus are called to become more and more holy (more "set apart" for God's work), none of them will reach perfection during this life. So what is the final hope for Christians who still struggle with sin? Also, what is the final hope for people who are devastated and hurt by those who have sinned against them in terrible ways? Here are three promises from God's word about the final end of sin:

Sin will be destroyed. The first big promise that we see—especially from the passage you just read—is that the devastation of sin will be completely absent from the new heaven and new earth, the eternal home for God and his people. There will be no place in heaven for those who have given their lives to intentional and rebellious sin; the apostle John even says that "nothing unclean" will be able to enter God's eternal place at all (Rev. 21:27). This is a picture that reminds us that sin will finally be destroyed. There will come a day when the effects of sin will no longer plague our lives. As God's people, we will finally be free from sin. We will not be even tempted to sin anymore, because we will be perfected and will live in the perfect presence of the good God forever.

Satan will be defeated. Revelation 20 makes clear that Satan, the great enemy of God's people, also will be finally defeated by the Lord Jesus Christ. Do you remember the very beginning of this chapter, when we learned about the entry of sin into this world? The promise that came to Adam and Eve, along with God's judgment, was that the "offspring" of Eve would one day crush the head of the serpent—Satan (Gen. 3:15). Jesus came to destroy Satan, sin, and death on the cross. Revelation 20 reminds us that this victory will be finalized one day. Satan will be destroyed; God's enemy, and the enemy of his people, will be no more, and God's people will live joyfully without the presence of sin for all eternity to come.

We will be made perfect. Finally, as we mentioned in passing above, God's people will finally be made perfect. Not only will the effects of sin be nonexistent in God's perfect place, but we will be freed from sin. The Bible talks about this as our being "glorified"—made perfect and set free from sin. This has not happened yet! While followers of Jesus are called to obedience and holiness, we will never reach perfection and glorification in this life. But we have this hope of a future day when God will complete his saving work in our lives and hearts. We will be perfect—set apart to worship and dwell with our God forever and ever.

So this is the picture that the Bible presents to us of the end of sin. God will finally wipe out this terrible infection that plagues our existence. There is great hope for God's people!

PRAY!

In this section of the chapter, you have learned about the final end of sin, as presented by the Bible. As you consider this, let this future vision of the new heaven and new earth—the place where there will be no more sin—be a source of hope to you each day. Be reminded of the good things that God has for all who love him, and set your hope on heaven as you say no to sin today. Right now, ask God to help you and strengthen you to do this.

REVIEW

In this chapter, we took another big step forward in our study of systematic theology as we tackled the doctrine of sin from a biblical perspective. Hopefully, as you read this chapter, you came to a deeper understanding of the seriousness and weight of human sin against the holy God. By God's grace, that should lead you toward more thankfulness and praise when you see how great Jesus's sacrifice on the cross really is.

Now we'll close the chapter by reviewing the important concepts and lessons that you have learned about sin. Here are a few key points for you to remember:

Definition of Sin

- We defined sin as any lack of conformity to the perfect will and character of God.
- It is important to define sin in relation to God because he is the perfect source of goodness, love, and truth.
- With this definition, we begin to understand that sin is very broad and very widespread (bigger than we might have thought).

Adam and Eve

- In the beginning, there was no sin in the world, and Adam and Eve lived in a perfect relationship with their Creator.
- Through Adam and Eve's disobedience, sin entered the world and immediately began to have devastating effects on creation.

Curse and Death

- After the sin of Adam and Eve, God cursed the earth because of it, and life became very difficult for human beings in a cursed and fallen creation.
- Sin necessarily brings death; Adam and Eve grew old and died (this would not have happened if they had not sinned).
- Sin brings death because it is fundamentally opposed to God, who is the giver and source of all life. This death is physical (all human beings die) and also spiritual (all sinners are condemned to eternal punishment if they do not repent and place their faith in Jesus).

Sinful Natures

- Because of sin in the world, every human being is born with a sinful nature.
- This sinful nature means that we are all prone to sin; we have a natural bent toward sin that we cannot overcome by our own strength.
- Because of our sinful natures, it is impossible for any human being to live a life that is free from sin or totally pleasing to God.

Total Depravity

- The concept of "total depravity" means that we are completely fallen—that every part of our lives (and our world) is tainted and infected by sin.
- Total depravity does not mean that we are all as bad as we possibly could be, but that sin has touched every part of our existence.
- Total depravity points to the fact that we stand completely guilty before the holy God and deserve only judgment from him.

Propitiation

- "Propitiation" refers specifically to the removal of wrath against sin.
- Jesus was the propitiation for our sins; he literally bore God's wrath against sin when it was poured out on him at the cross.

Christians and Sin

- The penalty of sin, for Christians, was truly paid by Jesus on the cross.
- In Christ, the power of sin is gone from the lives of believers; they are no longer slaves to sin, but are ruled by God's Holy Spirit.
- Christians begin to have new pleasures; their desires begin to conform to the desires of God, and they cease loving sin like they used to.

The End of Sin

- Revelation 21 gives us a picture of the final end of sin, when God will establish a new and perfect life in the new heaven and new earth.
- The defeat of sin and Satan was promised by God in Genesis 3—right after the fall of Adam and Eve.

> **Remember!**
>
> Look back at your memory verses for this chapter once more. Try to commit them to memory as you consider all you've learned about the doctrine of sin.

▲ PRAY!

As you end this chapter with prayer, ask God to help you see more clearly both the depth of your sin and the amazing grace and forgiveness that he has shown you through the work of his Son, Jesus Christ. Pray that this understanding of human sin would help you love him more—and rejoice more in the salvation that he has graciously offered to sinners who need it so desperately.

Chapter 6

THE DOCTRINE OF JESUS CHRIST

If you have never studied theology in this way before—according to systematized themes and categories—hopefully you are seeing the value of this method. This is not the only way to study biblical truth, but it is one way that helps us tie together all that the Bible teaches about particular subjects.

In this chapter, we are going to focus on the study of Jesus—Christology. Of course, we have talked about Jesus in every chapter of this book so far; he is absolutely essential to every topic and category of study in systematic theology! Still, it is necessary (and practiced by most theologians) to devote an entire theological category to Christology. Precisely because Jesus is so central to everything else we study in systematic theology, we need to be clear on who he is, what he has accomplished, and all he means to God's people and God's creation.

Even many scholars and historians who do not accept that Jesus is the Son of God and the Savior of the world still acknowledge him as one of the most influential people in history—if not *the* most influential. We mark our dating of the world on the basis of his life. The book about him—the Bible—is the most influential and widely read book of all time. Millions of people follow him and call him Lord. Faith in him has shaped many countries and world superpowers throughout history. As Christians, we believe that Jesus is the very Son of God—the eternally existent second person of the Trinity, and the Savior and Judge of all human beings. This chapter will be all about *him*.

It is important for us to begin by setting biblical Christianity apart from every other world religion in one important respect: Christianity rises and falls on the existence, death, and resurrection of Jesus Christ. In other words, it is all about a person—Jesus. Islam could exist without the prophet Muhammad; Hinduism could exist without its founder; Buddhism, as a system, could technically exist without the Buddha. Christianity, though, could not exist without Jesus; he is the very center and substance of Christian belief.

To put this in a slightly different way, if the bones of Jesus were somehow discovered, all of Christianity would be proved false, worthless, and a terrible lie. Everything for Christians hinges on the reality of Jesus Christ as a person, his death on the cross for sin, and his real, bodily resurrection from the dead. No other world religion is so tied to the existence and work of a real human (and divine!) person. Our religion is about a person; it is founded on Jesus.

In this chapter, then, you are going to seek to answer some very key questions about who Jesus is, how he came into this world, what he came to do, how he accomplished it, what he is doing now, and what he will finally do in accordance with God's great plan of salvation. Our goal is to let Scripture guide us to a clear summary of Jesus—his identity, his saving work, his present reign, and his final judgment of the world. We will then apply these great truths to our lives by considering how we ought to respond to Jesus. By the end of this chapter, you will hopefully have a much clearer picture of the Jesus the Bible presents to us: the eternally existent Son of God, who is the Savior of sinners and the King and Judge of all creation.

Remember!

Your suggested memory verses for this chapter are Colossians 1:15–20—a longer chunk than in earlier chapters. Do not worry; you will be able to memorize these verses, and they will become a great tool to have in your mind as you think about the identity of Jesus. As you read these verses, think deeply about all that they teach us about who Jesus is. Consider his identity and the saving work that he accomplished for God's people. Read them slowly several times.

He is the image of the invisible God, the firstborn of all creation. For by him all things were created, in heaven and on earth, visible and invisible, whether thrones or dominions or rulers or authorities—all things were created through him and for him. And he is before all things, and in him all things hold together. And he is the head of the body, the church. He is the beginning, the firstborn from the dead, that in everything he might be preeminent. For in him all the fullness of God was pleased to dwell, and through him to reconcile to himself all things, whether on earth or in heaven, making peace by the blood of his cross. (Col. 1:15–20)

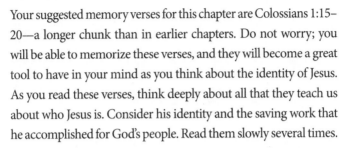

PRAY!

Pray to God that he would give you greater understanding of his Son—Jesus Christ. Ask him to remind you that your faith is built on Jesus and to make you excited and motivated to learn about your amazing Savior and Lord.

JESUS'S *IDENTITY*

We saw above that, like no other world religion, Christianity rises or falls with the person and work of its founder, Jesus Christ. But who is he really?

Eternal Existence

You are going to start your exploration of the doctrine of Christ at the beginning—which is really no beginning at all. You are going to consider what the Bible teaches about the eternal existence of Jesus Christ as the second person of the Trinity. You will be reminded that Jesus Christ has always existed, that he is fully God, and that he was active in the creation of this world. You are going to seek to see this glorious Christ as he truly is—in all his splendor, glory, and power!

📖 READ!

Take a minute to read John 1:1–18, one of the best passages in Scripture for summarizing Jesus's identity, his eternal existence, and his role in creation. Read this passage carefully and consider all the truths that it teaches us about this God who took on human flesh.

It is important for us to start our discussion about Christology with a reminder of who Jesus has always been—from before the beginning of time. If we do not start here, we can be in danger of not totally understanding the full wonder and power of Jesus's incarnation (becoming human), his death on the cross for sins, and his resurrection from the dead. Here are three important biblical truths that we need to grasp about Jesus:

Jesus has existed eternally. Since before time began, throughout eternity past (a concept that we cannot fully grasp with our human minds), he has existed as the second person of the Trinity, which we learned about in chapter 3. This is a term that we use to describe the God of the Bible, who presents himself to us as one God in three persons: God the Father, God the Son, and God the Holy Spirit. John 1 makes it clear that Jesus (the "Word") was in the beginning with God and "was" God (vv. 1–2). There has never been a time when Jesus has not existed, and he has reigned forever as the second person of the glorious Trinity.

Jesus was active in the creation of this world. John (and Paul, in Colossians) also makes it clear that Jesus had a part in the creation of all things. While we do not know exactly what role each person of the Trinity played in creation, we know that the triune God created, and it is therefore completely true to say, "Jesus created this world." So the very Jesus who died on the cross is the Creator of this world; all things were made by him and for him (Col. 1:16)!

Even though Jesus is fully God, he took on human flesh at a point in history. Finally, it is important to remember that Jesus Christ has not always had a human body. He has existed eternally as the second person of the Trinity, but there was a point in the history of the world (about two thousand years ago) when this divine person took on human flesh and became a man. This was a change; it was the first time that Jesus had taken on a body. Even after he returned to heaven, he kept this body, and will keep it for all eternity. He reigns now in his resurrected, glorified, and perfect body. He is God in human flesh—a concept that we will discuss in much more detail in the pages to come.

So our discussion of Christology is focused on the eternally existent second person of the Trinity—the very God who made this world. This is the Jesus that we are learning about.

▲ PRAY!

Pray to God the Father, asking him to continue to give you a right view of his glorious Son, Jesus, so that you will worship him in the right way. God has exalted his Son; he wants you to worship him and praise him as he truly is!

True Humanity

In addition to Jesus's eternal existence, the Bible clearly reveals another very important aspect about him: the amazing and profound reality that the Son of God actually became human. The implications of this mysterious truth are huge—they mean everything for the salvation of sinful human beings.

READ!

Read Hebrews 2:14–18 as you prepare to consider the humanity of Jesus Christ. Think deeply about this description of the way that Jesus was "made like" us in every way (v. 17); he became fully human! Jesus was exposed to "real life" on earth, with all of the struggles and temptations that human beings face. Therefore, he really knows and understands what you are going through today.

When we talk about the humanity of Jesus, we are talking about the doctrine of the incarnation. This word refers to God actually taking on flesh. The Bible teaches this doctrine very clearly. It is simple yet mysterious, and we need to do our best to understand it. Here are some important implications of this truth:

Jesus was (and is) fully human. Jesus was not a kind of "God ghost," who only appeared to be human, but was really not. He did not only take the appearance of a man. Jesus really *became* human; John makes that absolutely clear to us as he begins his Gospel, and the rest of the Gospel writers and the New Testament apostles make it clear as well. Jesus was born to Mary—a real human woman who was a sinner and needed God's salvation just like the rest of us. He grew up: from a baby, to a boy, to a man. He ate food and went to the bathroom. He got sick and tired. He faced the same temptations and struggles that we face.

There was, of course, one way in which Jesus differed from every other human being who has ever lived: he was perfect. Jesus did not sin. Because Jesus had no human father—the Holy Spirit caused Mary to become pregnant with him—he was born with no sinful nature. He chose freely not to sin, but to obey God perfectly. Jesus faced temptation; Satan tempted him for forty days in the desert soon after his baptism by John (Luke 4:1–13). Nevertheless, he never sinned.

Because of Jesus's sinless life, he is truly able to represent sinful humanity as our perfectly righteous advocate. The technical theological term for this is the "active obedience" of Jesus Christ, referring to the way he perfectly kept the law of God in our place without ever sinning. When Jesus gave himself up to death on the cross (an act of "passive obedience"), he died as the perfect substitute for God's people, both because of his perfect life and his sacrificial death. When we repent and put our faith in Jesus, we receive credit for his perfectly righteous *life* and we are forgiven because of his sacrificial *death*.

Not only *was* Jesus human; he *is* human, and will be human forever. When he rose from the dead, he rose with a glorified and perfected resurrection body—the first of the resurrected bodies that all of God's people will receive one day. Jesus reigns—even now—in his resurrected and perfected human body, and he will reign so forever!

Jesus can sympathize with us. What does it mean that Jesus was and is fully human? One important truth that the Bible teaches us is that, because of Jesus's humanity, he can sympathize with us. He is able to help us when we are tempted, writes the author of Hebrews, because "he himself has suffered when tempted" (Heb. 2:18). He is able to sympathize with the weaknesses of human beings because he became a human being. What an amazing truth this is; Jesus really knows what we are going through. He knows our pain, our struggles, and our temptations.

Jesus can save us. Finally, Jesus's humanity means that he really can save us. You see, if Jesus had not really become human, the sacrifice that he made would not really have been for human sin. He had to identify himself fully with the people that he came to save by truly becoming human. He became "flesh and blood," according to Hebrews, so that "through death he might destroy the one who has the power of death, that is, the devil" (Heb. 2:14). Jesus's incarnation—his taking on of human flesh—made him able to identify with sinful human beings and thus to be the final sacrifice for human sin.

⬤ PRAY!

Spend a few minutes thinking deeply about the real humanity of Jesus Christ. He did not just appear to be human; he really and truly became human so that he could save sinful human beings and reconcile them to God through his death. Thank God for this! Thank Jesus that he became like us in order to identify with us and save us.

Full Divinity

Just as the Bible clearly teaches the truth of Jesus's humanity, it also clearly teaches his divinity. Jesus Christ the man is also completely God. Christians must cling to what the Bible teaches—that Jesus, the Savior of sinners, is fully human *and* fully God.

█ READ!

Take a moment to read Philippians 2:5–11, focusing on all that this brief passage teaches about Jesus's descent in humility to become human, but also about his ultimate identity as the glorified Lord of all. Consider his amazing gift to sinful human beings and his eternal exalted reign as the glorious and holy God of the universe.

Here are two important truths that are related to Jesus's divinity:

Jesus never ceased being God. It is important to realize that Jesus, even during his time on earth, never ceased to be fully God. He chose to set aside the glories of his eternal reign for a time (as Paul talks about in the Phil. 2 passage that you read) and take on the weakness of human flesh, but he never ceased to be the God of the universe. This fact is proved by Jesus's miracles, such as when he calmed the storm (Mark 4) or raised Lazarus from the dead (John 11). Even in his humble descent to humanity, Jesus never stopped being fully God.

Jesus's divinity means our salvation. It is also important to understand that just as Jesus's humanity is necessary for our salvation (because it meant his full identification with human beings in their weakness and temptation), so his full divinity is necessary if we are to have any hope that he can save us from our sins. If Jesus were not fully God, he could never have actually paid the infinite and eternal price for sin that human beings deserve. Remember, as we saw in earlier chapters, that because God is infinitely holy, the sin human beings commit against him is infinitely weighty. This is important: only God himself could actually pay an infinite and complete price for sin. Jesus did this on the cross; he was able to do it because he is God.

Many problems arise when people affirm Jesus's humanity or divinity without affirming the other. Historically, many heresies (dangerous false teachings) have been built on assumptions that Jesus was either not quite fully human or not quite fully God. As you can tell from our discussion of Christology so far, we are intent on affirming that the Bible teaches two truths about Jesus extremely clearly: he was, and is, both fully human and fully God.

Here, for example, are two ancient heresies that people lean toward in their beliefs about Jesus even today:

- Docetism. This heresy taught that Jesus only appeared to be human; he was not really a man. Docetists had a problem with God becoming human, so they taught that Jesus was fully God but did not really take on flesh and blood. This is opposed to what the Bible teaches, as we have seen.
- Arianism. This heresy (picked up and continued, in some ways, by Mormons and Jehovah's Witnesses today) teaches that Jesus

was not the eternally existent second person of the Trinity. Arians teach, rather, that Jesus was created by God the Father, who then adopted him as a Son. This teaching is opposed to Scripture and what we are affirming in our doctrine of Christology.

As you continue to study Scripture and learn more about Jesus, keep these two biblical truths clearly in mind: Jesus was and is fully human, and Jesus was and is fully God. He has always been fully God; he became human and will remain human in his resurrected, glorified, and perfected body forever.

● PRAY!

Talk to God about your vision of Jesus and your thoughts about him. Confess the ways that you do not, daily, think about Jesus in a way that is exalted enough. Ask God to help you see Jesus as the God of the universe—the King who humbly chose to become human to fully save sinners for eternity.

JESUS'S *SAVING WORK*

For the past few pages, we have been focusing on *who* Jesus is—his identity. We have examined carefully what the Bible teaches about Jesus Christ as the eternally existent Son of God—the one who came to earth as a human being while still remaining the glorious and eternal God of the universe. It was natural for us to start with this careful focus on the identity of Jesus in this systematic theology category of Christology.

Now we will turn to considering *what* Jesus did and does—his saving work. We will begin by considering what the Bible teaches about his suffering and death—his sacrifice for sin on the cross. By the end of this discussion, you will hopefully have a better idea of the way that

Jesus humbled himself to death, as well as what that death actually accomplished for lost sinners.

Suffering and Death

Jesus's suffering and death on the cross is probably a topic that you have talked about—or at least heard about—many times. What happened on the cross is at the very center of the Christian faith, as it is the place where saving hope is found for lost sinners who need grace.

READ!

Read Matthew 27:32–61. Read this passage carefully, as it records the actual suffering, crucifixion, death, and burial of Jesus Christ. While this may be a familiar passage for you, try to see it with new eyes as we prepare to discuss the death of Jesus in a more theological way than perhaps you ever have before.

Here are a few key points that we need to affirm in a systematic theological study of the suffering and death of Jesus Christ:

Jesus really died. First, the Bible teaches that Jesus really did die. The fully human Jesus actually stopped breathing and became dead. While it is hard to understand how this could happen to the Creator of the universe , this is what the Bible clearly teaches. Jesus was crucified, perished, and then was buried in a tomb—as you saw in the passage that you read from the Gospel of Matthew. Jesus's human body experienced real physical death and lay in a tomb for three days.

Jesus's suffering was both physical and spiritual. Second, while Jesus's physical suffering was immense, terrible, and brutal, it was not nearly as severe as the spiritual suffering he endured on the cross. Jesus was not the only person ever crucified; in fact, two men were crucified with him on the day that he died. Jesus's greatest suffering was the spiritual agony of God the Father placing the guilt, shame, and punishment of human sin on him completely, then turning away from him in anger and wrath. This is why Jesus cried out from the cross *not*, "This hurts!" but, "My God, my God, why have you forsaken me?" (Matt. 27:46). The agony of being under the wrath of the Father was far worse than the pain from the nails that pierced Jesus's hands and feet. He was treated like a sinner by God himself and bore the terrible pain of separation from God, which is hell itself. Jesus went through this ordeal in order to save God's people.

Jesus's death really accomplished something. Finally, we need to understand that Jesus's death was not just an example to us or a beautiful picture of God's love, although it certainly was both of those things. It is vital that we remember that his work on the cross was efficacious, which means "effective." Jesus's death really did pay the full price for sin for God's people who believe in him and trust him. He really did fully bear the wrath of God. He really was the great substitute for sinners—the final sacrifice. God looked on this sacrifice of Jesus and accepted it as the full payment for the sins of his people. As we discussed earlier, Jesus represented God's people as their perfect substitute; he kept God's law perfectly without sin, so he was worthy to present himself as the spotless Lamb—the final sacrifice for sinners who would put their faith in him.

⬆ PRAY!

Spend a few minutes in prayer to God. Thank him that he allowed his only Son to suffer in your place to pay for your sin. Thank him that the suffering of Jesus was not only physical, but also spiritual, as he bore the wrath that should have been poured out on guilty sinners. Give him glory and praise, and thank the God who was willing to go to such lengths to save the people he loved.

Resurrection

Having considered the death of Jesus Christ on the cross, we'll now think about his resurrection. We'll examine the event itself, its significance, and its meaning for Christian life and hope today.

READ!

Read 1 Corinthians 15:20–28—just a portion of Paul's broad discussion of the resurrection of Christ and believers in this part of his letter to the ancient church at Corinth. As you read, consider the implications of Jesus's resurrection for believers that Paul points out here.

The resurrection of Jesus Christ is absolutely essential to Christian faith. In fact, Paul says—just before the passage that you just read—that if Jesus Christ has not really been raised from the dead, "then our preaching is in vain and your faith is in vain" (1 Cor. 15:14). In other words, for Christians, everything hinges on the fact that Jesus Christ really did rise bodily from the dead.

So what are the implications of Jesus's resurrection? What does it mean that Jesus did, in fact, rise bodily from the grave?

First, Jesus's resurrection means that his sacrifice for sin was complete and acceptable to God. If Jesus's death on the cross had not fully covered and paid for the sins of God's people, he would have stayed dead; there would have been more debt for sin that had to be paid. But the very fact that Jesus did not stay dead proves that no more punishment is needed for God's people; he truly paid the entire penalty for sin. One way to think about the resurrection, then, is that it is God's stamp of approval on the finished work of Jesus Christ on behalf of sinners. It is God's way of saying, "Done! The price has been fully paid. You can become alive again!" Jesus's resurrection is God's living proof that we can really be forgiven.

Second, Jesus's resurrection means that he will reign eternally. This is what Paul argues in Acts 17 and in 1 Corinthians 15. The fact that Jesus is risen from the dead is proof that he really is the eternal King and Judge; he has been raised in victory, and he will judge the world with all authority and power. Paul puts it this way in the passage you read above: "For God has put all things in subjection under his feet" (1 Cor. 15:27). The resurrection reminds us that Jesus rules over even death because he conquered death by rising triumphantly for all who follow him.

Third, Jesus's resurrection means that all who follow him and believe in him will one day rise in the same way. This is clearly what Paul teaches in 1 Corinthians 15. Jesus's resurrection is a kind of guarantee that the resurrection of all who put their trust in him will really happen! Paul calls Jesus the "firstfruits" of all those who have died and will one day rise again (v. 20). In other words, Christ's resurrection is the first visible sign of the great resurrection of all Christians at the end of time. The hope of Christians for resurrection and eternal life is firmly attached to the resurrection of Jesus Christ their Savior. The resurrection, then, is no small and insignificant doctrine.

PRAY!

Thank God for giving us the glorious hope of resurrection through the rising of Jesus Christ from the dead. Thank him for all that the resurrection of Jesus represents for us and teaches us about our hope for eternal life. Praise him for all that the resurrection means: sin is paid for, death is dead, and eternal life in Christ is certain.

JESUS'S *PRESENT REIGN*

In this chapter on Christology, we have looked back to consider the incarnation, death, and resurrection of Jesus Christ. In the next section, we will look forward to reflect on what the Bible has to tell us about the return, judgment, and eternal reign of King Jesus. These are very important directions to look because it is vital for us to know what Jesus has done and all that he will do in the future.

But it is also important to focus on what Jesus is doing right now. We will ask some basic questions and look at Scripture in order to see Jesus's present role in the world and in the lives of his followers.

READ!

Read Hebrews 10:11–25, a passage that describes Jesus's work on the cross as well as his present work as he waits to return in judgment and final victory to this world. Think about the finality of Jesus's work on the cross that is signified by the fact that he "sat down" when it was finished (v. 12). Think about him waiting to return for his final judgment and reign.

We can consider what Jesus is doing now by asking two simple questions:

Where is Jesus now? The question of Jesus's present location is a valid one because of what we have already learned about his humanity (Jesus has a risen and glorified human body that he will keep forever). So Jesus is literally in a place right now; in his physical human body, he exists somewhere. But where?

The Bible is clear that Jesus is sitting at the right hand of God the Father in heaven (Heb. 10:12; 12:2). Heaven is indeed a place, even though it is invisible to us. The Hebrews 10 passage makes clear that this is where Jesus is even now.

What is Jesus doing now? As Jesus sits in heaven at God's right hand, what is his current role?

First, Jesus is mediating for us before the throne of God. The Bible tells us that Jesus is a mediator. He was a mediator when he died on the cross to bridge the gap between sinners and the holy God. But he continues to be a mediator, making intercession to God on behalf of Christians (Rom. 8:34). This means that he continues to speak to God on our behalf, reminding him, in a way, of the blood that he shed for our sins.

Second, Jesus is ruling over the world (see Matt. 28:18). Even though sin is still very real in the world today, and Satan is seeking to do all the damage that he can, Jesus Christ is the risen King who has total power and authority over all things in creation. He is holding the very universe together, according to Colossians 1:17, and is in complete control of everything that happens in God's world.

Third, Jesus is waiting for the perfect and chosen time to return. Jesus told his disciples, in Matthew 24:36, that no one except God the Father knows the exact day or hour when he will return, and this will come at a time when no one expects it (v. 44). Peter tells us that God is waiting to send Jesus back to earth because he is patient; he is giving people time to repent and put their faith in him (2 Pet. 3:9). At some point, however, Jesus's waiting will end and he will return as the great Judge of the world; the Bible tells us that he is coming soon!

So when you think about Jesus now, think about him as the great and humble Savior. But also consider where he is and what he is doing right now. He is seated at the right hand of God the Father in heaven, where he is ruling over this world and mediating between you and God. And he is waiting to return in God's perfect timing to judge the world and everyone in it.

PRAY!

Thank Jesus for his role right now in your life! Thank him that he is reigning at the right hand of God the Father, mediating for you, and helping you know more about him. Ask God to help you remember Jesus's current role as you go about your day today.

JESUS'S *FINAL JUDGMENT*

It is good for us to focus on Jesus's earthly ministry; we have done that numerous times already in this book. That, in fact, is a huge focus of Scripture; we have four Gospels that tell us all about the life, death, teaching, and resurrection of Jesus. It is also good for us to remember that Jesus continues to work for his people today from the right hand of God the Father.

Yet even as we look back to what Jesus did and remember his present reign, it is important that we always look forward to keep in mind all that Jesus will do for God's people in the days to come. So we will focus now on the return and judgment of Jesus Christ, the eternal King. Jesus is not only the one who died and rose again, but is also the one who will come again to judge all of his enemies eternally and to take his people home to be with him.

READ!

Read Revelation 19:11–21. This is a picture of Jesus Christ coming in judgment and victory over his enemies, all those who have given their lives to sin and rebellion. Think about this picture in contrast with the way that we often tend to think about Jesus—as a humble servant and friend of sinners who laid down his life. Remember that the one who came once as the humble Savior will one day return as the mighty and conquering Judge of all the world!

The Bible makes it clear that Jesus came once to save sinners, but he will come again to judge sin and to eternally save all those who belong to him. The second coming of Jesus will be very different from the first! In his first coming, he came, ultimately, to die. When he returns, he will come to judge the world and reign forever in righteousness. With this in mind, here are three important points that the Bible teaches about the return and judgment of Jesus Christ:

Jesus will return to earth in glory and victory. The apostle John tells us, as his "revelation" begins, that Jesus is "coming with the clouds" (Rev. 1:7). In other words, his second coming will not be secret and humble. Unlike when he was born as a baby and laid in a manger, his return to earth will be dramatic, global, and powerful. Jesus will make himself known, when he returns, as the glorious God and the eternal Judge of all the earth.

Jesus will judge all people on earth. While we often think of God the Father as the great Judge (which is true), the Bible presents Jesus Christ himself as executing the judgment of God on all of his enemies at the last day (Acts 17:30–31). The passage that you read from Revelation presents a startling picture of Jesus as he rides forward on a white horse, trampling God's enemies in judgment and wrath. Jesus, the Bible teaches, will execute God's judgment on all who reject his salvation and rule. He is the gracious Savior, and he accepts all who turn to him in faith. But he will eternally judge all who reject his offer of salvation.

Jesus will reign as the eternal King. Finally, we see clearly that the Bible presents Jesus as the great King who will reign forever over God's people. Ultimately, every knee will bow and every tongue will confess that Jesus Christ is Lord (Phil. 2:10–11). The suffering Savior will be the glorious risen King.

PRAY!

Ask God to help you see Jesus in all of his true power, glory, and righteousness. He is the resurrected and glorious Lord who will reign forever over his people. Pray that God would make you ready to meet Jesus as the great King and Judge, face to face, as you follow him every day.

RESPONDING TO JESUS

As we wrap up this chapter, we will focus on applying all we have learned about Jesus to our lives as his followers. In other words, we will discuss the right response to Jesus if all of these things about him really are true. How should our lives reflect his identity, his work, and his role in the world both now and in the future?

READ!

Read Revelation 5—the entire chapter. Enjoy reading about this amazing scene in heaven, which shows clearly the worthiness of Jesus—the Lamb—to carry out all of God's purposes for salvation and judgment in the world. Pay careful attention to the response of the heavenly creatures to Jesus in this passage and consider how their response should shape our own response to his person and work.

Systematic theology is a wonderful discipline! It is good for us to carefully gather together categories of theology that we can then study carefully, seeking to put together all that the Bible teaches about them, in order to better understand God and his amazing work in this world.

Yet as noted earlier, one danger of systematic theology is that it can become an academic discipline that fails to connect with our hearts. In other words, if we are learning *about* God, but this learning never draws us nearer *to* God in relationship, then our study may be interesting, but it will not be eternally valuable in the way that we relate to our Creator.

What, then, should be our response to this Jesus we have learned so much about? Here are three appropriate responses:

Fear. Many people do not like to talk about fear in relation to the way that we approach God. Yet this is a concept that is found throughout the Bible; followers of God are called to fear him. This, of course, is a slightly different thing than the fear experienced by someone whose life is in danger—but it is not totally unrelated to that kind of fear. Jesus—the one who existed before time, who died and rose again, and who will return with infinite glory, judgment, and power—is a mighty King who is rightly to be feared. We should be in awe of him; our attitude toward him should be one of reverence. We know that he shows us great love and grace, but we also know that he holds all the power in the universe to judge all people everywhere. He is worthy of our fear, awe, and reverence.

Worship. It is this response, really, that we see highlighted in the Revelation 5 passage that you read. Jesus, we saw, is revealed to John as the only one who can open the "scrolls"—probably a picture of the purposes of God for judgment and salvation in the world he has made. As this is revealed, the living creatures and the elders (heavenly beings) immediately sing a song of praise to him, declaring his worthiness. The chapter then ends with everyone falling down before Jesus in total submission and worship. That should be our heart response to him: worship! When we see his power, worthiness, and glory, we should want to fall before him and praise his great name.

Love. Finally, as we think about the kind of Savior we serve, we should remember that fear and worship combine with love in our response to him. This is the mighty King and Judge who is also the Lamb that was slain—the suffering friend of sinners who laid down his life on a cross for them. Those who belong to Jesus have a deep love for him; they see him as their Savior, and they love him as the greatest friend for their hearts and souls. Jesus is clear that those who love him will keep his commands, so our obedience to him and his word is one clear sign that we truly love our Savior.

As you consider these responses to Jesus—responses that are based on who he is—check your own heart. Are you responding to Jesus in these ways?

PRAY!

Talk to God about your response to his Son. Are you falling down before him in worship? Do you seek to obey him and bring him praise every day? Confess your failures in these things to God and ask him to help you follow Jesus with fear, worship, and love today!

REVIEW

As we conclude this chapter on Christology, we can look back at many truths about Jesus Christ that we have learned. We have examined his identity as the eternally existent Son of God who was active in creation. We have discussed his incarnation, his saving work on the cross, and his resurrection. We have looked at his role now and anticipated his return to earth and his final judgment of the world. And we ended by applying the truths that we have learned in this chapter by thinking through the right responses to Jesus for those who truly want to accept him and follow him. The goal of that discussion was to remind you that you have not just been learning concepts in this chapter; you have been learning about a person. Here are a few key points for you to remember:

Eternal Existence

- As the second person of the Trinity, Jesus was active in the creation, so we can truly say that he created the universe.
- Jesus has no beginning and no end; he exists eternally and has always reigned as God over all things.

True Humanity and Full Divinity

- Jesus took a human body and became really, truly, and completely a human man. This is known as the incarnation. He will keep his glorified and resurrected human body for all eternity.
- Jesus remained fully divine—fully God—even as he took on a human body. Jesus is 100 percent God and 100 percent human, without any confusion or compromise.
- Both Jesus's humanity and his divinity were necessary for him to accomplish forgiveness and salvation for God's people on the cross; he identified with human beings in his humanity and was able to fully bear the infinite punishment for sin because of his divinity.

Suffering and Death

- Jesus really did die; his human body physically perished, and he was buried in a tomb.

- Jesus's worst suffering was not physical but spiritual, as God the Father turned his back on him in judgment and wrath.
- Jesus's death on the cross for sins was really effective; it was not just an example, but was the real payment of the full price of sin for God's people.

Resurrection

- Jesus truly rose physically from the grave after three days.
- The resurrection of Jesus Christ was God's stamp of approval on his work on the cross; it proves to us that the sins of believers really have been paid for and that the sacrifice was accepted by God.
- Jesus's resurrection is at the center of Christian hope because, as Paul says, Jesus is the "firstfruits" of all who follow him, for they one day will rise again as well.

Present Reign

- Right now, Jesus is seated at the right hand of God the Father in heaven, where he is reigning and ruling over the world with righteousness.
- Jesus is waiting for God's perfect timing for his return; God, in turn, is patient to give sinners time to repent.
- Jesus is mediating between sinful people and God the Father; he is pleading for them on the basis of the blood he shed on the cross.

Final Judgment

- Jesus promises to return one day—not to suffer and die, but to judge the world in righteousness and establish his eternal reign in the new heaven and the new earth.
- Revelation pictures Jesus as a conquering King and Judge who will save his people but also trample his enemies in judgment.
- The exact hour and timing of Jesus's return is unknown to us, but we should expect it and be ready for it.

Remember!

Can you say or write the suggested memory verses for this chapter perfectly? Consider the way that these verses have shaped how you think about Jesus Christ in your study.

⬆ PRAY!

As you end this chapter on Christology with prayer, thank God for all that you have learned about his Son—the great Savior of sinners and the eternal King and Judge of all the world. Thank him that he provided salvation through Jesus and ask him to give you strength to follow him and respond to him in the right way every day.

Chapter 7

THE DOCTRINE OF SALVATION

You have just finished a chapter on Christology—the study of Jesus Christ. It is hard to argue that any other category of systematic theology is more important than that one; for Christians, faith and life begin and end with the person of Jesus Christ. It is all about him!

Yet one could make an argument that, in terms of actual faith, belief, and practice, the chapter you are beginning now deals with the most important topic in this book. There is probably no more important question for human existence and destiny than this one: "How can I be saved?" Our goal in this chapter will be to answer that question clearly from Scripture as we dig into "soteriology"—the study of salvation.

Has anyone ever tried to tell you that all religions are basically the same? This is a very common opinion today in a world that has increasingly elevated the value of "tolerance." It will become more and more common for you to hear people say, "It does not matter what religion you accept; they all say basically the same thing and all lead to some kind of salvation. The important thing is that we simply get along and coexist." While Christians are certainly called to love and respect people of other religions, they must never compromise on the issue of salvation.

Why? Because, contrary to the popular view that all religions are fine and can bring salvation in different ways, we have the clear witness of the Bible, which says, "There is salvation in no one else, for there is no other name under heaven given among men by which we must be saved" (Acts 4:12). These words of Peter remind us of the bold claim of the Bible: salvation comes only through faith in Jesus Christ, God's Son.

As we pursue our goal for this chapter of discovering what the Bible has to say about salvation in Christ, we will take several steps:

- First, we will look at the witness of the Old Testament, which shows us how God pointed his people forward in many ways to the great salvation that he would provide for them.
- Second, we will look at what the Bible seems to present as the "order of salvation"—the progression of works of God, by his Holy Spirit, that lead to a person being saved.
- Third, we will look at a few theories of the atonement (what happened on the cross as Jesus died).
- Fourth, we will examine the biblical picture of what Jesus's sacrifice on the cross actually does for sinners, seeing the wonderful breadth of the way the Bible talks about his salvation.

We will end with a brief discussion on the importance of repentance and faith as we discuss the human role in the salvation that is described to us in Scripture. The goal is for you, by the end of this chapter, to have a much fuller understanding of God's amazing gift of salvation to sinners through Jesus.

Remember!

Your suggested memory verse for this chapter comes from Acts 4; it contains verse 12, which was quoted just above. These words were spoken by Peter as he and John bore witness to the Jewish council in Jerusalem after they had been arrested for preaching the gospel of Jesus Christ. Read these verses carefully several times, thinking about the bold statement that Peter was making with these words. Consider the implications for our understanding of salvation.

Let it be known to all of you and to all the people of Israel that by the name of Jesus Christ of Nazareth, whom you crucified, whom God raised from the dead—by him this man is standing before you well. This Jesus is the stone that was rejected by you, the builders, which has become the cornerstone. And there is salvation in no one else, for there is no other name under heaven given among men by which we must be saved. (Acts 4:10–12)

▲ PRAY!

Ask God to guide you, according to his word, as you consider his great salvation in this chapter. Pray that he would help you understand the wonder of his grace and mercy even more clearly. Ask him to give you a humble spirit to accept all that his word teaches about how sinful human beings can be eternally saved.

SALVATION AND THE OLD TESTAMENT

Later in this chapter, we will spend much of our time looking at New Testament texts because it is there that God's salvation through Jesus is explicitly explained and applied for us. Yet it would not be wise to jump straight to the New Testament when all of Scripture helps us understand lost sinners' need for God's great salvation and the kind of salvation it will be. So we first will sweep over the Old Testament in broad strokes in order to consider just a few of the many ways that these ancient Scripture passages began to define what God's salvation of his people would ultimately look like, all it would accomplish, and who actually would bring it about in this world.

📖 READ!

Read Deuteronomy 18:15–22. Consider carefully what Moses is saying; think about these words, which point to a prophet "like" him (v. 15) who would come in the future. Think about how this might relate to our discussion of the Old Testament teaching about God's salvation—and God's Son!

The Bible is all about Jesus. Jesus himself makes this clear in John 5:39, when he tells the Pharisees that the Scriptures (of the Old Testament) bear witness about him. Because of this truth, Christians see the gospel message—the death of Jesus for sins and his resurrection from the dead—as the central message of the entire Bible. The Old Testament points forward to Jesus and his work, and the New Testament explains and applies their significance.

Because the gospel is so central to Scripture, there are almost countless ways in which the Old Testament points forward to God's salvation through Christ and anticipates it for his people in beautiful ways. We will examine just four of these ways to see how the Old Testament Scriptures set up this doctrine for God's people long before Christ came to earth to actually accomplish it.

Adam and Eve—the promise of an offspring. As you probably know, just after the fall of Adam and Eve, God made a big promise in Genesis 3:15. He said that Eve's "offspring" would one day crush the head of the serpent—Satan. Bible scholars have long taken this to be the first gospel/salvation promise from God to his people in the Bible. It was a promise that his salvation, through a descendant of Eve, would be a final victory over Satan, sin, and death. God's salvation, in other words, would be a *victory*.

Noah—salvation from judgment. Through the life of Noah, who was saved from God's watery judgment on the evil earth through a boat that

God told him to build, God provided another vivid picture of what his salvation would be like for his true people. Just as there was only one safe place from God's judgment in the days of the flood (the ark), so there would be only one safe place from God's judgment on the whole earth on the last day (the cross of Jesus Christ). God's salvation, in other words, would be an *escape from judgment.*

Moses/law—sin required blood. Throughout the time when God's people kept the law of Moses and sought to worship God through the means he had given them, they performed many animal sacrifices for their sins. While the death of these animals never literally took away sins (Romans 3:25 tells us that God chose to overlook sins until he placed them on Christ), they were a vivid sign to God's people of one fact: sin required death and blood. God's salvation, in other words, when it finally came, would be a *final blood sacrifice* for the sins of his people.

Isaiah—a suffering servant. The prophet Isaiah, in chapter 53 of his long book of prophecy, looks ahead to a servant and Savior whom God would provide for his people (read this chapter if you have extra time). This servant would be stricken, abused, and punished for the sins of God's people (vv. 4–5). He would take all their sins on himself as a kind of substitute. God's salvation, in other words, would be about a Savior who would be a *substitute* to take God's wrath for the sins of his people.

So as you see, the Old Testament gave many hints about how God's salvation would be accomplished. When you start putting these hints— and all the rest—together, you begin to see a very full picture of God's great salvation—even from the Old Testament.

As we think about these hints, it is important to remember that Old Testament believers (such as Abraham, Moses, and David) were saved in exactly the same way that Christians are saved today. They looked ahead to God's provision of mercy through the Messiah—the promised one. We look back to the glorious cross of Jesus and have the privilege of knowing him by name. Every believer in every age has been saved by faith, as God has showed grace to those who trust in Christ alone for salvation.

⬆ PRAY!

Thank God for the way that he so obviously pointed his people forward to the salvation that he was going to provide in and through Christ by his death on the cross for sins and his resurrection from the dead. Pray that God would help you see his promise of salvation even more clearly, all over the Old Testament, as you read and study it in the future.

THE ORDER OF SALVATION

You have now seen just a few of the ways that the Old Testament pointed God's people forward to the great salvation that was ultimately unveiled and given fully through Jesus. Hopefully that helped you understand that God's plan to send his Son as the Savior of the world was not a "plan B"—something that God did because nothing else seemed to work! Rather, his salvation of sinners through Jesus was his careful and beautiful plan from the very beginning.

It is this idea of God's eternal plan in salvation that we will begin discussing now. We will look at several key doctrines by which we will lay out the order of salvation. This is a very important way of understanding salvation: it considers the sequential process of God's work to save sinful people. Here are the doctrines we will consider: (1) election, (2) regeneration, (3) justification, (4) sanctification, and (5) glorification.

Election

The doctrine of election is a very important—and very controversial—aspect of salvation. For this reason, we will seek to ground our discussion in the character of God and the truth of his word.

READ!

Read Ephesians 1:1–14, paying special attention to verses 3–5 and 11.
Think about what this passage is teaching about the doctrine of elec-
tion. Consider God's role, according to Paul, in human salvation as
you read.

Whether or not people believe what the Bible seems to teach about
God's election, or choice, to save certain people, they all (if they
take God and the Bible seriously) need to admit that this first step in
salvation has to begin with God. Even before he created the world,
he had a salvation plan centered on Jesus's death for sins on the cross
and resurrection from the dead. This is important: salvation begins
with God!

When we talk about election, or predestination, we are referring to God's sovereign choice from before the beginning of time
to save *some* people eternally through Christ. Ephesians 1 teaches
this very clearly. Therefore, election is the first step in the order of
salvation that we are learning in this chapter. So how should we
think about election?

First, we should remember that God can do whatever he wants,
and whatever he does is by definition right, just, and fair. Many critiques of the doctrine of election center around accusations that it is
somehow not "fair" for God to choose to save some and not others.
This is a dangerous critique because none of us actually wants fair
treatment from God, since that would mean that we would all go
to hell (if we take seriously what the Bible says about our sin)! The
critiques of election often assume, too, that our definitions of "just"
and "fair" are more important than God's. But he, and he alone,
determines what is right and just. He alone is God.

Second, we should see that the Bible really does clearly teach this
doctrine. In the passage you read from Ephesians 1, Paul makes two
statements that are very hard to avoid or misinterpret:

- "He chose us in him before the foundation of the world" (v. 4).
- "In him we have obtained an inheritance, having been predestined according to the purpose of him who works all things according to the counsel of his will" (v. 11).

It is difficult to get around the clear teaching of the Bible that God, before time, elected some whom he would save.

Third, we should see that human responsibility is never taken off the table in the teaching of the Bible. A common critique of the doctrine of election is that it somehow makes humans into robots who have no real choices but are simply controlled by God or by "fate." This is nowhere taught in the Bible. Scripture affirms that human beings make real choices as rational beings with real wills and full responsibility for their actions—and for their rejection or acceptance of God's word. The Bible never downplays human responsibility!

So to summarize this first step in the order of salvation, we can affirm, from Scripture, that the first part of our salvation happened before the world was even created. God made an eternal decree; he "elected" to save some people eternally for himself through the work of his Son, Jesus Christ. This means that salvation starts with God. If you are saved through God's grace and by faith in Jesus, it is because God chose you before the foundation of the world. This is an amazing thought, and it should make you fall down on your knees before God and thank him.

⬤ PRAY!

Think deeply for a few moments about God's sovereignty, power, and election. While we have seen that these realities about God do not rule out human responsibility at all, he is the one who conceives and executes the perfect plan of salvation in the lives of his people. Ask God to help you to trust him more and believe that he is the great God with the perfect saving plan.

Regeneration

The next step in the order of salvation is regeneration. As does election, this step reminds us that God is the ultimate and first "mover" in human salvation—it is ultimately *his* powerful work in the lives of human beings. By his grace, he makes the first move toward people who could never take the first step toward him because of their sinful condition.

READ!

Read Ephesians 2:1–10. Pay special attention to the human condition of all who are apart from Christ and consider what this condition means for the ability of human beings to choose God on their own. Then focus on the action in verse 5 (God "made us alive"). Consider the impact this verse should have on our understanding of salvation.

Regeneration refers to God's miraculous work, by the power of the Holy Spirit, to make people come alive spiritually. Because of regeneration, sinners are enabled by the Holy Spirit to repent of sins and put their faith in Jesus Christ. This is a doctrine that is clearly taught in Scripture, and we can see its necessity and reality in several ways.

First, we see that regeneration is necessary because of the human condition. Paul, in the passage from Ephesians 2 that you read, makes it clear that human beings are "dead" in sin (v. 1); in other words, they are not partially alive, but completely dead, and therefore unable to do anything good. In fact, Paul even says that they are followers of the "prince of the power of the air"—Satan himself (v. 2)! It would be impossible for any human being in this condition (all of us, apart from Christ) to choose to follow Jesus by his or her own will, power, or strength. The Bible reveals that we are incapable of repenting and believing on our own. So regeneration is necessary if anyone is to be saved.

Second, we see that regeneration happens completely by God's choice and action. In Ephesians 2:5, Paul describes how God makes dead sinners "alive together with Christ." This is a beautiful picture of regeneration.

Regeneration, then, is a step in salvation that comes *before* human beings actually repent of sins, believe in Jesus, and make a profession of faith in him. No one can turn to Christ with a heart that is dead; it is impossible for sinners who are following Satan to make a good choice on their own. Salvation is made possible for sinners because God acts powerfully to regenerate their hearts, to make them able to turn to him.

Here, then, is where we are so far in our order of salvation:

1. Election—God sovereignly chooses some, before the foundation of the world, whom he will save through Christ.
2. Regeneration—God works by his Holy Spirit in the hearts of dead sinners to make them "come alive" and respond in faith to Jesus Christ.

▲ PRAY!

Pray a simple prayer to God (if you have put your faith in Jesus as your Savior and Lord): "Lord, thank you for making me come alive!" Remember that, apart from the work of his Holy Spirit, you would have remained dead—not even able to wake up and choose Jesus—but by his grace, he regenerated you to make you able to repent of sin and turn in faith to his Son.

Justification

Justification is probably what most often comes to mind when you think about salvation. It is the act of being justified—declared righteous, forgiven, and saved—before the holy God on the basis of Christ's work on the cross, which is received by faith alone. We need to explore how justification happens and how it is received by sinful human beings who need it so badly.

THE DOCTRINE OF SALVATION

READ!

Read Romans 4:1–8. Pay attention to the way this passage speaks about how people are justified before God. Consider the way that Abraham was justified, according to Paul. Think deeply about Paul's summary statement in verse 5, which would have been shocking to legalistic Jews, who thought that they were justified by their works. Consider all that these verses mean for our understanding of how we are made right before the holy God.

The word *justification* is a legal term. It refers to someone being declared righteous—right and innocent of wrongdoing. So we should start by admitting that the very fact that sinners who are dead enemies of God can even hope for justification is amazing! Yet the Bible tells us that there *is* hope that sinners can be justified before God and saved eternally through Christ.

We have learned about election and regeneration already—the first two steps in the order of salvation. Now comes this next step—justification. It is important to understand that, while this step too is ultimately God's work, this is also the step in the order of salvation in which the human response is active, through faith in Jesus (which is, of course, the miraculous gift of God). Think about it this way: we have no role in our election by God or his regeneration of us. But after regeneration, we are saved through faith in Jesus.

So what do we need to affirm, from Scripture, about justification?

First, justification is purely on the basis of Jesus's work on the cross for sinners. How does God save sinners? How can he actually declare sinful people righteous? How is it possible that he "justifies the ungodly," as Paul says he does in Romans 4:5? The only way that God could do this was by punishing his own Son—fully God and fully man—on the cross for the sins of his redeemed people. Justification—eternal righteousness before God—could be secured for human beings only through the sacrificial work of Jesus Christ on the cross.

Second, justification is received only by faith in Jesus, not by any works that we do. Paul is very clear about this in Romans 4 (and in all of his other writings in the New Testament). Sinners *must not* come to God hoping or trusting that any of their works can somehow save them or make them right before God. None of our works could ever justify us or cancel out the infinite offense of our sin against God. The only way to be justified is, like Abraham, to accept God's offer of forgiveness and salvation by faith.

Third, justification really is effective, final, and complete through Jesus Christ's sacrifice. His death on the cross was not just a symbol of God's love for us. It really paid the full penalty of sin for all of God's people whom he chose for himself before the foundation of the world. This means that salvation depends not on us—our feelings, our good works, our abilities—but on the finished work of Jesus Christ for our sins on the cross, which was validated and confirmed by his glorious resurrection from the dead. Nothing can wipe away this justification that God has provided for us through his Son!

So here is where we are so far in our order of salvation:

1. Election—God sovereignly chooses some, before the foundation of the world, whom he will save through Christ.
2. Regeneration—God works by his Holy Spirit in the hearts of dead sinners to make them "come alive" and respond in faith to Jesus Christ.
3. Justification—God declares sinners to be righteous on the basis of the finished work of Jesus Christ on the cross—a work that sinners accept through faith.

▲ PRAY!

Spend a moment thanking God that you have the hope of justification before God. In Christ, by faith, God sees you as righteous and holy before him. This is an amazing gift! If you have repented of your sins and put your faith in Jesus, then thank God for what he has given you. If you have not done this, consider whether or not you want to do so.

There is only one way to be justified before the holy God—through faith in Jesus, his Son!

Sanctification

Sanctification is the step in the order of salvation that follows justification. In this discussion, we will define this word and explain how both God and Christians work at this important process. During this discussion, you should take time to evaluate your own heart and life in order to see whether you are experiencing this part of salvation.

READ!

Read Ephesians 4:17–32—a passage that is full of teaching about what sanctification should look like in the lives of followers of Jesus Christ. As you read, think about the specific instructions and commands that Paul gives to the Ephesian believers. Consider, also, the grounds for those commands (see vv. 20–21, 23–24, and 30). Look at your own life as you consider this teaching from the apostle Paul.

Very literally, sanctification refers to the process of becoming holy. In the Old Testament context of the law and sacrifice, the priests would sanctify themselves through careful cleansing and washing rituals. This symbolized that they were setting themselves apart for the holy and pure purpose of worshiping to God.

To put it in a different way, sanctification is the process by which a person "grows into" his or her justification. Let's think about this carefully.

When God justifies a sinner by the grace of Jesus and through faith alone, that person stands righteous before God. If he or she died the moment after receiving Christ, he or she would be in the presence of Jesus immediately. Justification is the once-for-all saving work of God for sinners through the finished sacrifice that Jesus made on the cross for sins.

After justification, though, much spiritual growth often needs to happen in the lives of new Christians. They may need to learn to walk as children of God—to actually begin living out their justification and acting in accordance with God's word. Sanctification describes this process of Christians becoming more holy, more set apart for God's work, and more like Jesus.

We should note three important facts about sanctification:

First, sanctification is God's work. In other words, the process of becoming holy is not one that Christians have to engage in all by themselves! God gives his Holy Spirit to dwell in believers when they put their faith in Jesus Christ as Savior and Lord, and the Spirit helps them grow in holiness in countless ways. Sanctification is part of salvation because it is God's work by the power of the Holy Spirit.

Second, sanctification includes human effort. Unlike justification, sanctification does have a human element. Even though the Holy Spirit gives Christians strength to obey, change, love, and grow, Christians are still called to give effort to the pursuit of holiness, growth, and obedience. That is why Paul can give the kind of commands that he does in Ephesians 4. Sanctification is powered by God, but Christians are called to work at holiness as well.

Third, sanctification is not complete until heaven. As the process of sanctification moves forward in believers' lives, the characteristics of godliness should, and must, increase. However, this process will never be perfectly complete in this life (we will explore this further in the next section).

So now we have learned about four of the five steps in the order of salvation. Here is where we have come so far:

1. Election—God sovereignly chooses some, before the foundation of the world, whom he will save through Christ.
2. Regeneration—God works by his Holy Spirit in the hearts of dead sinners to make them "come alive" and respond in faith to Jesus Christ.

3. Justification—God declares sinners to be righteous on the basis of the finished work of Jesus Christ on the cross—a work that sinners accept through faith.

4. Sanctification—God continues to make justified sinners more and more holy as they strive to grow in their obedience by the power of the indwelling Holy Spirit.

PRAY!

Think about the process of sanctification in your life. As you follow Jesus Christ as your Lord, do you see yourself becoming more like him? Are you experiencing more and more hatred of sin and love for God, his word, and his people? Talk to God about these things. Ask him to help you work hard to grow in him, even as his Holy Spirit helps you do this. If you do not yet know Jesus as your Savior, talk to God about this. Ask him to show you how you can follow him.

Glorification

Salvation, as we have seen, began before time as God sovereignly elected to save some by the grace of Jesus Christ. Moreover, salvation will go on into eternity, as God's people will enjoy him and his glorious salvation for endless days ahead. This discussion, then, will focus on the great hope that God's people have for the life to come—the future of their salvation. This step in the order of salvation is called glorification.

READ!

Read 1 Corinthians 15:35–49. Read this passage carefully; read it twice if you have time. Think carefully about what Paul is teaching about the resurrection of the dead and the resurrection bodies that Christians will receive. Think about the hope that the Bible offers for life after death—this glorified state that is to come.

Glorification refers specifically to the perfection of God's redeemed people in every way. The Bible teaches us that we will be made glorious both physically and spiritually.

First, we will be *physically* perfected. This is the aspect of glorification that Paul focuses on in the passage from 1 Corinthians 15. The bodies that we have now are good gifts from God, but they also grow sick, age, and die; we are mortal. One day, though, Christians will be given new, perfect, immortal resurrection bodies. They will be physical bodies, but they will be perfected—not able to grow sick or weary, or to die. As we have seen, Paul tells us that because Jesus has been resurrected in this way, we too will experience this kind of resurrection.

Second, we will be *spiritually* perfected. Do you remember, in our discussion of sanctification, that we said that sanctification is never complete in this earthly life? We learned that while Christians should be becoming more and more like Jesus throughout their lives, their sanctification will not be perfect until heaven. Well, this will indeed happen one day, after death. The moment we die, we will be with Jesus—spiritually present with our Savior and freed from sin. At the resurrection, in our glorified bodies, we will experience a world that is not infected with sin. We will no longer give in to temptation because we will be freed from the very presence of sin. We will not sin in anger, lust, hatred, envy, or greed anymore. When Jesus has made an end of sin, Satan, and death, we will finally know what a glorified and totally sanctified state of life is like!

Because of this future hope of glorification, there is a certain way that we can talk about our salvation in Jesus Christ. We can say that it is "now and not yet." Here is what we mean:

- Our salvation is *now*. We have been justified and saved by God by grace through faith in Christ. Our salvation is secured!
- Our salvation is *not yet*. We are still waiting for the end—the last step—of our salvation; we are waiting for the final resurrection,

when we will finally be glorified and perfected to serve Jesus forever in the new heaven and new earth.

So you have now come through the five steps of the order of salvation that we have been learning. Just to review, here is where we have come:

1. Election—God sovereignly chooses some, before the foundation of the world, whom he will save through Christ.
2. Regeneration—God works by his Holy Spirit in the hearts of dead sinners to make them "come alive" and respond in faith to Jesus Christ.
3. Justification—God declares sinners to be righteous on the basis of the finished work of Jesus Christ on the cross—a work that sinners accept through faith.
4. Sanctification—God continues to make justified sinners more and more holy as they strive to grow in their obedience by the power of the indwelling Holy Spirit.
5. Glorification—God will finally perfect and glorify his redeemed people, giving them resurrection bodies and completing their sanctification.

▲ PRAY!

Thank God for the amazing eternal future that he has in store for all his people. Thank him that, if you follow Jesus Christ, you have a glorious eternity ahead of you that includes a resurrected body and life with your Savior in the new heaven and new earth. Ask God to give you assurance that this great future is really ahead.

ATONEMENT THEORIES

Our study of the order of salvation has shown that salvation starts with God and ends with God; it began before the foundation of the world and will continue into eternity forever and ever. If you have not thought about the greatness of God's salvation of human beings before, hopefully this study is moving you and causing you to praise him greatly!

Now we need to focus very specifically on what Jesus did on the cross. Because Jesus's death on the cross is so central to how the Bible presents salvation to us, it is good for us to make sure that we understand all that it really means.

To begin, we will focus on three main theories of the atonement—different ways of looking at Jesus's work on the cross. Our goal is to see what certain people tend to emphasize about Jesus's death and ultimately move toward a full understanding of the cross and its central meaning.

READ!

Read Colossians 2:13–15 (especially v. 15) and Philippians 2:1–11, both of which connect to one atonement theory that we will discuss. As you read these passages, consider what Paul (the author in both cases) is emphasizing about Christ's death on the cross. Think about how—based on these verses alone—you might understand the death of Jesus to function for God's people.

It is good to get a picture of what people tend to focus on as they consider the cross of Christ and his death there. So we will now move through the three most prevalent atonement theories and explain why it is important to understand them.

The Christus Victor *theory.* This theory of the atonement suggests that, above all, Jesus's death on the cross was about winning a battle over the forces of Satan and God's enemies. Christ, the "Victor," triumphed over the forces of evil through his death on the cross, winning a great victory by humbly dying. You can see how this theory could come about through focusing only on verses such as Colossians 2:15, which depicts Christ "triumphing" over God's enemies through the cross.

Victory certainly is a real aspect of what Jesus did on the cross; he did defeat Satan, sin, and death forever through his sacrifice. But that was not the only thing that happened through his death.

The moral exemplar theory. Another theory of the atonement suggests that, above all, Jesus's death on the cross was about giving God's people an example of love, sacrifice, humility, and service to others. You can see how this theory might emerge from focusing primarily on passages such as Philippians 2:1-11, which does indeed call God's people to look to Jesus's example of serving and loving others, and emulate it. According to this theory, Jesus's sacrifice is mainly about calling God's people to lay down their lives for God and his people.

This is a real aspect of what Jesus did on the cross; he did give a great example of love and sacrifice to God's people, which we are called to follow. But this is also not the only thing that Jesus did through his death on the cross.

The substitution theory. This theory of the atonement suggests that, according to many passages in Scripture, Jesus's death on the cross was a sacrificial and substitute death in the place of sinners. This theory teaches that, above all, Jesus died to substitute himself to really pay for the sins of God's people and to bear God's wrath in their place. As you can tell, the teaching in this chapter adheres most closely to this theory of the atonement (we will talk more about this below).

Jesus accomplished many things at the cross. He *did* triumph over Satan, sin, and death, so there is truth in the *Christus Victor* theory of the atonement. He *did* give his people an example of love and sacrifice, so there is truth in the moral exemplar theory. But Jesus also really did substitute himself as the sacrifice for God's people's sins. We must not lose that as the central aspect of Jesus's death on the cross!

⬥ **PRAY!**

Think through all that Jesus accomplished on the cross. Thank God that his death was much more than a victory over Satan or just an example to us. Thank him that his death really was a substitution for God's people. Because it was, we can know that our sins really can be forgiven and taken away. Praise God for Jesus's sacrifice and ask him to help you always remember it!

WHAT WAS ACCOMPLISHED AT THE CROSS?

As we approach the end of this chapter on soteriology, we need to take an even closer look at the cross of Jesus Christ and all that was accomplished there. You will be examining a few of the ways that the Bible talks about the work of Jesus. By the end of this discussion, you hopefully will have a greater picture of the God who saves sinners through the gracious gift of his own Son.

📖 **READ!**

Read Colossians 1:15–23; read it two times all the way through. Think about the main way that this passage is teaching us about salvation through Christ. Consider Paul's focus in this section of his letter and the way that he is trying to show the beauty of God's salvation.

In this last portion of our discussion of salvation, we are seeking to answer a simple yet complex question: What *is* salvation? Another way to phrase this question is to ask, "What exactly happened at the cross of Jesus?" The goal of this final part of the chapter will be to help you understand some of the different ways that the Bible talks about human salvation and see the "bigness" of the salvation that God offers to sinful human beings through his Son.

Here are some of the main ways the Bible describes what happened when Jesus died on the cross:

THE DOCTRINE OF SALVATION

- Reconciliation. This is the particular aspect of Jesus's death on the cross that Paul highlights in the passage from Colossians 1 that you just read. By Jesus's death, according to Scripture, God "reconciles" sinful human begins to himself. The cross is the only way in which sinful human beings can be brought back into a right relationship with the holy God—for that relationship has been infinitely damaged by sin.

- Redemption. Many times in the New Testament, the work of Christ on the cross is described as "redemption." This word literally refers to a kind of "buying back" from slavery; in Bible times, you could "redeem" a slave or a servant through the payment of a price. So when Jesus died on the cross for God's people, he literally redeemed them; he "bought them back" from slavery to sin.

- Substitution/sacrifice. The whole sacrificial system of the Old Testament pointed forward to Jesus. Throughout the Old Testament, God's people were instructed to sacrifice various animals as "substitutes" for their sin, which God chose to accept until Jesus came to be the final sacrifice. Jesus, then, is presented to us in the Bible as the ultimate substitute; his death is really and truly the final sacrifice for the sins of God's guilty people.

- Propitiation. We learned about this word in chapter 3 and again in chapter 5; do you remember it? Literally, propitiation has to do with the removal of wrath. Paul uses this word in Romans, and the apostle John uses it in his first epistle. Jesus's death on the cross is presented to us in Scripture as the way that God chose to pour out his wrath against sin—not on his people, but on his Son in their place.

- Justification. Finally, the Bible presents the cross of Jesus Christ as the place where God really justifies sinners; he declares sinners righteous because of what Jesus has done. This is a legal word that, in Christianity, refers to the right standing that comes to sinners before the holy God on the basis of Jesus's work. The cross, then, is about full justification for sinners who would otherwise stand guilty and condemned before the holy God.

There are, of course, more ways to explain what happened on the cross. But these are some of the central ways that the Bible describes Jesus's work. Hopefully you are at least seeing how huge God's salvation to sinners in Christ really is. The right response is a heart filled with repentance for sin and faith in Jesus Christ as the only true Savior of sinners.

PRAY!

Ask God to give you a properly big view of the salvation that he has offered to sinners through his Son. Think carefully about the reconciliation, redemption, sacrifice, propitiation, justification, and more that Jesus's death accomplished for God's people. Pray that God would give you a heart that is filled with thankfulness for all that he has done for you through his Son.

REVIEW

You have learned much in this chapter about God's great salvation through Christ. Hopefully you have come to see more clearly his greatness in this salvation—from beginning to end. We'll end the chapter by reviewing the concepts and lessons that you have learned. Here are a few key points for you to remember:

Salvation and the Old Testament

- The Old Testament pointed God's people forward to a full picture of his salvation, which would be fully revealed in his Son, Jesus Christ.
- From the very moment of the fall of Adam and Eve, God promised ultimate victory over sin, Satan, and death through the "offspring" of the woman (Jesus).

- The ark of Noah pointed to the fact that salvation from judgment was needed.
- The law of Moses pointed to the fact that a final sacrifice for sin was needed.
- Isaiah pointed God's people toward a suffering servant who would bear their sin.

Election

- God chose to save some people before the foundation of the world, according to the apostle Paul in Ephesians 1.
- The doctrine of election in no way cancels out human responsibility anywhere in the Bible.
- Salvation starts with God, who had a sovereign plan for salvation even before he created the world.

Regeneration

- Because of total depravity, human beings are unable to choose God by their own strength, power, or goodness.
- Regeneration refers to God miraculously making humans "come alive" so that they are able to repent of sin and put their faith in Jesus.
- Regeneration is God's action by the power of his Holy Spirit.

Justification

- Justification is an act of God, who freely declares sinners to be just on the basis of the work of Jesus on the cross.
- Justification is a legal term, indicating that sinners can actually be declared righteous and just before the holy God.

Sanctification

- Sanctification refers to the process of becoming more holy, more like Jesus, and more set apart for God's work.

- Sanctification is the work of the Holy Spirit, but human beings also work hard at their sanctification as they follow Jesus.
- Sanctification will not be fully completed in this life.

Glorification

- Glorification is the final step in salvation; it refers to the resurrected and perfected state of the believer in Jesus Christ.
- Glorification will mark the completion of sanctification.
- Glorification reminds us that our salvation is now and not yet.

Atonement Theories

- The *Christus Victor* theory of the atonement sees Jesus as primarily triumphing over Satan at the cross.
- The moral exemplar theory of the atonement sees Jesus's work on the cross as mainly a great example.
- The substitution theory of the atonement sees Jesus as the real substitute for sinners on the cross.

The Cross

- There are different ways in which the Bible describes what Jesus did on the cross, including reconciliation, redemption, sacrifice, propitiation, and justification.
- Through these descriptions of Jesus's death and the salvation that God brings through it, we should have a very full and big picture of all that God accomplished through his Son.

Remember!

Can you say or write your memory verses for this chapter perfectly? Do so right now. As you do, consider again the bold affirmation of the apostles that salvation is found in Jesus—and in no other name under heaven!

PRAY!

Ask God to give you strength and wisdom to understand his salvation well. Pray that he would help you to see the beauty of all that he has done for sinful human beings through Jesus. Then pray for boldness to share this great salvation with the world. Ask God to make you courageous as a witness to the only Savior of sinners.

Chapter 8
THE DOCTRINE OF HEAVEN AND HELL

We come now to the category of systematic theology about which there may be more confusion than any other—heaven and hell. We have many questions to answer and misconceptions to correct! But doing so will be time well spent because of the deep truths about God himself and the wonderful salvation he has provided for us that we can learn by considering heaven and hell.

As has been our goal throughout this book, we will seek in this chapter to base all that we say on the teaching of the Bible as we examine key points that it makes about the eternal destiny of human beings—those who trust Jesus Christ as Savior and those who reject him. Hopefully, by the end of this chapter, you will have a much better grasp of what we can know—from Scripture—about these important doctrines.

In this chapter, we'll seek to do the following: (1) examine and correct misconceptions about heaven and hell; (2) try to understand what heaven and hell can teach us about God (there is actually much for us to learn since both places are connected to the character of God); (3) dig into the question of what heaven and hell actually are; (4) seek to answer some common questions about heaven and hell; and (5) make some applications of the truths of heaven and hell to our lives.

It is good for you to be aware of a few important ways to approach this discussion:

- You should begin to think more often of your own eternal destiny and the eternal destiny of others. The Bible is extremely clear that heaven and hell are very real places, not just theological ideas. Also, as you learn the concepts and lessons of this chapter and become convinced of the reality of heaven and hell, you should think more often about the need to share the gospel with others. Every human being you know and see is bound for either heaven or hell.
- It is important to remember that heaven and hell—as destinations—are based on different responses to Jesus. We will come back often to the importance of accepting Christ as Savior and Lord. The response to God's Son truly determines the eternal destiny of every human being.
- We will be careful to ground much of our conversation about these difficult topics in the character of God. Hell is not an easy concept to talk about. In one sense, we should not be able to discuss it without sadness in our hearts as we think about people who have rejected God and his Son, Jesus Christ. Yet we will try to see how God's just and righteous character leads us to our belief in this truth.

Remember!

Your suggested memory verses for this chapter come from Revelation 22—the very last chapter in the Bible. These words are the apostle John's description of the great vision Jesus gave to him of the eternal glories of heaven that are ahead for followers of Christ. Read these words slowly and carefully, thinking about the great promises that are contained here.

Then the angel showed me the river of the water of life, bright as crystal, flowing from the throne of God and of the Lamb through the middle of the street of the city; also, on either side of the river, the tree of life with its twelve kinds of fruit, yielding its fruit each month. The leaves of the tree were for the healing of the nations. No longer will there be anything accursed, but the throne of God and of the Lamb will be in it, and his servants will worship him. They will see his face, and his name will be on their foreheads. And night will be no more. They will need no light of lamp or sun, for the Lord God will be their light, and they will reign forever and ever. (Rev. 22:1–5)

PRAY!

Pray simply that God would help you begin thinking more often about your eternal destiny and that of others. Ask him to help you become even more convinced of the truth of the gospel so that you want to share it with people around you.

MISCONCEPTIONS ABOUT HEAVEN AND HELL

Because there is so much confusion and incorrect teaching about both heaven and hell, we will start by digging into some of the most common false beliefs about both places. As always, we want to counter false ideas about these doctrines with the truth of the Bible.

READ!

Spend a few minutes reading through Revelation 21:1–8. Think about how this passage can remind us of how we should be picturing and thinking about heaven. Consider the hope that this passage offers to Christians as they consider the world that God is preparing and their role in it.

The most common misconceptions about heaven and hell have to do with their nature and purpose. There are many false ideas about what they will be like and what will happen there, but the word of God gives us clear pictures in both cases.

Heaven

Here are a couple of common misconceptions about heaven:

Heaven is a spiritual place but not a physical place. This is a bit tricky because there is a sense in which heaven—as it exists right now—*is* a spiritual place. It is a real place (Jesus is there with his resurrected physical body!), but believers who have died are with Jesus in spirit only since the resurrection has not yet happened. But the heaven that we are talking about—the one that will last for all eternity—will be a very physical place. Christians will dwell in this place with physical resurrection bodies. In other words, heaven will not just be heaven; it will be a new heaven and a new earth. We will talk more about this below.

Heaven will be boring. This misconception comes from the popular depictions of heaven with clouds, angels, and harps. If it were our eternal destiny to sit around on clouds all day playing harps, that might indeed be boring (unless you really enjoy playing the harp). Heaven, though, will be an eternal existence of joy, feasting, and growing in the knowledge of God and his new creation. There will be nothing boring about it!

We will go deeper into these truths later in this chapter.

Hell

Here are three common misconceptions about the doctrine—and reality—of hell:

Hell is where Satan reigns. Often in popular literature, movies, and cartoons, Satan (usually pictured with horns and a pitchfork) is portrayed as ruling over all of the people who are in hell. This portrayal is usually fairly mild, with Satan acting as a kind of taskmaster for people who are in hell. However, the Bible is clear that Satan will not have any special or exalted place for eternity—even in hell. Revelation 20 shows Satan finally cast into the lake of fire; he, too, will suffer the eternal punishment of divine wrath because of his rebellion against God and his hatred of God's people.

Hell is a place of destruction, not punishment. Often, in order to make the concept of hell seem more acceptable, people teach that hell is ultimately not punishment but destruction. In other words, they try to make the argument that the Bible presents hell as simply the final death of people who reject Christ. This is not what the Bible teaches. Jesus and many of the apostles clearly use the language of "eternal punishment" to describe hell. The Bible clearly teaches an eternal, conscious punishment for those who reject Jesus Christ. We will discuss this more later.

People in hell will get a second chance. In popular literature and thinking, there is often a tendency to teach that the doors of hell are locked from the inside—that even people in hell will always have a chance to repent and turn to Jesus. The Bible does not teach this; it says that every man and woman lives once, and after this life he or she stands in judgment before God (Heb. 9:27). We all will be judged eternally on the basis of what we do with Jesus Christ in this life, and there will be no second chances.

⬤ PRAY!

Ask God to give you an accurate understanding of both heaven and hell as you carefully study his word and listen to it. Pray that he would help you understand more and more his glorious and gracious character and the importance of responding in faith to his Son, Jesus Christ, now.

WHAT HEAVEN AND HELL TEACH US ABOUT GOD

We have seen that the word *theology* literally means "God talk." When we engage in theology, we are talking together about God and things that relate to God. As surprising as it may sound, this is true even for the doctrines of heaven and hell. Both heaven and hell are very connected to the character of God. Because we want our theology to be not just an academic discipline, but also something that draws us nearer to God, it is appropriate that we consider what these doctrines teach us about God even before we get into the details about them.

Heaven and God's Character

First we will see how the hope of heaven, as presented to us in Scripture, points to the grace, mercy, and generosity of a loving God.

READ!

Spend some time reading and thinking about the following passage: 2 Thessalonians 1:5–12. Read this passage carefully two times through, if you have enough time. Consider what it says about God's character in relation to his people (the "saints"), how he loves and cares for them.

The concept of heaven—the fact that it is a real hope for Christians, according to the Bible—offers an important lesson about God's character and heart toward his people.

Do you remember the doctrine of "aseity," which we learned about in chapter 3 when we considered the doctrine of God? There we learned that God does not need anything at all; he certainly does not need a heaven filled with redeemed people in order to fulfill something that is lacking in who he is! Yet God ordained and planned not only the redemption and salvation of his people, but also a glorious existence for them in a new heaven and a new earth! This points us to an amazingly gracious and generous God—one who has richly and generously provided an eternal inheritance for sinful people who need him desperately.

Just listen to the words of Jesus as he told his disciples about the good place that he was going away to prepare for them: "Let not your hearts be troubled. Believe in God; believe also in me. In my Father's house are many rooms. If it were not so, would I have told you that I go to prepare a place for you? And if I go and prepare a place for you, I will come again and will take you to myself, that where I am you may be also. And you know the way to where I am going" (John 14:1–4).

This is an amazing gift of God! Jesus promised his disciples that when he went away, he would prepare a place for them—a place in God's new heaven and new earth (God's "house" for his people). The hope and existence of heaven, then, point us to these truths about God's character:

- God is generous. He delights in giving good gifts to his children, and he is preparing an eternal place for them that is far beyond the greatest joys and pleasures of this world.
- God is gracious. God not only saves his people from sin and death, but he graciously provides them with an abundant and perfect eternal home with him.
- God is loving. God really does want to share eternity with the people whom he created and loves; he delights in them and wants them to sing his praises.

It is good for us to remember that the existence of heaven points us to a God who delights in giving gracious and generous gifts to the children he loves and has redeemed through the work of his Son, Jesus Christ.

PRAY!

Spend some time simply thanking God for his grace, mercy, love, and generosity—all of which are revealed in his planning of eternal joy and pleasures for his people. He did not have to plan things this way. Yet he chose to show grace to sinners through his Son, Jesus Christ, and chose to include us in his eternal plan. Praise God for this!

Hell and God's Character

The existence of hell also teaches us about God's character. God saves some people, but he also judges eternally those who reject him and his offer of salvation through his Son; the Bible clearly teaches this.

READ!

Take a minute to read the same passage that you read just above: 2 Thessalonians 1:5–12. This time, though, focus on what is said about those who oppose God the Father and his Son, Jesus Christ. Consider deeply how God will interact with that group of people, according to this passage. Think about how these verses can help us form our understanding of the doctrine of hell—and how it relates to the character of God.

How does the reality of hell—eternal punishment, as defined by the Bible—inform our understanding of the character of God? It teaches us the following:

God is just. The fact that there is a place of eternal punishment reminds us that the Creator God of the universe is just. Because he is absolutely righteous, he must justly punish all sin. In fact, if God were not to completely punish all sin, he would cease to be God, for he would no longer be righteous. The justice of God demands that he deal completely with all sin and rebellion against his holy character. The fact that there is a hell means that God will deal with sin in an eternal and final way.

God is wrathful toward sin. The doctrine of hell also teaches us that not only is God just, but he also executes his wrath on sinners. Sin angers God; for this reason, he not only ensures that the consequences are paid, but actually personally executes his wrath against the people who commit sin by sending them to hell if they refuse his offer of salvation through Christ. This truth is demonstrated in all of the Bible.

God has provided one way for salvation. Finally, the fact that hell exists as a place of eternal punishment reminds us that God has provided one way for salvation—the way that Jesus Christ, his Son, paved through his sacrificial death on the cross. The violence and horrible nature of hell remind us of the eternal consequences of rejecting the one great and clear offer of salvation that the God of the universe has given to sinful men and women. He will not accept any human being who rejects this offer.

When we consider passages such as the one you read from 2 Thessalonians, it is often difficult for us to understand the terrible wrath of God against sin. At such times, we have to continue to affirm that God is just, that his wrath is rightly poured out against sin, and that his one offer of salvation through his Son is not to be ignored. This is what the doctrine of hell teaches us about the God of the universe.

PRAY!

Pray along the following lines:

- *Ask God to help you understand his justice even more clearly as you consider your own sin and need for the death of Jesus.*
- *Pray that God would help you be more urgent about sharing the gospel with people who are facing his wrath if they never trust Jesus.*
- *Ask God to make you even more thankful for the grace of Jesus Christ, which spares you from his wrath if you trust him!*

WHAT ARE HEAVEN AND HELL?

Let's now begin examining both heaven and hell more carefully. What *is* heaven? What *is* hell?

Heaven

As we begin our discussion about heaven, we will consider a brief narrative from the story of Jesus's crucifixion in Luke's Gospel. This account reveals something interesting about heaven.

📖 READ!

Read Luke 23:32–43 carefully, focusing on the conversation that Jesus has with the criminal who looks to him in trust and belief. Note what Jesus says to him; consider what that means about heaven now and in the future.

As we compare the passage from Luke 23 with other parts of the Bible, we see that there is a way to talk about heaven right now and a way to talk about heaven in the future.

Heaven now. Based on what we see in Scripture, heaven right now is a real place where God dwells and rules with the risen Lord Jesus at his right hand. The very fact that Jesus could say to the criminal who was crucified with him that he would be in "paradise" with him "today" (Luke 23:43) tells us that there is a place—which we call "heaven"— to which God's people go when they die. We know that those who go to heaven now do not yet have their resurrected bodies; Paul makes it clear to us that the physical bodies of those who die wait in the ground for the resurrection from the dead (1 Cor. 15). But the Bible is insistent that when believers die, they are *immediately* with Jesus in heaven.

So heaven right now is a real place that is separate from this earth. The souls of believers are there, present with Jesus, and waiting for the resurrection of their physical bodies to the glorified state.

Heaven in the future. In the future, after the resurrection, heaven will still be a place, but it will be far different than it is now. The apostle Peter makes it clear that this present earth will one day be "dissolved"— burned up as by fire (see 2 Pet. 3:10)—and will be no more. John tells us that God will make a new heaven and a new earth—a place for God's people to dwell forever with him (see Rev. 21). This new heaven and earth will not be separated as they are now; heaven and earth will actually be one. God will dwell in the midst of his people, and believers in Jesus will walk, run, worship, and celebrate in a physical heaven/earth with glorified resurrection bodies. This new heaven and earth will be like this earth in some ways—but far greater, more beautiful, and perfect.

So in the future, heaven will still be a real place, but it will be heaven and earth all rolled into one. The old earth will be gone forever.

There are many things about the new heaven and earth that the Bible does not tell us; we will talk more about that later. But the Bible does tell us what is most important. The hope of Christians is that they will live forever in the presence of Jesus, worshiping and serving him. There will be no more death, pain, tears, or sin; life will finally be perfect and good with God in his place.

PRAY!

As you pause to pray, thank God for giving us enough information about heaven to give us reason to hope boldly in the new heaven and new earth—and in life forever with him. Pray that he would help you think more often about eternity so that you are motivated to follow him and tell others about his great salvation.

Hell

As we turn our attention from heaven to hell, we have to remember that this is a topic that we should never take lightly. We need to treat what the Bible teaches us about hell seriously because it emphasizes the seriousness of sin and the great holiness of the Creator God. Also, any discussion of hell should motivate Christians to share the gospel with people who do not know Jesus yet.

READ!

Read Matthew 25:31–46—a passage in which Jesus describes the final judgment that will come when he returns to earth. Pay attention, especially, to what Jesus says about the eternal punishment of hell in verses 41 and 46. Think about how Jesus's words teach us about hell; consider how he warns people to respond to him in faith and obedience.

What does the Bible teach us about hell—this place of punishment for all who reject God and his salvation through Jesus?

First, the Bible tells us that hell is a place. The passage that you read from Matthew 25 speaks of the "eternal fire prepared for the devil and his angels" (Matt. 25:41). Jesus points to a place of punishment where Satan will be thrown—as well as people who do not follow Jesus and love others in his name. John speaks of the "lake of fire and sulfur" into which Satan will be finally thrown at the last judgment of Jesus Christ (Rev. 20:10).

Second, the Bible teaches that hell is a place of "eternal punishment" for those who have sinned against the infinitely holy God. That is the exact phrase that Jesus uses in Matthew 25:46, and he uses similar phrases at other places in the Gospels. There is no hint in Scripture of hell being anything other than a final and everlasting judgment for Satan and all who reject the offer of salvation through Jesus Christ. It is not a final destruction or a mere end of existence.

Third, the Bible teaches that hell will be a place where no one will experience the grace and love of God toward his people. Those in hell will know God's presence in a way, but they will be experiencing the wrath of God against sin without any of his grace and love. So, there is also a very real sense in which hell will be eternal separation from God—from all of his goodness, grace, and love. Even those who do not know Jesus in the world today cannot fully imagine an existence without some experience of God's grace and presence; life on this earth is *full* of God's grace every day. Even the fact that we have breath and life is an example of God's "common grace," which he gives to all people. Hell, though, will be the full experience of God's wrath without his gracious and kind presence. It will be eternal torment.

It should be difficult for us to speak about these weighty truths without tears coming to our eyes and our hearts being moved to share the gospel of Jesus Christ with those who do not yet know him. As we have seen in earlier chapters, Peter reminds us that God is waiting patiently to bring his final judgment on this world because he wants more people to repent and turn to Jesus (2 Pet. 3:9)! Would you be a part of God's saving work today? Would you be courageous to share the life-giving eternal message of Jesus Christ with those around you?

⬆ PRAY!

Ask God to help you take sin more seriously, consider his holiness more deeply, and see the wonder of his salvation through Jesus even more clearly! A consideration of God's wrath and the seriousness of sin should make us cry out to God for mercy as we put our faith in his Son.

COMMON QUESTIONS ABOUT HEAVEN AND HELL

Because there are so many false ideas about heaven and hell, even in the Christian world, we will now seek to answer a few common questions that emerge as people think through these doctrines. This section will involve more application of biblical principles since the Bible does not tell us *everything* about heaven and hell. Yet as we read Scripture and apply its truths, we can draw good conclusions about what eternal life in the new heaven and new earth will be like for God's people. Sadly, Scripture also helps us do the same for the eternal destiny of those who reject Jesus.

Heaven

We'll first wrestle with common questions about heaven. The Bible gives us clearer answers for some of these questions than for others, but all of them can be answered to some degree through biblical principles and truths.

📖 READ!

Read Matthew 22:23–33—the account of Jesus's interaction with the Sadducees, who try to stump him with a question about heaven and the resurrection (in which they actually do not even believe). Consider Jesus's words about heaven (and about marriage as well).

Here are some common questions about heaven that believers often ask:

What will we do in heaven? Many people wonder what we will actually do all day long in heaven for all eternity. While the Bible does not go into much detail about the actual activities of people in the new heaven and new earth, we know that everything will be done in worship to the Lord Jesus Christ. However, it is probably not right to see eternity as one big worship service—at least as we define such a service today. It is not wrong to think about jobs, work, feasting, and even fun explorations of God's creation. All of this will be done under the rule of Jesus and for his glory!

Will there be animals in heaven? This is a question that we cannot perfectly and finally answer, but it does seem logical to think that, in a new earth, there could be perfected animals for God's glory and the delight of human beings. The best way to answer this question is to note that the joy that animals bring us here on earth will be perfectly completed and satisfied in eternity with Jesus. We simply cannot yet know what that experience of joy will look like.

Will we recognize other people in heaven? It seems to be a good principle that in heaven, we will not know *less* than we do here on earth. So it seems right to assume that we will recognize loved ones, family members, and brothers and sisters from our churches when we see them in heaven. We will join together to share stories of God's grace and will delight in worshiping and praising the Savior together as his unified and redeemed people.

Will people who are married in this life still be married in heaven? Jesus clearly addresses this question in his reply to the Sadducees in the passage that you read above. His answer is no! In heaven, marriage will be no more. Why is this? It is because marriage was always meant to point us to the deepest marriage, the one between Christ and his church (see Eph. 5:22–33). Human marriage is not the end goal in and of itself; it is meant to point us—and the world—to the ultimate perfect union between God and his people through Christ Jesus (see Rev. 21:1–2, where God's people are presented to him as a "bride adorned for her husband"). When that union is perfectly fulfilled in heaven, human marriage will no longer be necessary, because the greater marriage will have begun—and it will continue forever.

Will it be possible to sin in heaven? This is another question for which the answer is a resounding no! This should be deeply encouraging to us. In our resurrected and perfected bodies, our sinful nature will finally be gone. Sin and death will be eternally defeated by Jesus, and we will not be able to sin anymore, nor will we even be tempted to sin. Our life in the new heaven and earth will be, finally, a perfect existence and an unstained relationship with God and other people.

Staying focused on Jesus. In the midst of all of these questions about heaven, it is important for us always to stay focused on the main thing— the eternal hope of Christians, Jesus Christ. We should ask ourselves, "What am I looking forward to most about heaven?" If our hearts are rightly worshiping, then the answer should be God. He is our goal, our prize, and our treasure. All the other blessings of heaven are just added gifts on top of dwelling forever in the presence of our Creator and Savior.

◐ PRAY!

Ask God to give you strength and wisdom to keep learning from his word as you seek to know more about heaven, hell, and eternity. Thank him for making so many things clear to us, and ask him for patience and faith with regard to the questions that you still have. Most of all, pray that he would help you stay focused on Jesus himself as the true and final hope of Christians.

Hell

Now let's turn our attention to some common questions that people ask about the doctrine and reality of hell. As with the questions we considered about heaven, many of these questions are not specifically addressed in Scripture, but we can apply biblical principles and truths to reach careful and thoughtful answers. Perhaps you have personally wrestled with some of these questions or will one day be able to help a friend wrestle with them as you are guided by God's word.

▨ READ!

Read Luke 16:19–31—Jesus's parable about the rich man and Lazarus (a different Lazarus than the one whom Jesus raised from the dead). While this is a parable, it is appropriate to assume that Jesus's teaching about hell and eternity in this passage reflects reality. Consider what he is teaching. What is his main point? What are we learning about hell and eternal punishment?

Here are some common questions about hell that often trouble believers:

Will Satan rule hell for all eternity? In Revelation 20, we see Satan himself being thrown into the eternal lake of fire (v. 10). He will not have a "reign" in hell, but will be judged and eternally punished along with all who have rejected God's rule and God's word. This is the best understanding that we can gain from Scripture on this subject.

Will the presence of earthly friends provide any comfort in hell? You may have heard people say, jokingly, concerning the possibility of spending eternity in hell, "That's all right; I will be with my friends." Sadly, there will be no comfort in hell from being with people they loved on earth. The torments of being under God's wrath and eternal punishment will be so horrific and painful that even the presence of other human beings will not help at all. Also, those relationships, which on earth had at least some hints of God's "common grace" in them, will now have nothing but sin, death, and punishment attached to them.

Will God be present in hell? This final question is a challenging one, especially since many people today like to define hell as "the absence of God." That is not completely accurate because God, being omnipresent, is everywhere and reigns over all. It is probably better, given the teaching of the Bible, to say that hell is the experience of the overwhelming wrath of God against sin without any experience of his grace or love. We simply cannot even imagine what that would be like. Hell will include the presence of God, but it will be manifested only in his terrible wrath against sin.

▲ PRAY!

If you belong to God through faith in Jesus Christ, thank him that you have a certain hope of escape from his judgment. If you are not sure that you have a relationship with God, spend some time talking to him about it. If there are Christians in your life whom you trust, talk to them as well. This is the most important matter in the entire world, as it concerns your eternal soul!

IMPLICATIONS FOR CHRISTIANS

You have put in a great amount of work and done much learning in the area of systematic theology. You have studied what the Bible says about God, salvation, human beings, sin, and more. Hopefully you have discovered many new truths about these categories as we have looked carefully at the teaching of Scripture about them.

As you continue to learn, though, the goal should be not merely to amass information and knowledge about God, but to continue growing closer to him in faith through a vibrant relationship with his Son, Jesus Christ. That is what the final pages of this chapter are designed to help you do. By taking time to apply the truths we have been learning about the doctrines of heaven and hell, you will be reminded that theology must be a matter not just of the head but also of the heart.

📖 READ!

Read 2 Corinthians 5:1–10, which focuses on the contrast between our earthly dwelling (the "tent" of our physical bodies) and our eternal heavenly dwelling with Christ. Consider the descriptions of the groaning now (v. 2) as Christians wait for the day when they are "at home" with the Lord (v. 8). Notice that the Spirit is the guarantee of the good things that are to come for those who belong to Jesus Christ (v. 5).

What are some implications of the doctrine of heaven and hell for Christians?

First, these doctrines should remind us constantly of the seriousness of human sin against the holy, infinite, and eternal God. The very existence of hell—the need for justice and wrath to be satisfied eternally—reminds us that human sin is deathly serious. It must be paid for—either by Jesus on the cross or by sinners themselves for all eternity in hell. All that we have learned about hell in this chapter should make us take the sin in our hearts and lives extremely seriously. God really does hate sin, and all sin that is not covered by the blood of Jesus Christ will result in his wrath and judgment.

Second, though, the reality of heaven points us again and again to the amazing, generous grace of our loving God. As we learned, God did not have to create humans, redeem them, or give them an incredible future inheritance in the new heaven and new earth. God does these things out of the freedom of his will—from sheer delight and joy at showing grace to lost sinners who need him. When we read passages from the Bible that point to the eternal inheritance that Christians have in Jesus Christ, our response should always be wonder over God's undeserved favor toward us.

Third, our conversation about heaven and hell should remind us of the need for us to have an eternal perspective on life. We need to pray that God would give us more and more of an eternal view as we live every day. It is difficult, in the midst of everyday life, to think carefully about eternal things, but that is what Christians are called to do! This chapter should move us to consider deeply the eternity that is coming—both heaven for believers and hell for those who reject Jesus. This kind of consideration should motivate us to share the gospel with others as well!

Finally, the things we have considered in this chapter should remind us of the brevity of our existence on this earth. Whenever we discuss eternity, we should be reminded that every human being will die after a relatively short lifespan. The Creator God, though, has offered eternal life to weak, mortal human beings. Only in this way can we have hope for more than a short life that can be taken away so quickly.

Hopefully this chapter has enabled you to look toward eternity in a new way as you have considered deeply all that lies ahead for those who love Jesus and for those who reject him.

⬆ PRAY!

Ask God to help you to think more often about life with an eternal perspective. If you know Jesus through faith, pray that he would help you think with more assurance about your eternal future. As you think about hell as well, pray that God would give you more passion and urgency to share the good news of the gospel with people who need to hear it!

REVIEW

In this chapter, we have seen that the Bible speaks very openly and candidly about the reality of heaven and hell, and we would do well to think more often about the eternal destiny of human beings. Now we'll review the concepts that you have learned in this chapter. Here are a few key points for you to remember:

Heaven and God's Character

- The reality of heaven points to the generosity of God, who not only saves sinners, but provides them with a rich eternal inheritance.
- The reality of heaven also points to the grace of God, who gives sinners unmerited favor and eternal life with him.
- Heaven reminds us that God really does want to dwell with his people forever—that he truly desires an eternal relationship with the people he has created for his own glory.

Hell and God's Character

- The reality of hell points to the justice of God; he is perfectly righteous and just, and he will not let sin go unpunished.
- The reality of hell also points to the wrath of God against sin; he really is angered by sin, and he will pour out his wrath against it for all eternity upon those who reject Jesus.
- The reality of hell points to the finality of God's offer of salvation through his Son, Jesus Christ. Hell reminds us that God truly has provided for salvation, and he will not be happy if his Son is rejected and scorned.

What Is Heaven?

- Heaven now is a spiritual place; it is not the final heaven that John looks forward to in Revelation 21.
- In the future, heaven will be a different real place—a physical new heaven and new earth, which believers in Jesus will experience with resurrection bodies that are perfectly glorified.
- Heaven (the new heaven and new earth) will be the final dwelling place for God and his redeemed people, where they will live together in perfect relationship forever.

What Is Hell?

- Hell is also a real place, where the Bible teaches that those who reject Jesus will experience spiritual and physical punishment for sin.
- Hell is not so much the absence of God as it is the full experience of his wrath against sin—without any of his mercy or grace.

Common Questions about Heaven

- Heaven will not include human marriage, as human marriage is meant to point to the perfect eternal relationship between God and his people.
- In heaven, there will be no more sin; the sinful nature in human beings will be destroyed, and God's people will finally be free to live in right relationship with both God and others.
- Heaven will be far from boring! It will be the eternal experience of worshiping God—learning from him, working for him, serving him, and enjoying his marvelous new creation.

Common Questions about Hell

- Even Satan will be thrown into the lake of fire (see Rev. 20); we should not think of him as "ruling" in hell for eternity.
- The Bible speaks of a final judgment for all people; it does not point us toward second chances for those who reject Jesus Christ in a final way.

- Hell will be a place of eternal punishment, not a place of final destruction (where people simply cease to exist).

Remember!

Can you say or write your suggested memory verses for this chapter perfectly? Do so right now. As you do, consider the glorious future hope of which John's vision reminds Christians.

◢ PRAY!

As you end this chapter on heaven and hell in prayer, ask God to give you an eternal perspective on this life as you consider all that is ahead for those who love Jesus and for those who reject him. Pray that he would help you think more often of the Christian eternal hope, which comes through faith in Jesus Christ alone. Ask him to help you be more excited and passionate about sharing the hope of the gospel with people who need to hear it.

Chapter 9

THE DOCTRINE
OF THE CHURCH

Hopefully, if you are a follower of Jesus Christ, you are involved in some kind of local church community. As you will
learn in this chapter, local churches have been the primary
way that the gospel of Jesus Christ has been taught, lived
out, and passed on since the resurrection and ascension of
Jesus Christ. Although the church can often seem weak and
imperfect, the Bible actually makes clear that it is God's main
focus of work and witness in the world today! In this chapter,
therefore, we are learning about something that is very near
to the heart of God—the church.

The formal name for this category of systematic theology is "ecclesiology"
(the study of the church). It is important to note that this doctrine is especially and immediately applicable to you—if you do follow Jesus—because
church life should be at the very center of your spiritual life and your relationships with other believers in Jesus. Hopefully this chapter will give you
a clearer understanding of several key points about the church, including:

- How the church started. We will look at the formation and development of the church in the days following Jesus's resurrection and

ascension. It is important to start here so that we have a clear picture of how we got to our current experience of church today. We will seek to understand exactly what the church is—how God views it and what he means for it to be in the lives of Christians and in the world he has made. Interestingly, while many people talk about the church a lot, very few of them can give a clear definition of what the church actually is! It is much more than a building, as we will see.

- The universal church and the local church. We will aim to clarify the important distinction between the universal and the local church. You have probably already noticed that, even in this initial discussion, we have talked about the church broadly and also about local churches specifically. There is both a difference and a connection between these two concepts.

- Church sacraments. We will seek to understand what the Bible teaches about the sacraments, then take a close look at the two Protestant sacraments—the Lord's Supper and baptism.

- Church government. There are numerous ideas about how churches should be led or governed—there are congregational, pastor-led, and elder-led types. We will seek to determine which is the most scriptural model.

- Marks of the church. Many Bible scholars agree that there are three marks of a true church of Jesus Christ—the preaching of the word of God, the administration of the sacraments, and the proper exercise of church government/discipline. We will examine the biblical arguments for these marks.

- Implications. Finally, we will seek to sum up what all of this means for believers who are members of the church of Jesus Christ.

All in all, our goal in this chapter is to give a clear picture of what the Bible teaches about God's church—the body that he has called out for himself and set up as his main mode of witness and work in this world. It is not a perfect institution, but it is dear to God, and Christians everywhere are called to love it and care for it.

Remember!

Your suggested memory verses for this chapter come from the apostle Paul's epistle to the ancient church at Ephesus. As you read these verses, think about the way in which Paul describes the church of God. Consider the "foundation" that he attributes to the church. Look at the way he says believers should be growing together. Is this how you usually think about the church? Why or why not?

So then you are no longer strangers and aliens, but you are fellow citizens with the saints and members of the household of God, built on the foundation of the apostles and prophets, Christ Jesus himself being the cornerstone, in whom the whole structure, being joined together, grows into a holy temple in the Lord. In him you also are being built together into a dwelling place for God by the Spirit. (Eph. 2:19–22)

PRAY!

As you dive into this new category of theology, spend some time devoting your study to God. Pray in the following ways:

- *Ask God for wisdom as you learn about the church and seek to see all that his word has to say about it.*
- *Pray for humility, that God would reveal areas in which you need to change the way you think about the church in general or your local church specifically.*
- *Ask God to give you strength and courage to be a servant of the church of Jesus Christ, if you are indeed a follower of him.*

CHURCH BEGINNINGS AND DEFINITION

Let's begin with the beginnings of the church in the first days following Jesus's resurrection and ascension. We will also move toward a basic definition of the church. Our goal here is to get a big-picture perspective on the nature of this eternal institution.

READ!

Read 1 Corinthians 1:1–3. Read this short passage several times, noting all that you can learn from it about Paul's view of the church at Corinth and its relation to the overall church of Jesus Christ.

Before the ascension of Jesus and the days of the apostles, the church (at least as we think about it now) did not exist. God has always had people for himself, of course, but the Jews met in the temple to worship God through sacrifice. By Jesus's time, there were synagogues as well—local places of worship and teaching where Jews could gather.

But after Jesus's ascension into heaven, he sent his Holy Spirit with special power to anoint the apostles (those who had been with him and learned from him) to preach the gospel and to help many people follow Jesus. Acts 2 records the first explosion of believers, as many people decided to put their faith in Jesus and become part of this early church.

The church became known as such in these first days because the word *church* (*ecclesia* in Greek) simply means "gathering" or "assembly." The early church was the gathering of followers of Jesus Christ. These gatherings began to be localized in certain towns, as followers of Jesus organized together and began meeting for worship, prayer, teaching, the Lord's Supper, and fellowship.

From Paul's greeting to the Corinthian believers that you read just above, we can see an important way that we can understand the early church—and the way that Paul thought about it. Here is how he described this gathering of believers: "To the church of God that is in Corinth . . . called to be saints together with all those who in every place call upon the name of our Lord Jesus Christ" (1 Cor. 1:2).

Did you see? Paul writes to *the* church—the real church of God, which is located (at least in part) in the city of Corinth. The believers in this local church are "saints" along with those who worship Jesus in every other part of the world. (We will talk more about this distinction and connection between the local church and the universal church in the next section.)

So as the gospel spread, God saw fit to establish local churches through the leadership, witness, and ministry of Jesus's apostles. The Holy Spirit inspired these apostles to write letters—epistles—to these churches in order to help them know how to worship God well and get along with each other. So the church grew and grew and grew. Now, there are local churches of Jesus Christ all over the world!

In the New Testament, God says some amazing things about the church—even some things that surprise us. The church, with all of its faults and weaknesses, still remains God's chosen weapon and witness in this world. Jesus died for his church and loves it dearly. So, then, should every Christian.

We might define the church, then, as simply the "gathering of the people of God." But we still have a lot of work to do to clearly explain how a local church connects to the church of God in all the world.

⬤ PRAY!

Spend some time asking God to continue to teach you about his love for his people, who make up the church. Thank him for calling his people to hold on to the gospel, teach others about Jesus, and shine as witnesses in this world through the work of the church. Ask him to help you be a stronger and more courageous member of the church of Jesus Christ.

THE CHURCH UNIVERSAL AND LOCAL

Even a few pages into this chapter, you have probably been able to tell that there are at least two ways that we talk about the church as Christians. We talk about churches—local gatherings of Christians in specific places (these are the kinds of gatherings that began to spring up in the early years after Jesus's ascension, as we saw from the passage in 1 Corinthians that you read and considered above). But we also have made some comments about *the* church—the church from a global perspective. We'll now dig into what we mean when we use this term in these ways.

The Universal Church

Let's now turn to Scripture to unpack what it teaches us about the universal church and see how this concept should relate to our thinking about God and his great work of salvation for his people. We'll then shift our focus to the local church.

READ!

Read Revelation 7:9–17—John's vision of the great multitude of the universal church gathered before the Lamb—Jesus—in white robes. Look at the description of this group. Notice what they are doing and how they are praising Jesus. Remind yourself that this day is really coming!

We'll begin by defining the universal church, then we'll look at its significance.

Definition. What do we mean when we talk about the universal church of Jesus Christ? The universal church consists of *every believer in Jesus Christ for all time.* In other words, this is a way of talking about the church that includes every man, woman, and child who has put his or her faith in Jesus Christ from the beginning of time and in every part of the world. It is a huge, multiethnic gathering of people that will not finally be brought together until the last day. The passage that you studied just above, from Revelation 7, shows the universal church to be a multitude of people from all nations who have been washed in the blood of the Lamb and will spend eternity in praise and worship to him in heaven forever!

The Bible is very comfortable talking about the church in this way. In Revelation 21, for example, the entire people of God (the universal church) is presented as a "bride" coming down out of heaven, adorned for her husband (v. 2). This is obviously a final picture of the gathering of all the people of God throughout the world and throughout the ages.

Significance. What is the significance of seeing the church in this way? Why is it important to acknowledge that we are part of a universal church—a great, cosmic, eternal gathering of people redeemed by the blood of Christ?

First, it is important for us to remember that, in Christ, we are part of something bigger than ourselves. Our faith in Jesus is personal, but it is also a faith we share with brothers and sisters with whom we will one day gather before the throne of the Lamb. When we come to Christ, we are joining this multitude that will praise him forever.

Second, it is important for us to remember that we are connected to believers in other parts of the world. Even though we place a kind of priority on our local churches where we live, believers elsewhere are saved through faith in Christ just as we are, so they also are part of the universal church. We should pray for these believers, support them, and recognize our common bond in the gospel of Jesus Christ.

If you belong to Jesus, you are part of something very *big*. You are a member of a great multitude—a universal church—that will gather to praise the Savior forever and ever. That is something to look forward to!

⊘ PRAY!

Take a minute to ask God to help you see the big picture of his work in the church in all the world. Then take a moment to pray for the universal church as it is represented around the world today:

- *Pray for Christians who are being persecuted for their faith in various parts of the world.*
- *Pray that the church would be bold to witness to the truth of the gospel everywhere.*

• *Pray that God would strengthen his church and keep her faithful until Christ returns.*

The Local Church

Having examined the concept of the universal church, we now will zoom in quite a bit in order to focus on the local church. This concept is central to the teaching of much of the New Testament, as many of the letters from the apostles were written to the early local churches that began to grow during the years following Jesus's ascension. From the very beginning of the Christian era, the Bible was clear that the work of the gospel would be centered in local churches of Jesus Christ. God chose to let his work and word go forward through these gatherings of believers in him. This is still true today!

📖 READ!

Read Titus 1—a chapter that contains some very practical instructions from the apostle Paul with regard to the proper governance and rule of local churches. As you read, pay attention to Paul's words in verse 5 (about appointing elders in every town). Then consider the specific instructions and requirements for leaders in the churches that Paul puts forward (vv. 6–9). Think about how all of this chapter is pointing us to Paul's assumptions about Christian faith being lived out in the context of local churches in specific places.

In a very real sense, when a believer puts his or her faith in Jesus Christ, we can say that this person has joined the church of Jesus Christ—the universal gathering of believers. Yet there is another step that we see in the Bible. In the New Testament, believers lived out their faith not just as "floating members" of the universal church, but as real members of local churches in the cities and towns where they lived. The apostles assumed this and wrote epistles (inspired by the Holy Spirit) to these local churches. Therefore, we need to understand what a local church is and why is it important for Christians.

Definition. As we see what the Bible teaches us about the local church, we can come to define it this way: *a localized manifestation of the universal church of Jesus Christ.* In other words, it is biblically appropriate and accurate to talk about local churches in the same category as the universal church. They are not different things; they are just localized "arms" of the universal church.

The New Testament authors—the apostles—do not really have a category for a believer in Jesus Christ who is not living out his or her faith in the context of a local church in his or her town. In fact, it would be impossible to actually obey much of the New Testament if we were not involved in local churches along with other believers!

Explanation. All of this is not to say that everyone in every local church is actually part of the universal church! The universal church, remember, is made up of all *genuine* believers in Jesus Christ. Can there be people who are part of local churches without actually knowing Jesus in a saving way? Of course! But this does not mean that the local church is not still the primary way that believers in Jesus live out their faith and involvement in the universal church.

This fact has led some people to talk about the universal/local distinction in a slightly different way:

- The *visible* church is the church that we see—members of local churches who gather together for worship.
- The *invisible* church is the true (universal) church that is made up of true believers in Jesus Christ.

While we cannot always completely tell who is part of the invisible or universal church, we still are called to live out Christian faith in the context of the local church.

Application. All this means is that the local church—the local body of believers—is the main way that Christians connect with the universal body of Jesus Christ. Membership, involvement, service, and witness within the local church are the ways in which Christians today are called to live out faith in Jesus with other believers. The Bible does not have a category for a "churchless" Christian, even if that Christian claims to be part of the universal church of Christ through faith. From the earliest days of the New Testament, Christians practiced their faith in local churches. This is God's way for his work to move forward in this world.

◔ PRAY!

Take a minute to ask God:

- *To continue to give you love for a local body of believers, if indeed you follow Jesus Christ as Savior and Lord.*
- *To help you see the local church as your primary involvement and place of service and ministry.*
- *To give you strength to serve the church of Jesus Christ all the days of your life.*

CHURCH SACRAMENTS

One of the most important aspects of church life is the celebration of the sacraments—the Lord's Supper and baptism. But despite this importance, there is much misunderstanding about the sacraments among believers. Hopefully by the end of this discussion you will have a better understanding of the meaning and importance of the sacraments in your life as a Christian and as a member of Christ's universal and local church.

We'll start by seeking to define what the sacraments are and the purpose they serve within the church and the lives of believers.

Definition. The word *sacrament* literally means "holy thing." So when we talk about the sacraments, we are talking about worship practices that are holy—set apart in a special way for God. As Christians think about the Lord's Supper and baptism as sacraments, they mean the following:

- These practices were instituted by Jesus in a very special way—unlike any other part of corporate worship.
- These practices are special ways in which the Holy Spirit promises to work in the lives of his people in the church.
- Because these are holy practices instituted by Jesus, he has "attached" his presence to them in a special way.
- These practices are ways in which God communicates his grace to his people in the church. This is not his "saving" grace; baptism cannot save a person from sin! But God's gracious presence and blessing is given to his people through these sacraments in a very real and special way.

So we can define a sacrament as a *physical sign of an invisible reality of God's Holy Spirit.*

Institution and purpose of the sacraments. Because the sacraments were instituted by Jesus Christ, we see that they were given by him to his followers, who would practice them chiefly in the context of the community of believers in Jesus Christ—the church. We therefore believe that the Lord's Supper and baptism are meant to be practices that are done in the church—under the rule of elders and pastors, and in the context of a local church community.

The purpose of the sacraments is to serve as signs of spiritual realities to God's people in the church. They are also very real ways in which God seals the work of belief, by his Holy Spirit, in his people's hearts.

The Lord's Supper

The first of the two Protestant sacraments that we will consider is the Lord's Supper.

CHAPTER 9

🔖 READ!

Read 1 Corinthians 11:23–34. This passage contains some careful instructions from the apostle Paul regarding the practice of the Lord's Supper (or Communion). As you read this passage carefully, focus on Paul's teaching about the Supper. Note how seriously he takes it; consider his instructions for why and how it is to be celebrated.

From the passage you just read from 1 Corinthians and from the Gospel accounts of Jesus's last meal with his disciples, we know that the Lord's Supper is a special spiritual meal that Jesus instituted (or established) for the good of his people. As Scripture teaches us, the Lord's Supper is:

- a symbolic—not literal—meal of bread (which symbolizes Jesus Christ's body) and wine (which symbolizes Christ's blood)
- a meal that is to be regularly celebrated by Christ's followers
- a sacrament to which Christ has attached himself in a special way
- something that is to be taken very seriously, since it is a very real partaking—"feasting"—by faith on the body and blood of Jesus
- a meal that is to be taken only by Christians, who have put their faith in Jesus and are part of the church

Local churches of Jesus Christ all around the world celebrate the Lord's Supper, although different churches distribute and practice it in different ways. It is important to realize that while the truths about the Lord's Supper that we have just described are central and important, neither Paul nor Jesus defines exactly how the Lord's Supper is to be celebrated. The Bible does not insist, for example, that you use bread and not crackers, or wine and not grape juice. But the centrality and importance of this sacrament in the life of the local church is extremely obvious from the Bible. It is a way for God's people, in the context of the local church, to remember Jesus's death and partake—by faith—in his body and blood. In this, God gives real grace to his people as they follow him.

⬤ PRAY!

Thank God for giving us such a wonderful sacrament—the celebration of the death of Jesus Christ, his Son, for our sins. Ask him to help you think more deeply about the meaning and power of this sacrament. If you celebrate the Lord's Supper regularly (and you should, if you are a follower of Jesus Christ), ask God to help you approach it with the proper reverence and worship next time you take it.

BAPTISM

The other Christian sacrament, in addition to the Lord's Supper, that Jesus Christ gave to his people is baptism. While there are varied convictions and opinions about how this sacrament is to be practiced and applied in the church today, there is no doubt that baptism is an important sign of Christian faith and worship.

◀ READ!

Read Matthew 28:16–20—the passage that is known as the "Great Commission" of Jesus Christ. As you read, focus on the specific commands and call that Jesus gives to his disciples in this passage. Notice how baptism is linked to Jesus's call to them to "make disciples" of all nations (v. 19). Note, also, how they are to baptize the people who believe in him (v. 19).

What does baptism mean? What does it signify? What does it accomplish?

By means of physical "washing" with water, baptism is a visible symbol and sign of the washing of sinners with the cleansing blood of Jesus. It also is a sign of the Holy Spirit cleansing God's people and making them new.

In the Old Testament, the sign of circumcision was placed on every male who entered God's community, according to God's law. This was the sign that they belonged to the people of God, even though circumcision did not, of course, guarantee their personal faith in him.

Most Christians agree that baptism is the new covenant sign of belonging to the family of God—the church.

There are two major views on how we are to understand baptism in the Protestant church today:

- Credobaptists (those who hold to believers' baptism) see baptism as a sign that should accompany the entrance of a person into the invisible church through a profession of faith in Jesus Christ. Those who hold to this position wait to conduct a baptism until a person has confessed Jesus as Savior and expressed a desire to be baptized and follow him.
- Covenantal paedobaptists (or those who hold to infant baptism) see baptism as the covenant sign that should be put on any child of believing parents who are part of the visible church. While they do not believe that baptism saves the infant or takes away sins, they do believe that it marks the child as a covenant child and is a real means of grace in that child's life as he or she grows up in the covenant community—the church.

No matter what one believes about the mode and timing of baptism, there are some important points about this sacrament that are demanded from Scripture. These are:

- Baptism is to be administered only once. Unlike the Lord's Supper, this is a one-time sacrament in the life of a person in the church.
- Baptism is to be done in the name of the Father, the Son, and the Holy Spirit, according to the command of Jesus Christ.

Baptism is to be administered with water, which is the physical sign that the Bible gives us for this sacrament. While some advocate for different ways in which the water is applied to the one being baptized, the actual sign of water is absolutely crucial, as it signifies the cleansing blood of Jesus Christ.

Baptism is extremely important. It is the sign and seal that Jesus Christ himself commanded to be attached to all members of his body, the church—whether as infants or as professing believers. It is a holy practice—a sacrament—that he has committed to his people for their benefit and use.

⬢ PRAY!

Ask God to help you better understand the beauty of the sacrament of baptism. Pray that he would help you see that, while it does not save a person, it is a sign and seal of God's amazing work of washing away, by the blood of Jesus Christ, the guilt of sinners. If you follow Jesus and have not yet been baptized, talk to someone today about taking this sign on yourself.

LEADERSHIP IN THE CHURCH

If we look around at different churches today, we find almost countless models for church leadership and government. There are certainly biblical principles and truths for how the church is to be governed, but various denominations and traditions have very different ways of applying those principles and truths. Our task in this section of our study of ecclesiology is to see what the Bible tells us about church leadership.

⬛ READ!

Read 1 Timothy 3—a chapter in which Paul lays out some clear qualifications and guidelines for the men who should lead Christ's church. As Paul describes the required character for elders and deacons, consider his words very carefully. Think about these marks of character that he describes.

Here are some of the most popular forms of church government today:

- Congregational—churches that are led primarily by the congregation of people, who usually make decisions by voting together and appointing representative leadership.
- Led by one pastor—churches that have a "solo" or "senior" pastor who basically runs the church and makes all the decisions.

- Led by elders—churches that have a body of elders who fulfill the qualification for eldership as defined in 1 Timothy 3 and together lead the church forward in faith, vision, discipline, teaching, and authority.

While there is some room for varying models of church government within Christian churches that really love Jesus and believe the Bible, it seems that the Bible—through passages such as 1 Timothy 3, Titus 1, and others—puts forward a model of church government that is elder-led (specifically with a "plurality," or group, of elders). In other words, the Bible seems to place a big emphasis on godly men who serve as elders of local churches in order to lead the people of God well, teach them the gospel, exert spiritual discipline and authority, and guard against false teaching and behavior.

As we think through the role and function of biblical elders, here are just a few key points that we should consider:

- Biblically, the roles of elder and pastor seem to be the same. While some elders in the church may be paid as pastors and others may work elsewhere and yet lead in the church, "elder" seems to be the biblical label for any man in this kind of position of spiritual authority.
- As we see in Scripture, the main roles of an elder seem to be the preaching of the word, the leadership of the congregation, the exercising of spiritual discipline, the administration of the sacraments, and the defense of the church and the gospel.
- While no elder is perfect, the Bible (in 1 Tim. 3 and Titus 1) lays out very strict qualifications regarding the character of the men who are to rule the church of Jesus Christ. Also, the Bible reserves this role of spiritual leadership and authority for men only (though women are equal in dignity with men and can exercise leadership and teach within certain contexts).

Many churches have deacons as well; this is another role that is biblically defined in parts of the New Testament, including the passage from

1 Timothy 3 that you read just above. That role of church leadership has similar character qualifications as for elders, but it does not seem to include the aspect of teaching, as the elder role does. Therefore, it is probably right to understand the role of deacon as one of service, not of spiritually authoritative preaching and teaching of God's word.

This is, of course, only a very small start toward an understanding of church government; you will learn much more as you join a church and become involved in its life and vision. But for now, here is a summary of what we have discussed:

- Biblically, it seems that elder rule is the model for local churches.
- The roles of elder and pastor, biblically, are the same.
- Elders who lead God's church are responsible for preaching, discipline, leading in the sacraments, and guarding the truth and life of the gospel in the church.
- Deacons are ordained servants in the church who do not have a teaching role.

PRAY!

Thank God for establishing a model of leadership and government for his church. Pray that he would make you a person with the kind of character that is described in 1 Timothy 3; that is, godly character that every follower of Jesus should seek to have! Then pray for Christ's church around the world. Pray that it will have godly leaders. Ask God to protect pastors and elders from sin, and make them faithful as they follow him and lead his church.

THE MARKS OF A TRUE CHURCH

At this point, we need to bring some of what we have been learning together and talk about the marks of a true church. This is an important issue to discuss today, for we live in an age when many Christian schools and Christian ministries are doing much of the work that used to be done only by local churches. So it is important to ask, "What *is* a church, anyway?" That is the question we will seek to answer by looking at several marks that ought to be true of any biblical church.

📖 READ!

Read 1 Timothy 4:11–16—a passage that records Paul's careful instructions to Timothy about his leadership in the early church at Ephesus. Note what Paul calls him to do. Consider what these instructions might mean for our understanding of the marks of a local church, as well as what churches everywhere should be devoting themselves to in life and worship together.

What marks a true local church and sets it apart from a Christian organization, or even a group of Christians who are meeting in someone's home for worship and prayer? While Christians certainly can gather at any time for worship, there are some clear marks of a true local church that the Bible provides for us. Here they are:

Preaching of the word. First, we see that a true local church of Jesus Christ includes a commitment to the diligent and faithful preaching of the word of God. It is very difficult to read the epistles from Paul to Timothy (1 and 2 Timothy)—a young pastor in the early church at Ephesus—and not see the centrality of the preaching of the word in the church. This calling is central to any pastor's work and to the well-being of the local church of Jesus Christ.

Administration of the sacraments. Second, a true local church practices and celebrates the two sacraments that we have learned about in this chapter—the only two sacraments that were instituted by the Lord Jesus Christ. A local church should be baptizing—infants and/or believers—with water in the name of the Father, Son, and Holy Spirit. Also, a true local church should be regularly celebrating the sacrament of the Lord's Supper—the spiritual "meal" for Christians, which was instituted by Jesus to remind them of his sacrificial death on the cross for their sins. Local churches should be practicing these sacraments, but institutions that are *not* churches should *not* be practicing them. They are to be practiced under the guidance, leadership, and spiritual authority of biblical elders in local churches.

Church government and discipline. Finally, a true local church is to have a biblical form of government and discipline, which we have argued should come in the form of at least some type of elder rule. While this certainly can take different forms, the biblical principle is for godly men to have a role in leading the congregation, teaching and protecting it, and exercising spiritual discipline, if necessary, when people fall into sin. A true local church is to be under the care of more than one (and hopefully several) godly elders who govern according to God's word.

Other church practices. While the three marks above are the main ones that define a local church of Jesus Christ, there are other church practices that the New Testament seems to describe as basic and standard for the church today. These practices include prayer, public reading of Scripture, fellowship, giving, and singing.

While there could be a local church, biblically defined, without some form of singing, for example, this is often an important part of worship, and the Bible presents early churches to us as congregations that sang together as part of their worship.

Hopefully you now have a better picture of what a church is, biblically defined. We'll wrap up this chapter by thinking together about how Christians are to apply the truths that we have been learning about the doctrine of the church.

▲ PRAY!

Spend a minute presenting the following requests to God:

- *Pray that he would lead you to involvement and service in a healthy church, if indeed you want to follow Jesus and grow in him.*

- *Pray that he would help you serve and lead in a local church more and more as you grow and mature in your faith. Ask him to show you your gifts and your role in the body of Christ so that you can build up the believers around you.*

IMPLICATIONS OF THE DOCTRINE OF THE CHURCH

As you look back on what we've discussed so far, hopefully you can see the beauty of the church of Jesus Christ even in the midst of its weakness and imperfections. While God's people are not yet perfected (as they will be one day), the church is still God's primary way of moving his work in this world forward by the power of his gospel and the work of his Holy Spirit.

Now we need to work on applying some of the truths that we have learned in this chapter by considering the right role and place of the local church in the lives of Christians today. We will seek to draw some important conclusions about all that we have learned so that you will be reminded—again—that systematic theology is not just for your brain, but for your heart and life as well.

READ!

Read Titus 2—a beautiful part of Paul's letter to Titus, which has much to teach us about the way the local church is to function as a place of fellowship, teaching, training, and mentoring. Consider what Paul says about the roles of the different generations as they interact with one another for the glory of Jesus Christ.

As we consider some of the big-picture implications of all that we have been learning about the church in this chapter, hopefully you will begin to see that the truths about the church of Jesus Christ should have a real impact on the way that you live out your faith, if you have indeed trusted Jesus Christ as Savior and Lord. What should we conclude about the church and its role in the lives of Christians?

God loves the church. The first major conclusion that we should draw from this chapter of study is that, clearly, the church of Jesus Christ is dear to God's heart. Paul, in Ephesians 5, reminds us that Christ died sacrificially for God's church (v. 25). Peter calls the church the "household of God" (1 Pet. 4:17). We have been reminded that, in the midst of its weakness and imperfections, the church is nevertheless the main way that God has chosen to advance the work of his gospel in this world. Through the foundation of the apostles in the first days following Jesus's ascension to the growth of the church throughout the world, this is God's plan for spreading the good news of his Son.

There is no universal without local. We can also conclude, based on all that we have seen through the teaching of the New Testament writings, that there does not seem to be any category in the minds of the apostles for a Christian who is part of the universal church (through faith in Jesus Christ) without being invested in a local church (a local gathering of believers in Jesus Christ that displays the marks of the church). The local church, then, is the place where faith in Jesus Christ is actually lived out—practically and tangibly—by believers in Jesus Christ. In fact, the Epistles of the New Testament would not even make sense if believers were not living out faith, worship, and fellowship in local churches that met regularly for worship and teaching. You could almost say that if someone is not invested in a local church, there is simply no way to tell whether he or she is really a member of the universal church.

The primacy of the church. The very practical conclusion to this discussion is that the local church is to be a central priority in the lives of followers of Jesus Christ around the world. As you think about your walk with the Lord Jesus Christ in the years to come, consider this: Will you make the local church a priority in your life? Will you give your life and time to building up believers in Jesus Christ at a local church near you? Will you love the church the way your God and Savior loves and cherishes it?

⬆ PRAY!

Ask God to give you a deep love for his church—just as he has love for his people. Pray that he would give you strength, courage, and commitment as you grow older to live out your faith in Christ and your love for him in the context of a local body of believers, where you can exercise your faith and serve others in the name of Jesus.

REVIEW

In this chapter, you have learned much about the church—what it is and why it has such significance in the lives of followers of Jesus Christ. To help you firmly grasp these truths, you're encouraged to spend a few minutes reviewing the concepts and lessons that you have learned in this chapter. Here are a few key points for you to remember:

Church Beginnings and Definition

- From the earliest days following Jesus's resurrection and ascension, local churches began to spring up, filled with followers of Jesus Christ who had believed the apostolic gospel.
- In the early days of the church, God spoke through apostles, who wrote epistles (letters) to the early local churches to instruct them in their faith and in how they ought to live for Jesus.
- The word *church* comes from the Greek word *ecclesia*, which means "gathering."

The Universal Church

- The universal church is made up of all believers in Jesus Christ from every age and every place.

- Revelation 7 gives a picture of this great multitude of believers gathered in praise of Jesus forever.
- The universal church is also sometimes referred to as the "invisible" church; people enter through faith in Jesus Christ, and it can sometimes be difficult for us to determine whose faith is genuine and whose is not.

The Local Church

- The local church is the localized manifestation of the universal church; it is not a completely separate category, but a real part of the universal church.
- It is possible that not every single person in every single local Christian church is actually a believer in Jesus Christ.
- The New Testament assumes that followers of Jesus Christ live out their faith in the context of local churches with other believers.

The Sacraments

- A sacrament is a holy practice that was instituted by Jesus Christ and given to the church in the context of worship.
- The Lord's Supper is a spiritual meal that is designed to help believers in Jesus celebrate his death for sin on the cross.
- Baptism is a sign of belonging to God's covenant people; it is to be done once, with water, and in the name of the Father, the Son, and the Holy Spirit.
- The sacraments are meant to be celebrated in the context of local churches under the leadership of elders/pastors.

Church Leadership

- The biblical model of church government—based on what we see in passages such as 1 Timothy 3 and Titus 1—is elder rule; the church is to be led by elders/pastors who demonstrate godly character and can teach God's word well.

- Elders are to be responsible for preaching, the administration of sacraments, and church discipline and leadership.

Marks of a True Church

- The three main marks of a local church are (1) preaching, (2) the celebration of the sacraments, and (3) church government and discipline.
- While there are many Christian organizations and ministries today, we need to be clear about what actually defines a local church.

Remember!

Can you say or write your suggested memory verses for this chapter perfectly? Do so right now. As you do, consider one more time the amazing way that the apostle Paul describes the church of Jesus Christ.

⏶ PRAY!

Thank God for choosing to redeem people for himself through the death of his Son and for ruling over his church in this world until Jesus returns. Pray that God would help his church to be even more faithful, steadfast, and courageous for the gospel in this world! Ask him to help you be an important part of his church locally as you serve and follow Jesus Christ.

THE DOCTRINE OF ANGELS AND DEMONS

You've come a long way in your exploration of "God talk." By now, you should be in the habit of looking to Scripture to shape the way that you form beliefs and think about various subjects.

In this chapter, you are going to dive into the systematic category of angels and demons—in other words, the spiritual realm. This topic fascinates some people; they obsess over angels and demons, and think often about their influence and impact in the world. Other people, though, never think about the reality of the spiritual realm; they function almost as if angels and demons—spiritual beings—do not exist. The proper Christian response is probably somewhere right in the middle of those two extremes. We need to acknowledge what the Bible teaches about the reality of the spiritual realm, but we also need to guard against obsession about it; after all, God is the one whom we worship and trust.

As we begin our detailed examination of what the Bible has to say about these topics, here are a few big-picture principles that Christians who believe the word of God should keep in mind:

The spiritual world is real. First, if you have never acknowledged that angels and demons—and a complex spiritual realm—exist, you need to do that now. The Bible is clear that angels are servants of God who have acted (and still act) in God's world according to his will at various times and places. Demons, too, are mentioned in the Bible often; they are servants of Satan and oppose the work of God in this world. As you will see in your memory verses for this chapter, these demons are referred to in the New Testament as "rulers" and "authorities."

The spiritual world is powerful. Second, we need to admit that there is real power in the spiritual world. While God is ultimately in control of all things, the power in the spiritual realm is greater than human power. This means that Satanic forces and demonic powers are not things to be trifled with or taken lightly. While we can always trust God as the most powerful being in both the spiritual and material worlds, we should not assume that spiritual powers are things we can handle on our own.

Christians need to understand the spiritual world. Third, because the spiritual world is very real and powerful, we therefore should seek to understand it as best we can, according to the Bible. That is the goal of this chapter. We do not want to obsess over the involvement of angels and demons in this world, but we do want to examine carefully what Scripture teaches about the spiritual world. Then we can seek to apply right thinking and good biblical doctrine to our lives as we follow Jesus and understand reality in light of his good word.

Jesus is King. Finally, in all of our study and thinking about the spiritual world, we should return again and again to the lordship and rule of Jesus Christ—the great King of the universe. In Scripture, he is declared to be over all rulers and authorities; in fact, he conquered Satan himself, in a final way, through his death and resurrection! While it is good to understand and take seriously the power of Satan and his forces in this world, we should always remember that the Savior we follow has already conquered and will finally have eternal victory over sin, death, Satan, and all of his followers.

Remember!

Your suggested memory verses for this chapter come from Paul's conclusion to his epistle to the ancient church at Ephesus. Read them through several times and think deeply about what they are saying. Focus on how Paul acknowledges the reality of Christians' struggle against spiritual powers and authorities—demonic forces. Paul does not pretend that these powers do not exist! But he does recommend a kind of "armor" that Christians can put on to withstand their attacks.

Finally, be strong in the Lord and in the strength of his might. Put on the whole armor of God, that you may be able to stand against the schemes of the devil. For we do not wrestle against flesh and blood, but against the rulers, against the authorities, against the cosmic powers over this present darkness, against the spiritual forces of evil in the heavenly places. Therefore take up the whole armor of God, that you may be able to withstand in the evil day, and having done all, to stand firm. (Eph. 6:10–13)

PRAY!

As we prepare to dig into what the Bible says about the spiritual world, spend a few minutes talking to God in prayer about the following points:

- *Ask him to give you wisdom as you search his word for truth about angels and demons.*
- *Pray that he would protect you from fear and enable you to trust Jesus as the great King and Ruler of all.*

• *Ask God for strength to learn how to put on his armor as you struggle to stand strong and live for him in this fallen world.*

GOD AND THE SPIRITUAL REALM

Before we begin thinking in depth about angels and demons, it would be wise for us to consider God's relationship to the spiritual realm. Our goal here is to correct some erroneous thinking that can sometimes lead people to believe that God is in the midst of an equal struggle against the evil forces of the demonic world. We will return to the doctrine of creation in order to see God as his word presents him to us—as the sovereign ruler and Lord of all creation, including the spiritual world!

READ!

Read Genesis 1:1–2 and John 1:1–5; they are both brief, so read them at least twice all the way through. As you read, consider the foundational concept for this chapter: that God is the Creator of all things—even demons, and Satan himself. Think of the amazing power of the triune God—the Father, the Son, and the Holy Spirit—who existed from all eternity totally on his own, in perfect peace and unity. Think what this means for our attitude toward—and understanding of—angels and demons.

The two Scripture passages you just read properly set God apart from the beings of the spiritual realm. This is good for us. You see, the fact that the God of the Bible is the eternal Creator of the universe rightly shapes our view and understanding of the spiritual world, as powerful and frightening as it sometimes seems to us! So let's think about what the doctrine of creation reminds us about God in relation to angels and demons.

God is absolutely unique and distinct from the rest of the spiritual realm. The Bible, and particularly the doctrine of creation, reminds us that God is absolutely distinct from his creation—even the spiritual realm. Satan, as powerful as he is, is a created being; demons, too, are created by God. Long before angels and demons ever existed, the God of the Bible was reigning supreme and secure in himself. Satan could never hope to stand against God. However, God has chosen to allow him to act in powerful ways for a time.

God is absolutely sovereign over the spiritual realm. As we noted above, some people mistakenly believe that the world is in the midst of a power struggle between God and Satan. They think of God and Satan as two almost equal beings—God working for good, and Satan fighting against him for the advance of evil. This is a form of "dualism"—the belief that there are two equal forces in the universe (good and evil) that are in constant battle and tension with one another. But this is *not* the teaching of the Bible!

Scripture is clear that God alone is absolutely "sovereign" over the spiritual realm. The word *sovereignty* refers to the complete control—the ultimate power—of God. He is the Creator and Ruler of all angels and demons; they can do nothing apart from his will, and he can stop the work of Satan himself in an instant. We should never think of our God as anything other than the one who is all-powerful, all-knowing, and completely in control of everything that happens in this world—and above it and below it too!

God's people have nothing eternally to fear from the spiritual realm. For God's people, these truths mean that they have nothing to fear—ultimately and eternally—from demons or even from Satan himself. This does not mean that they will not experience the effects of sin, demonic attacks, or terrible things in this sinful world (which is under the influence of the devil in large ways). But it does mean that Christians can have hope that, if they truly belong to Christ, God's Holy Spirit dwells within them in a real way. This is the actual Spirit of the living God of the universe, at whose presence even the demons tremble with fear!

So as we move into the following discussions about angels and demons, remember that God, the Creator, reigns as the eternal Ruler of the spiritual realm. He created every human and every spiritual being; they are all under his control and absolute sovereignty.

● PRAY!

Spend a minute asking God to help you see him in all of his power, might, and glory. Pray that he would remind you how truly great and wonderful he is—how high and exalted above every part of creation that he has made. Then ask him to protect you from all fear and despair as you trust that you truly belong to him—and are guarded by him—through faith in Jesus Christ and the indwelling of his Holy Spirit.

ANGELS

We now turn our attention to angels, which the Bible depicts as beings of great magnificence. Hopefully observing the power and splendor of these beings and of the spiritual realm will point us to the infinitely greater power and splendor of the Creator God!

What Are Angels?

We're first going to consider what the Bible has to teach us about the essence of angelic beings—what they actually *are*. While God's word does not offer us a detailed description of how and when God made the angels, or of what exactly they look like, we can nevertheless gather truths and principles from various Scripture passages that teach us about these beings that are in eternal service of God.

● READ!

Read Matthew 22:29–33 and Revelation 22:8–9, which give us glimpses of the essence of angelic beings. Read both of these brief passages at least twice through and consider what they have to teach us about angels.

You have probably seen pictures, movies, or cartoons portraying angels, but it's likely that none of them portrayed angels in any way close to what they are actually like! What does the Bible say?

Angels are created beings. First, the Bible is clear that angels, like humans, are created and living beings, made by God. In Psalm 8, the psalmist points out that human beings have been made "a little lower" than the angels and "crowned . . . with glory and honor" (v. 5). Angels, then, have greater glory and honor than humans; it is noteworthy that the natural human response to these beings when they appear is first fear and then worship. Nevertheless, angels were created by God, and therefore are less than God. They are another kind of living being that God made.

Angels are eternal, nonmortal beings. Jesus makes it clear that angels—unlike human beings—are eternal and nonmortal (they do not share in human institutions such as marriage, for example; see Matt. 22:30). Angels were created by God to live forever; they do not grow old and die. While it seems that angels can certainly take on physical form, they are spiritual beings.

Angels are servants of God. Primarily, angels were created by God to be his servants (we will talk much more about what their service looks like in the next section). You saw this in the passage from Revelation 22 that you read just above. John was tempted, as we discussed above, to bow down and worship the angel who was showing him this vision of heaven. The angel stopped him, though, reminding him that, although glorious, he was nothing more than a "fellow servant" of God with John (v. 9). Angels are not to be worshiped; they are servants of God, who alone is worthy of worship and praise.

Angels dwell in heaven with God. Angels, unlike human beings, never have lived on earth and never have been subject to the fall in the same way that human beings are. Angels, then, do not have sinful natures; they are not guilty of sin, rebellion, and death. We know this because they are portrayed (in Rev. 4, for example) as dwelling closely with the holy God in heaven. Sinful beings would not be able to do that! So the permanent dwelling place for angels is in heaven with God.

⬤ PRAY!

Spend a minute simply praising God for his wisdom, power, and might demonstrated in his creation of angels. These beings are so wonderful that when human beings have seen them at various points in history, they have often been tempted to worship them! Also, praise God that he is far more glorious than angels, and that these heavenly beings reflect his glory and splendor in just a faint way.

The Purpose of Angels

Now that we have considered what angels are, we are going to dig a bit deeper into their purpose, as we see it revealed in the Bible. We will identify several of the chief roles that we see angels filling in Scripture as they obey God and help his work to move forward in the world he made. While we are not certain about the work of angels in the world today, we can look at how they have worked throughout the history of God's people.

▬ READ!

Read Luke 1:26–38—the account of the angel Gabriel's visit to Mary to tell her about her pregnancy and the coming birth of Jesus Christ. As you read this passage, note Mary's response to the angel, as well as Gabriel's response to her and his words of announcement. Consider what this passage has to teach us about the purpose of angelic beings in God's plan and work in the world.

In the previous section of this chapter—about the essence of angels— we saw that, above all, the Bible presents angels to us as servants of God. This was the point that the angel in Revelation made clear to John when John attempted to worship him (Rev. 22:9). But what do these servants do? What is their purpose? In the Bible, we see them acting in several key ways:

- Announcement. This is the purpose that you saw in the passage from Luke that you read just above. The angel Gabriel (one of the few angels who is named in Scripture) was sent to Mary to announce the coming birth of Jesus Christ, God's Son. The angels had a busy season, as another heavenly messenger (perhaps Gabriel again) was sent to Mary's soon-to-be husband Joseph as well (Matt. 1:20–21). God was clearly using this angelic servant to make important announcements to his people about his coming salvation and powerful work in the world through his Son. We also see angels making announcements to people in the Old Testament from time to time.
- Protection. At various points in the Bible, angels are presented to us as God's means to protect his people. Psalm 91:11–12 mentions this protective role of angels. Likewise, in Daniel 6, after his deliverance from the lions' den, Daniel explains to the king of Babylon that the lions' mouths were shut by God, who sent his "angel" to take care of him (v. 22).
- Worship. Revelation 4 and 5 make it clear that, among other purposes that angels fulfill, one seems to be simply worshiping God and singing praises to him in heaven. Revelation 4, in particular, shows us a scene from the throne room of heaven, which John sees as a part of his vision. In this scene, he sees angels singing praises to God continually (v. 8).
- Provision. At various times in Scripture, angels are shown to provide for the needs of God's people—even in tangible ways. In the life of Jesus, in fact, when he was in the wilderness being

tempted by Satan and went without food for forty days, we are told that angels were "ministering" to him (Matt. 4:11).

- Carrying out God's purposes. There are other ways in which angels carry out the purposes of God in the pages of Scripture, including guarding the garden of Eden, defeating God's people's enemies in battle, and rescuing righteous people from a city about to be destroyed by God's judgment (see the story of Lot in Genesis 19). Clearly angels do God's bidding and carry out his purposes in this world, whatever they may be.

As noted earlier, we are not sure how angels function today, but we can be sure that God is still using these faithful heavenly servants to carry out his work in the world—probably in ways that we will not fully understand until we meet them in heaven.

⊙ PRAY!

Thank God for using his angels to move his work in this world forward and to care for his people in so many ways.

The Christian Response to Angels

Having learned about the essence and purpose of angels, we can now think about the right relationship that Christians are to have with them.

Think back to our discussion above about the ways that some people in the world today seek to relate to angels. We saw that some people tend to be overly obsessed with them, talking about them a lot and even focusing on them in a borderline worshipful way. Other people act as if angels and the spiritual realm do not even exist at all. Hopefully, based on what we've discussed so far, you can see why both of these responses are a bit unbalanced—and unbiblical.

Another common idea is that there is a "guardian angel" for each person, but this is not taught in Scripture. That does not mean it is not possible for people to have individual angels "assigned" to them, but the Bible does not explicitly teach anything about this.

Our goal is to work toward the right way for Christians to think biblically about angels and properly relate to them. As you will see, the biblical response to these heavenly beings is somewhere between worship and obsession on the one hand, and a total denial of their existence on the other. Christians can learn from Scripture how to relate to angels as they follow the great God and Savior of the world.

READ!

Read Daniel 10:1–14. Focus on Daniel's interaction with the angel— particularly his response of fear and awe. How does the angel respond to Daniel's fear? What seems to be God's purpose in sending this angelic messenger to his servant Daniel?

What should be our response to angelic beings as we seek to live for Jesus Christ in this world?

We should worship and thank God because of angels. First and foremost, the existence, work, and purpose of angels throughout history and now (though we do not always see it) should drive us to give more praise and worship to God himself. John's response to the angel in Revelation 22 reminds us that angels are beings with beautiful and terrifying glory, yet they do not even begin to compare in glory and power to the almighty God of the universe.

We should see angels as our fellow servants. Second, we should—as the angel said to John in Revelation 22—see angels as "fellow servants" of God with us. We should recognize that, as they are made for God's purposes, actions, worship, and service, they stand alongside us in service and praise of him.

This means, of course, that Christians are not to pray to angels or worship them in any way. God alone is worthy of worship; prayer should be directed to him alone, in the name of Jesus Christ alone. As glorious and powerful as angelic beings may be, they are to be seen as servants of God, who is the Creator of them and us.

We should look forward to sharing heaven with angels. Finally, as we look ahead toward eternity, we should be hopeful for the day when we will share heaven with angels and join in praise and worship of the Father, Son, and Holy Spirit with them! We know from Revelation 4 that angels are praising God in heaven constantly; we also know that they are spiritual beings who do not die. So we can biblically assume that these angelic beings will be with us in the new heaven and the new earth; they will be our worship "partners" as we live eternal lives in praise and worship of our great God.

⏶ PRAY!

Ask God to give you a right attitude toward angels, who are truly fellow servants of God with us. Pray that:

- *God would help you to see his glory through the work and actions of angels in Scripture.*
- *God would help you be grateful for these wonderful fellow servants of Jesus.*
- *God would give you great hope and expectation for praising him with the angels for all eternity.*

DEMONS

You have been learning about angels—the glorious heavenly beings that were created by God to sing his praises and accomplish his purposes in the world. Now we will shift our focus toward demons—spiritual beings who also were created by God but who serve a very different purpose than that of God's angels.

What Are Demons?

Our goal in this section is to get to the essence of demons—to determine biblically what these beings are and where they came from.

📖 READ!

Read James 2:18–19 and 1 Timothy 4:1–3. These two brief passages both mention demons in passing. As you read, consider what we can learn about the essence of these spiritual beings from what James and Paul say.

Here are summaries of some of the basic biblical teachings about demons:

Demons are spiritual beings created by God. It is extremely important to begin, as with angels, with the fact that demons were created by God. Since nothing exists that God did not create, the logical conclusion is that God made the demons to be his good servants—like the angels. The passage from James that you just read confirms this, as it seems clear that demons have right beliefs about who God is; they have known about him from the beginning of their existence, even though they chose to rebel against him!

While the Bible is not explicit about exactly how the demons were turned toward evil, it seems likely that they are fallen angels who followed Satan in his rebellion against God and pursuit of evil. So demons were created by God, but turned against him in hatred, rebellion, and destruction.

Demons, like angels, are spiritual beings; they do not have physical bodies. They therefore do not live, grow old, and die like human beings, but exist in a spiritual state. Because of this, they have significant power and influence in the world, although not nearly to the extent of the almighty Creator God, who rules over them (and at whose name they tremble).

Demons are fallen, evil, and in the service of Satan. The very essence of demons, according to Scripture, is evil to the core. While we do not know when their rebellion—their "fall" from heaven—actually occurred, we know that demons are now completely fallen, desperately evil, and in the service of the prince of demons—Satan himself. We will learn more about Satan specifically in the pages to come.

Demons are under the judgment of God and bent on destruction. Because the demons are fallen and evil, they are under the judgment of God; Jesus Christ will finally judge all evil—including the evil of Satan and his demons, and they will be thrown into the lake of fire forever (see Rev. 20). The demons know this! They know that their doom is sure, and they are therefore desperately wicked and bent on destruction. One way that they seek to destroy, according to 1 Timothy, is through deception—leading people away from the true gospel of Jesus Christ. We will learn more about this just below.

Demons, then, are spiritual beings—fallen angels of sorts—who were created by God but followed Satan in his rejection of God's rule. They are under the judgment of God and are desperately evil—bent on destroying as many people as they can before the final judgment. But while they have significant power and spiritual influence, they tremble at the name of Jesus and at the power of God.

⬆ PRAY!

Ask God to make you very aware of the reality of demonic powers in this world. Pray that he would help you to discern the real spiritual struggle that exists, but also to never lose hope in Jesus Christ as the one who is powerful and mighty, and who will finally overcome all evil.

Who Is Satan?

Now that we have thought about demons, we will take a closer look at the one who is called the "ruler" (or "prince") of this world (John 16:11) and the "prince of demons" (Matt. 9:34)—Satan. Scripture presents Satan as a real being, so we need to examine what the Bible tells us about him. Our goal is not to become obsessed with the person of Satan, but we should not ignore his existence, power, and influence.

READ!

Read Revelation 20:7–10. Read this passage at least two times and consider the very end—the destiny of Satan, the great accuser and enemy of God's people. Think about the hope that this passage should give to God's people even as we consider the power and influence that Satan so obviously possesses in this world today.

Here are a few aspects of the person of Satan—his origin, his purpose, and his ultimate destiny:

Satan's origin. The Bible does not give us a detailed account of Satan's rebellion against God and fall from heaven. Jesus mentions it in Luke 10:18, but he offers little detail. We know that Satan was an angel of God, created by God to serve him. We know also that by the time Adam and Eve ate the forbidden fruit in the garden of Eden, Satan already had fallen, for he was already committed to opposing God and his people. Satan, then, is a powerful spiritual being who was created by God as an angel, but who infinitely and completely rebelled against God's rule. He is the most powerful of all demonic beings, although his power does not begin to compare to that of God.

Satan's purpose. As we observe Satan's activities in Scripture, we see him doing the following against God's plan and God's people:

- Deception. Satan, above all, is a liar. From his first appearance in the garden of Eden (in the form of a serpent), his goal has been to lie to God's people and to turn them away from the truth of God's words. It is no wonder that Scripture refers to him as the "father of lies" (John 8:44).

- Accusation. Satan also is active in throwing accusations at God's people and provoking them to feelings of guilt, even though they are truly forgiven and redeemed by the blood of Christ. In fact, Satan is called the great "accuser" in Revelation 12:10 because of the way he seeks to oppose the truth of the gospel by trying to tell Christians that they are not really forgiven through Jesus's blood.
- Attack. Satan is pictured in Scripture as launching various attacks on God's people and God's purposes in the world. Revelation 12 gives an imagery-filled account of Satan's history in the world— opposing Jesus himself and also God's people since he knows his time is short. Like his demons, he is bent on destruction, and is bitter with rage at his coming judgment and destruction.

Even though Satan has great power, we should also see clearly that he is limited. He is not equal to God; he is not even close. In fact, the last battle in Revelation pictures an unnamed angel binding Satan (Rev. 20:2)! There is no comparison between Satan and God. He is a powerful fallen angel who is bent on destruction. But he is just that—a spiritual being, created by God, who will one day be judged by God. Until that day, though, God has seen fit in his sovereignty to allow Satan to work his evil purposes.

Satan has been called the "ruler" (or "prince") of this world (John 12:31; 14:30; 16:11). This world is his domain, and he thinks he owns it. Although he does have influence and power here, he is under the ultimate control of God. We see from the story of Job, for example, that Satan cannot even touch God's people without God's permission!

Satan's destiny. In the passage you read just above, you saw the eternal destiny of this great enemy of God's people. As Martin Luther put it in his great hymn, "A Mighty Fortress Is Our God," "Lo! his doom is sure." Satan knows this day is coming; he will one day be cast into the lake of fire—the eternal place of punishment for all who oppose God's rule. So in the meantime, his goal is to create as much deception, destruction, and evil as he can. His time is short; Jesus has already secured his demise through his death for sins and resurrection from the dead. One day soon, Satan will be punished forever.

PRAY!

Ask God to protect you from fear of Satan even as you acknowledge his reality and his powerful presence in this world. Pray that God would make you strong in his word and strong in your faith in Jesus Christ. Ask him to help you hope in the final victory of Jesus Christ the Lord!

The Purpose of Demons

Let's now return our focus to demons as we examine together their purpose and actions in this world, according to Scripture. Our goal is to think rightly about these evil spiritual beings—especially their ultimate fear at the name of Jesus Christ. James tells us that the demons accurately discern God's identity and power—so much so that they "shudder" (or "tremble") at the thought of him (James 2:19). Even so, they are servants of Satan who oppose God; they will be judged eternally for their willful rebellion against him.

READ!

Read Mark 5:1–20—a passage that records the influence of demons in the life of one man, whom Jesus healed and freed. As you read this account carefully, note the effect that the demons had on this man and even their influence on the herd of pigs! Think about the purpose of the demons in this narrative.

Below are several ways in which demons act in this world:

Deception. You read 1 Timothy 4:1–3 earlier in this chapter; in this passage, Paul warns Timothy about false teachings that are opposed to the gospel. Interestingly, Paul does not stop at simply identifying these teachings as false—he actually says that people who believe false things about Jesus are following the "teachings of demons" (v. 1). This makes sense, as demons are in the service of Satan, who is the father of lies and the king of deceit.

There is an important point to be made here. The Bible seems to be suggesting that demonic influence actually lies behind false religions—any belief that opposes the gospel of Jesus Christ, the Son of God. People who reject Jesus have not just chosen a different religion. They are actually deceived by Satan and are serving him and his demons. In other words, there is no neutral belief in the universe. Every man or woman either believes in Jesus or believes some form of the teachings of demons, which are lies and deceit.

Possession. In many accounts in Scripture, we see that demons can possess people, taking control of their bodies, minds, and hearts. One such account is found in the passage from Mark 5 that you read above. The goal of such possession is total destruction and damage to the person being possessed (we can see that the demons' goal is only destruction through what happens to the pigs that Jesus sends them into). Only Jesus could conquer the control that the demons had over the life of the man in Mark 5. They had consumed him, and Jesus needed to break their hold on his life.

It is important to note that the Bible nowhere suggests that demons are able to possess Christians—those who, through faith in Jesus, have the indwelling of God's Holy Spirit. Demons would not be able to coexist with the Spirit in a believer. Demons, then, are able to possess only those who do not follow Jesus and are therefore living in sin, exposing themselves to demonic influence in their lives and hearts.

Various attacks. The Bible also shows us that demons can launch various attacks in this world. While believers in Jesus cannot be possessed and controlled by demons because of the indwelling presence of the Holy Spirit, they can be influenced by the attacks of demons. While we do not know exactly what demonic attacks look like today, it seems biblical to assume that such attacks may be at the root of various evil things that occur in our world. God, in his sovereign plan, has allowed the influence of Satan and his demons to continue in this world until the day of his final judgment through the Lord Jesus Christ.

Demons, then, are spiritual beings in the service of Satan, who seek to deceive, possess, and attack people in order to oppose God's purposes and God's people in any way they can. God's people, though, can be confident and secure in the power of Jesus Christ and in the presence of God's Holy Spirit with them and in them.

⬥ PRAY!

Ask God to help you realistically acknowledge the power of demons in this world. But pray also that he would protect you from any fear or despair, based on your assurance that Jesus is Lord and Savior.

The Christian Response to Demons

We'll end our discussion of demons by examining the proper response to them, according to the Bible. How should we think about demons? How should we guard ourselves against their attacks? How should we remind ourselves of their eternal destiny? What is our ultimate hope in the midst of real spiritual warfare and demonic activity?

⬥ READ!

Read 1 John 4:1–6. Read carefully and thoughtfully, focusing on how the passage teaches followers of Jesus Christ to be discerning about the "spirits" (v. 1). Consider also the encouragement that this passage gives to Christians as it reminds them of the great power of the one who is "in" them (v. 4)—power that exceeds that of Satan himself!

What is to be our ultimate perspective on these spiritual beings that oppose God and his people? Here are a few principles that should guide Christians in answering this question:

We should acknowledge the struggle. First, it is important that as we read and study what the Bible has to say about demons and the spiritual world, we acknowledge that the struggle is real, intense, and dangerous. This is exactly what the memory verses for this chapter have been pointing you toward—you are engaged in a real struggle that is bigger than flesh and blood! God claims every part of this world as his, and Satan and his demons oppose God's work at every step. The work of demonic powers is constant, and it is important that we do not act as if this work does not exist.

We should beware of demons' deception. Second, based on the passage that you just read from 1 John, it is good for Christians to be on guard against the deceptions and lies of Satan and his demons. Remember, deception is one of their primary functions; they delight to deceive people with words and teachings that are opposed to the life-giving gospel of Jesus Christ. When John calls believers to "test the spirits" (1 John 4:1), he is urging them to compare every teaching or impulse that emerges in the world against the truth of the gospel—that Jesus Christ is the Son of God sent to be the Savior of all who believe. We should remember that demons are constantly pursuing the deception and destruction of people by turning them away from Jesus, so we should be watchful.

We should remember Jesus's power. John's words to Christians, in the midst of his warning about testing the spirits, are very encouraging. He reminds them that "he who is in you is greater than he who is in the world" (1 John 4:4). One thing that you must remember, if you follow Jesus Christ, is that the Holy Spirit of God is indwelling you, and his power and might far outweigh that of the most powerful demon—even

Satan himself! Jesus can squash the efforts of the demons with just a word, and that power makes these evil spirits tremble. While we need to acknowledge the power of evil in the world, we should never imagine that it compares to the power of Jesus Christ—the risen and conquering King.

We should take comfort in the promise of the final judgment. Finally, as we consider demons' work—their lies, evil, and attacks in this world— we should take comfort in the fact that there will be a final reckoning. Jesus will return to this earth as the Judge and will make all things right. Satan and his demons will be thrown into the lake of fire (Rev. 20:10), death and sin will be finally defeated, and God's people will dwell with him in a new heaven and new earth that is free from the influence of sin and evil. This should be a great comfort for Christians as they continue to struggle to follow Jesus now.

⏶ PRAY!

Ask God to make you strong—truly strong—in faith in Jesus Christ. Pray that he would give you wisdom and discernment to "test the spirits" in order to hold on to the truth of the gospel. Finally, ask him to remind you to truly believe that he who is "in you" is greater than he who is "in the world," if you are truly following Jesus Christ as Savior and Lord.

REVIEW

In this chapter, you have studied the systematic theology category of angels and demons, seeking to bring together much of what the Bible teaches about the spiritual realm. Hopefully you now have a more biblical perspective on the essence and purpose of angels and demons, as well as an even deeper hope and belief in the power and victory of Jesus Christ, the great Lord and Savior. He is supreme and sovereign, and he will finally judge Satan himself forever!

As we bring this chapter to a close, you are encouraged to look back over the chapter and review the concepts and lessons that you have learned. Here are a few key points for you to remember:

God and the Spiritual Realm

- Scripture affirms that God is the Creator of angels and demons—and of Satan himself. God is ultimately distinct from every other spiritual being because he alone is eternal and uncreated.
- Angels and demons are created beings even though they are spiritual and have a different kind of "glory" than human beings.
- Dualists have a mistaken view that God and Satan (or good and evil) are two equal and competing forces in the universe.

Angels—Essence and Purpose

- Angels are spiritual beings whom God created to act as his servants in this universe.
- We are not to worship angels (according to Rev. 22, among other passages), but we are to see that God uses them to do his work in this world.
- The Bible presents angels as glorious beings who point us to the far greater glory of God himself.
- Angels announce, protect, and do various other tasks in the world, as commanded by God.

Demons—Essence and Purpose

- Demons are, as best we can tell from Scripture, fallen angels who were created by God and who chose to follow Satan in his rebellion against God's rule and God's word.
- Demons are spiritual beings, not fleshly physical beings.
- Demons seem to be intent primarily on deception in this world, although the Bible shows us how they also are active in possession and in various other kinds of evil attacks and influences in this world.

- Ultimately, demons are bent on destruction and on opposing the work of God and his gospel in the world.

Satan

- Satan is a fallen angel who rebelled against God's rule at some point in time before the fall (we do not know when).
- While Satan is incredibly powerful, he is a created being, and his power does not compare to that of Jesus Christ.
- Revelation 20 gives us a picture of the end, when Satan will be finally judged and thrown into the lake of fire.
- Satan knows his time is short, so he has given himself to creating evil and destruction in this world, of which he is sometimes called the "ruler" (or "prince").

Responding to Angels

- Our right response to angels is not to worship them, but to see them as "fellow servants" of God with us.
- We should praise God for these heavenly beings who serve him and look forward to singing his praises along with them in heaven someday.

Responding to Demons

- We should "test the spirits," according to 1 John 4:1, and be ready to expose the lies and deceptions of demons that oppose the gospel truth of Jesus Christ.
- We should not be terrified of demonic activity because we know that he who is in us (the Holy Spirit) is greater than he who is in the world (Satan).

Remember!

Can you say or write your suggested memory verses for this chapter perfectly? Do so right now. As you do, consider one more time the way in which these verses acknowledge the presence of the spiritual battle, but also remind believers in Jesus Christ about their strength and hope in his "armor."

▲ PRAY!

As you end this chapter with prayer, talk to God in the following ways:

- *Thank him for what you have learned from his word about angels and demons.*
- *Ask him to help you acknowledge and be more aware of the reality of the spiritual battle that is going on constantly in this world, which is under the influence of Satan in many ways.*
- *Praise him that he has secured final victory over Satan, and for his people, in the death and resurrection of Jesus Christ.*
- *Pray that he would remind you that, if you follow Christ, he who is in you is greater than the prince of this world!*

Chapter 11
THE DOCTRINE OF LAST THINGS

In this chapter, you are going to wade into a very difficult and complex area of systematic theology, one that is the subject of constant debate and study. Do not be nervous; we will do our best to examine Scripture carefully and stay focused on the big picture even as we examine different viewpoints and perspectives on the subject matter.

Our topic of study for this chapter in systematic theology is "eschatology" (the study of the end times). Obviously, this chapter will take us mainly into the biblical book of Revelation, which is the primary place where we see the Bible's teaching about this doctrine. As you may know, there are many viewpoints about the exact timing and meaning of the events that Revelation predicts, as well as about the symbolism and metaphors that this apocalyptic book uses. Our goal in this chapter is to lead you to some clarity regarding these different viewpoints so that you can begin studying Scripture on your own and come to your own conclusions.

As we begin, we will focus on some general principles that will be important for you to keep in mind as we study several perspectives on the end times. Here are those principles:

Different viewpoints are permissible. It is very important to say at the outset that different viewpoints on the timing of the events described in Revelation, the meaning of various symbols and metaphors, and even the level of symbolism that one attaches to numbers and pictures are permissible. In other words, we are saying here that faithful, Bible-believing Christians who love Jesus *still may disagree about many points in Revelation.* Some people believe that a literal "antichrist" will come; others do not. Some people believe that Jesus will take his people from this earth before the "great tribulation"; others affirm that Christians will endure through the tribulation. There are points of disagreement about the topic of eschatology, but these points do not mean that people are not seeking to faithfully believe the gospel and the word of God. There is room for different viewpoints among God's people on these issues.

Certain truths are essential. While what we have just said above is true, there are certain truths that Revelation puts forward—basic biblical truths—that all Christians must affirm if they truly believe the Bible. Every Christian should believe, for example:

- that Jesus Christ will really return physically in glory to judge the world
- that there will really be a final physical resurrection and judgment of every human being
- that God will really establish a new heaven and new earth, where his redeemed people will dwell with him—and that unbelievers will face punishment in hell for all eternity
- that Satan will really be finally conquered and judged, and sin will be no more

There are other central truths, of course; these are just examples that all Christians must affirm.

Christians should work toward conclusions. Finally, while there are central truths that we must all affirm and different viewpoints on eschatology that are acceptable, it is important that Christians study the Bible carefully and *form their own conclusions* about what the Bible is teaching. In other words, it is not enough to say, "Jesus wins in the end; that is all we need to know about eschatology!" The Bible does affirm that Jesus wins in the end, but it says much more. In this chapter, our goal is to study the Bible carefully and help you form beliefs about what it teaches about the last days.

Remember!

Your suggested memory verses for this chapter come from the book of Revelation (of course!), and they give a picture of the final hope of God's people in the new heaven and new earth. This is the true hope of all Christians, no matter what position they take on when and how the events of the last days will occur. Read these verses slowly, thinking deeply about their meaning.

And I saw no temple in the city, for its temple is the Lord God the Almighty and the Lamb. And the city has no need of sun or moon to shine on it, for the glory of God gives it light, and its lamp is the Lamb. By its light will the nations walk, and the kings of the earth will bring their glory into it, and its gates will never be shut by day—and there will be no night there. They will bring into it the glory and the honor of the nations. But nothing unclean will ever enter it, nor anyone who does what is detestable or false, but only those who are written in the Lamb's book of life. (Rev. 21:22–27)

PRAY!

As you prepare to dig into eschatology, spend some time asking God for wisdom as you study his word in the coming pages. Ask him to help you stay focused on the big picture of Christ's return and judgment as you also seek to form right beliefs about the last days according to the Bible.

APOCALYPTIC LITERATURE

Before we move too deeply into the study of eschatology, it will be good to get better acquainted with apocalyptic literature, which is the biblical genre to which books such as Revelation, and parts of Daniel and Zechariah, belong. We need to get a decent idea of how this genre works before we begin referencing passages from Revelation. This is because, when we come to this genre, we can sometimes feel as though we are on unsteady ground. This is certainly one of the more difficult genres of Scripture to navigate.

READ!

Read Revelation 12:1–6—the passage that records a "sign" of a woman and a great dragon that John saw in heaven. Consider the difficulties in this passage; it is a wonderful example of apocalyptic literature! What questions do you have about the meaning of John's words?

We will begin by pointing out several characteristics of apocalyptic literature and explaining how they tend to function in books such as Revelation. Here are some features you should expect when you study apocalyptic books or passages:

- Graphic imagery. You just read from Revelation about a "dragon" who represents Satan in his attack on Jesus Christ and all of his followers in this world. In apocalyptic literature, the images often present not what someone *looks* like physically, but what someone *is* like. Jesus, for example, is pictured in Revelation in ways that would look strange if we took every description literally;

THE DOCTRINE OF LAST THINGS

the language is telling us what Jesus is like, not giving us a literal physical description.

- Cosmic drama. The events and predictions of apocalyptic literature are almost always very global in their focus. In other words, when you step into apocalyptic literature, you deal with issues that pertain to all of humanity and creation. These issues include judgment, the return of Christ, the defeat of Satan, and the eternal reign of the followers of Jesus. The drama is cosmic—global and huge.

- Future focus (usually). Much of apocalyptic literature has a bent toward the future; we learn, in Revelation for example, about many of the things that will "soon take place" (Rev. 1:1). Yet apocalyptic literature, broadly, is about the "revealing" of the hidden and mysterious purposes of God. Sometimes this can involve his purposes in the present or even in the past. The passage that you read above, for example, looks back into the past to explain Satan's attack on Jesus's work when he came to earth; it then stretches forward into the present.

These are just a few aspects of apocalyptic literature that you should expect to find in your study. Don't be intimidated or frightened; it will just take some hard work and careful study to get a better grasp of these passages.

It is important to note that everyone sees at least *some* symbolism and metaphorical language in a book such as Revelation, even people who claim to take it very literally. There are simply some things that must be taken figuratively; (for example, very few people understand Revelation to be teaching that God has literal, physical "bowls" of wrath lined up in heaven, ready to be poured out on the earth).

The goal, as we look into apocalyptic passages to form our beliefs about eschatology, is to let the Bible speak and to find our way to the right answers based on a good interaction with and understanding of the apocalyptic genre.

⬤ PRAY!

Spend a minute asking God for wisdom as you tackle the genre of apocalyptic literature. Pray that he would help you understand his word more and more, especially in this particularly challenging genre! Ask him to give you understanding and faith as you study these portions of the Bible.

KEY TERMS OF ESCHATOLOGY

Also before we dig into the various views on eschatology, it will be helpful to introduce several key terms that will come up often in the following pages. Hopefully a basic familiarity with these terms will help you better understand our discussion about eschatology.

▨ READ!

Read as much of Matthew 24 as time permits (read the whole chapter if you can). As you read, consider the parallels between this Olivet Discourse of Jesus and the passages from Revelation 12 that you read above.

In our study about the different viewpoints on eschatology, we will reference some unique terms that people use in discussions about this topic. In this section, you are going to get a bit more acquainted with these terms. It is important for you to be able to define these terms carefully and have a general sense of how people from different eschatological viewpoints understand them.

Tribulation. The tribulation generally refers to the time of trouble, persecution, violence, and suffering that is presented in Scripture as directly preceding the return of Jesus Christ and the final judgment of the world. While the Bible certainly points to this concept generally, it is not absolutely clear about how we should understand it.

Many Christians understand the tribulation to be a literal seven-year period, near the very end of the world, that will either begin or end with the "rapture" of believers in Jesus to heaven. Others believe that the great tribulation has already happened—at some point in the first century. Finally, still others take the tribulation to be a symbolic way of talking about the general suffering and violence that began in the world after Christ's ascension and will continue until his return.

Rapture. The concept of the rapture refers to the "taking up" of believers to be with Jesus. While all biblical Christians of course believe that God's people will one day be taken up to be with Jesus forever in the new heaven and new earth, there are different opinions as to how and when—and in what stages—this will actually happen. Some suggest that there will be a "secret" rapture before the great tribulation, when believers will suddenly be gone from earth. Others believe in a final rapture, which they link with the final judgment and return of Christ. Ultimately, the hope for all Christians is that they will one day be "caught up . . . in the clouds" with Jesus (1 Thess. 4:17); we simply are not certain exactly how it will happen.

Millennium. The viewpoints we are going to learn about are deeply grounded in varied understandings of the "millennium." The millennium refers to the thousand-year reign of Christ on earth, which is described especially in Revelation 20. There are varying interpretations with regard to whether or not this should be taken to be a literal or figurative reign of Christ on earth, whether or not the thousand years is a literal time period or a symbol of fullness, and even whether or not Christ will return before or after this millennium. But the Bible does describe this reign of Christ very clearly, so every Christian needs to wrestle with its meaning.

Antichrist. If you have extra time after you finish this chapter, read through Revelation 13. The "beast" that is described in verses 1–10 is often referred to as the antichrist—a person or being who will have a great role in opposing the gospel of Jesus Christ and deceiving many people who follow him. The second beast (vv. 11–18) is sometimes seen to be a different person, who is linked with the first beast in deception and opposition to God's people. These beings seem to be separate from Satan (the "dragon"), yet they are under his control and influence. Christians disagree on whether this chapter describes a real person, a "spirit" that is in the world in every age, or perhaps a past political ruler who persecuted God's people. Nevertheless, again, every Christian should wrestle with what the Bible is teaching in this passage.

▲ PRAY!

Thank God for his rich word, which gives us many details about Christ's return and judgment on earth, and the hope of eternal life for those who believe in him. Ask him for help as you continue to study his word and seek to understand it well.

PERSPECTIVES ON ESCHATOLOGY

We're now ready to begin moving into the discussion of several different viewpoints and perspectives on eschatology—the study of the "last things" of this earth. Obviously every viewpoint that we will present in this chapter cannot be completely correct! But it is important for you, as you begin study in this subject, to understand the different perspectives that people have as they interpret Scripture in this area.

In general, the different perspectives on eschatology are separated by the way they understand the millennium, which is the term that has been given to the one-thousand-year reign of Christ on earth. There are four main perspectives/viewpoints on how this millennium relates to our understanding of the final days of this earth, and we will focus on those views in this section. They are:

- dispensational premillennialism
- historic premillennialism
- amillennialism
- postmillennialism

These viewpoints interpret Revelation in different ways and come to different understandings about two main activities that relate to the millennial reign of Christ:

1. when Christ will return in relation to the millennium
2. when the rapture ("taking up") of believers to heaven will happen in relation to the millennium

Dispensational Premillennialism

We'll begin our survey of the different eschatological views with a look at the perspective of dispensational premillennialism.

READ!

Read Revelation 20:1–6—one of the main passages in Scripture that describes the millennium. Focus on what this passage tells us about this thousand-year period and what will happen during it. Think about the way in which symbols and metaphors are used in apocalyptic literature, including this passage.

Here are some of the basic teachings of the dispensational premillennial viewpoint:

General approach. In general, dispensational premillennialists hold to a very literal view of much of what is taught in Revelation and other apocalyptic passages in the Bible. They love Jesus, take the biblical text very seriously, and study it carefully in order to interpret it faithfully. People who hold this perspective see the thousand-year reign of Christ presented in Revelation 20 as being a thousand literal years on earth rather than a symbol for a "fullness" of time. They also look at passages such as Revelation 7 and see the 144,000 people from Israel there as a literal group of ethnic Jews who turn to Christ rather than as a picture of the fullness of true and spiritual Israel (all believers in Jesus Christ).

Return of Christ. The premillennial approach expects, based on Revelation 20, a return of Jesus Christ to earth "pre"—or before—the millennium. Therefore, people who hold this perspective believe that the Bible teaches that Jesus will return to earth and reign with some of the believers on earth for a literal thousand-year period, then the final battle against Satan will happen and the final judgment will come. Dispensational premillennialists and historic premillennialists generally agree about the timing of Jesus's return (before his reign on earth).

Tribulation and rapture of believers. Most dispensational premillennialists, though, believe in a secret rapture of believers that will occur before the tribulation, which is the seven-year period of trial, trouble, and persecution that is described in Revelation and in Matthew 24. So adherents of this perspective are described as "premillennial and pretribulation" because they believe that Jesus's return to earth will happen before the millennial reign on earth, but that believers will be raptured before the tribulation, which will come upon the earth in the final days of God's judgment.

Critiques. Here are the main two critiques of this eschatological viewpoint:

1. It sees a significant discontinuity (or "break") between the work of God in the lives of ethnically Jewish people and the lives of non-Jewish believers in Jesus Christ. Therefore, adherents focus intensely on the Middle East today because they believe that God still has a special purpose for ethnic Israel. The critique

of this is that it misses the biblical idea of "spiritual Israel" put forward by the apostles—that the church of Jesus Christ around the world is the new Israel, composed not of ethnic Jews primarily, but of the entire multiethnic people of faith.

2. It takes many passages far too literally in a way that does not take account of the way in which the genre of apocalyptic literature uses symbols and figurative language. Opponents of dispensational premillennialists suggest that it does not minimize the truth of Scripture to say that some symbols in apocalyptic literature are not meant to be taken absolutely literally.

PRAY!

Pray for the following requests as you continue to study eschatology:

- *Ask God for diligence and discipline as you seek to interpret his word carefully and accurately.*
- *Ask him for patience as you continue to work through difficult texts and concepts.*
- *Pray for faith as you relate to God personally through the study of his word.*

Historic Premillennialism

Now we'll turn our attention to historic premillennialism. While there are some similarities between this viewpoint and dispensational premillennialism, there are some important distinctions too.

READ!

Read Revelation 7:9–17—a wonderful passage of hope that gives us a picture of the great multitude of followers of Jesus Christ who are saved through the washing of his blood. Take careful note of what the angel tells John about their participation in the tribulation (see v. 14). How might this verse contribute to a historic premillennialist understanding?

Here are some of the basic teachings of the historic premillennial viewpoint:

General approach. Both historic premillennialists and dispensational premillennialists can also be described as "futurists." This means that, in general, both of these groups see much of what is written in Revelation as describing events that will happen in the future, in the last days of earth. This futurist approach is in contrast with amillennialists, whom we will learn about in the next section.

While historic premillennialists take much of Revelation in a futurist way, they are not as tightly literal in their interpretation as dispensational premillennialists in general. Many historic premillennialists, for example, are comfortable thinking about the millennial reign of Christ as not a literal thousand-year reign, but as a reign for a fullness of time. They can see the number one thousand as symbolic of fullness, which would be very consistent with the way numbers are used in apocalyptic writings elsewhere.

Still, historic premillennialists do take things such as the millennium and the tribulation to be literal events, even if they do not need to last literally a thousand years or seven years.

Return of Christ. Historic premillennialists hold that, in accordance with a literal interpretation of Revelation 20, Christ will return to earth before his millennial reign on earth with believers. They look for a great return of Christ, a period of time when he will reign visibly on earth with great power, and then a final judgment of all people who have ever lived before his great throne.

Tribulation and rapture of believers. Historic premillennialism differs from dispensational premillennialism, though, in the timing of the rapture of believers in relation to the great tribulation. Historic premillennialists hold that, according to Revelation 7:14 (and other places in Scripture), it seems that believers in Jesus Christ will be present for at least some of the tribulation and will have to endure it by faith in Jesus Christ. They reject the idea of a secret rapture, which is put forward by dispensational premillennialists, and affirm that the final rapture of believers will be after the tribulation and before the final judgment of Jesus Christ.

Historic premillennialists also object to the dispensational separation between ethnic Israel and spiritual Israel (Jewish people and the global church of Jesus Christ). They do not see a special role for ethnic Israel in the last days, as they understand God's work as having broadened to include spiritual Israel or true Israel—that is, all of God's people who are "children of Abraham" through faith in Jesus Christ. Revelation 7:1–8 is, for them, another picture of the true church of Jesus Christ in all of its fullness, not a picture of a literal number of 144,000 ethnic Jews.

Critiques. The main critiques of the historic premillennialist viewpoint come from amillennialists, who suggest that they still take too literal an approach to apocalyptic literature. We will examine more the purely symbolic and figurative approach that is put forward by nonfuturist proponents—amillennialists—in the next part of our discussion.

▲ PRAY!

Continue thinking deeply about these perspectives on the millennium and on eschatology. Ask God to give you wisdom as you interact with his word. Wherever you land in your personal understanding of these things, pray that God would help you take his word very seriously as you study it.

Amillennialism

Next we turn to the amillennial perspective. This viewpoint is very common in evangelical churches today, so it is important to understand it well.

📖 READ!

Read Revelation 20—the entire chapter. As you read, consider some of the different ways that various parts of this chapter could be interpreted based on some of the approaches we have discussed so far in our study of eschatology. This is a good passage to be familiar with as you continue to study this subject.

Amillennialism literally means "no millennium." This label for the viewpoint comes from the fact that proponents of amillennialism take apocalyptic literature—particularly Revelation—very figuratively and metaphorically. They are not futurists, as are premillennialists, and they see most of what is described in Revelation as describing past, present, and ongoing spiritual realities in figurative ways. Here are some of the basic views of the amillennial viewpoint:

General approach. The general approach of amillennialists is to see the apocalyptic genre of Scripture as working in an essentially nonliteral way. For those who hold to this viewpoint, numbers, events, and even individuals that are presented by the book of Revelation should often be taken to represent real spiritual realities, but not necessarily real events or people.

This approach to the text comes out, for example, in the amillennial view on the millennium. Amillennialists do not read Revelation 20 as something that will happen in the future, with Christ returning to earth and literally reigning here for a time. Rather, they see the millennium as a figurative picture of what is happening right now as Christ reigns over the earth from the right hand of God as the risen Lord and Savior. Likewise, they regard the binding of Satan that is described in Revelation 20 as a metaphorical holding back (to some extent) of Satan's influence in the world through the death and resurrection of Christ, allowing the gospel to grow and flourish in the world.

Amillennialists apply a similar interpretive philosophy and approach to many other pictures and scenes in Revelation.

Tribulation and rapture of believers. Like the millennium, amillennialists see the tribulation as a figurative description of the time of trouble in the "last days," which began after the ascension of Christ. Therefore, they argue that the last days began during the time of Acts and that we are still living in them. They see the signs of tribulation all over the world today, in various wars, sufferings, and instances of persecution.

Amillennialists do, of course, hold to a real rapture and a real return of Christ to earth. They simply do not take much of Revelation to be presenting things that will actually happen in the future—in the last days that are still to come, directly preceding the return of Christ.

Critiques. There are certainly some strong points to the amillennialists' position. They have a system for interpreting the events and pictures of Revelation in certain ways, and in general, this approach is consistent. They see apocalyptic literature as giving symbolic pictures of true spiritual realities—realities that are current and all around us. This enables them to stay very focused on the big picture—the death of Jesus, his resurrection, and his eventual return.

The main critique of this position is that it can tend to oversymbolize large portions of books such as Revelation, which do seem to describe real events, real people, and real occurrences that are still to come. Sometimes, too, the tendency for proponents of amillennialism can be to oversimplify the Bible's teaching on the last days, which certainly is undeniably rich, complex, and descriptive.

⬥ PRAY!

Ask God for wisdom to understand his word well and believe what it says. Pray that he would give you patience as you work through different eschatological viewpoints and a clear focus on the centrality of Jesus Christ, the Savior, in all of them.

Postmillennialism

Finally, we will look at one last perspective on eschatology and the teaching of Revelation: postmillennialism. This perspective was much more prevalent in the Christian world at other phases in church history than it is today, but some people still hold this viewpoint.

■ READ!

Read Ephesians 2:1–7. As you read this wonderful passage, which recounts the movement from death to life and from sin to salvation, pay special attention to verses 4–7, as these are key for the way that postmillennialists view the current situation of Christians, who are spiritually "raised" and will reign with Christ on earth.

Interestingly, postmillennialists have major agreements with both premillennialists and amillennialists on at least a few points.

- Postmillennial Christians agree with premillennialists that much of Revelation is to be taken fairly literally—as real events with real people acting in real times and places. They believe, then, in a real millennium, a real visible reign of Christ on earth, and a real presence of a person who is called the antichrist.
- Postmillennialists also agree with amillennial Christians that much of what Revelation describes has already happened— through the death and resurrection of Jesus Christ, and in the years immediately following his ascension (mainly in the first century AD).

How does the postmillennial perspective put this all together? Here is what it looks like:

General approach. We have already mentioned that postmillennialists agree with premillennialists that much of Revelation is to be taken as speaking of real events, real people, and real places. But they disagree in seeing many of these events as taking place not in the future but in the past—in the years following Jesus's ascension to heaven. The antichrist, then, is seen as Nero or one of the other Roman emperors who brutalized the Jews and persecuted God's people. The tribulation is seen as a great time of suffering during the first century.

But postmillennialists disagree with amillennialists by affirming that the millennium is referring to a real visible reign of Christ on earth that is still to come.

Timing of events. Because postmillennialists affirm that much of Revelation (basically everything up to chap. 20) has already happened, they urge Christians to see that nothing else major needs to happen before the visible earthly reign of Christ—the millennium. They therefore seek, by God's grace and power, to "usher in" the millennial reign of Christ on earth through sharing the gospel and building Christ's kingdom on earth. Postmillennialists (or at least some of them) have a very real hope that the millennial reign of Christ has perhaps already begun; in that case, things on earth will get gradually better and better (or more influenced by the Christian gospel and the church) as more and more people follow Jesus and he begins to rule more visibly and powerfully in this world.

Critiques. The major critiques of the postmillennial position involve a real look at the present state of this world and other descriptions of the last days in Scripture. First, people look at the world today and see the gospel growing, but they also see evil growing in terrible and awful ways. It seems that God is active, but Satan is active as well. Second, people look at parts of Scripture, many of which seem to bear witness to the fact that things on earth will be increasingly troubled as the last days approach, even as the gospel continues to go forth. Many premillennialists and amillennialists argue that the postmillennial position does not fit with human experience or with other descriptions of the last days in Scripture.

⬛ PRAY!

Pray that God would give you more faith—and more expectation—as you look for Jesus's return to earth, however it happens! Ask him to help you think more often about Jesus's judgment of this earth so that you remember to serve and follow him now.

BIG-PICTURE TRUTHS ABOUT ESCHATOLOGY

We began this chapter by encouraging you to work hard to study the Bible and come to your own conclusions about what you believe about eschatology. Hopefully you have at least taken some first steps toward forming your own position. In your reading of this chapter, you should have been studying the biblical texts carefully and considering how well the different viewpoints interpret God's word. You need to think these things through for yourself.

Even so, there are some big-picture truths that Christians from every eschatological viewpoint must affirm to be true if they really take God's word seriously. As we talk about some of these things, our goal is to establish some boundaries for orthodox positions on the end times. The fact is, we will share heaven with people who disagree with us on earth about how the end times are actually going to unfold.

📖 READ!

Read Acts 17:22–31—a record of a sermon that the apostle Paul gave to the men of Athens, who met constantly at a city center called the Areopagus. Take special notice of how Paul concludes this evangelistic sermon in verses 30–31, and how his conclusion reminds us of some very central truths about the last days.

As you are forming thoughtful conclusions about what you believe the Bible teaches about the end times, you should be comforted to know that there are big-picture truths that you can hold to and have confidence that you are remaining faithful to Scripture.

Above, we referred to "orthodox" positions on theological questions. What do we mean? An orthodox position is basically a belief or doctrine that is widely accepted—in this case, by biblical Christians. As we noted earlier, all of the positions on the millennium and the timing of Christ's return that we have studied fall within the boundaries of what we could call "Christian orthodoxy." In other words, premillennialists, amillennialists, and postmillennialists all truly believe the Bible, follow Jesus, and sincerely practice a true Christian faith. We believe this is true because the Bible is simply not completely clear on some of the issues we have discussed; there is room for different interpretations.

However, this raises the question of the big-picture truths that all Christians—regardless of their eschatological framework—must affirm to be true. What are some of these central and core beliefs about the last days that must be affirmed no matter what one believes about the nature of the millennium?

1. Jesus will return. All biblical Christians affirm that Jesus Christ will return bodily to this earth, both to judge it and to take his people home to be with him in the new heaven and new earth. He will reign forever as the great Savior and resurrected King of God's people.

2. Judgment will come. All biblical Christians believe that the Bible teaches one final judgment, at which all humans who have ever lived will stand, and from which all people will go away either to resurrection life in the new heaven and new earth or to eternal punishment in hell.

3. Resurrection life is real. All biblical Christians believe that followers of Jesus will truly be resurrected from the dead and will enjoy eternal life in a physical new heaven and new earth in glorified physical human bodies. Those who do not follow Jesus will also be raised, but they will face eternal judgment and punishment in hell under the wrath of God.

4. Satan will be defeated. All biblical Christians believe that Satan—and all of his demons—will also be judged and thrown forever into the lake of fire by Jesus Christ. At this point, sin and death will be forever defeated, and eternal life will continue forever for God's people in the presence of their Savior and Lord.

5. Jesus is the only hope. All biblical Christians affirm that the only hope for "standing" in the day of final judgment is to be washed and covered by the blood of Jesus Christ, which is received by faith alone in him. This is true for all Christians, no matter their views on the end times!

● PRAY!

Ask God to keep you focused on the main things—the big picture—as you continue to learn about the doctrine of eschatology. Pray that he would help you to believe the things that the Bible absolutely affirms as true and take them to heart as you look forward with hope to Christ's return.

APPLICATIONS OF ESCHATOLOGY

You have almost completed what has been perhaps the most challenging chapter so far in your study of systematic theology ("God talk"). The category of eschatology is not an easy one, especially as you begin to try to navigate all of the viewpoints on the last days, with their different approaches to Scripture. Hopefully you have heard clearly the call to study God's word diligently in order to form your own positions on these subjects, but also to stay focused on the main things—the big-picture truths that every biblical Christian should affirm.

With this last point in mind, we will use the final pages in this chapter to examine some of the key applications that Christians should be making to their lives as they study the doctrine of eschatology.

READ!

Read Revelation 1:1–3. This passage is just three short verses, so read it at least twice—once silently and once out loud. Think about how John's introduction to the book of Revelation helps guide us in our overall application of the doctrine of eschatology.

Hopefully you have gained new knowledge in this chapter. But knowledge about God does not necessarily imply a growing relationship with him. As we have noted before, the study of God is meant to engage the heart; we should be changed as we study and learn about our God and should be constantly applying the truth of his word to our lives as we follow him. So in this chapter's final pages, we will seek to pull together some main applications that should emerge for God's people through the study of eschatology.

Study Revelation. The apostle John gives us our first application—one that we have been putting into practice in this chapter! As he begins to record his vision in the book of Revelation, he tells his readers that they will be "blessed" if they read and hear the words that he is writing (Rev. 1:3)! So as we think about applications from this chapter, the first should be a call to study Revelation for ourselves so that we will continue to know and understand God's word more clearly and fully. Will you commit to studying Revelation and hearing its words carefully?

Obey Jesus. Second, though, John calls his readers to "keep" the words of his prophecy that he records (Rev. 1:3). This means, quite simply, that it is important for people to obey the words of Jesus Christ, the Savior and King of the universe.

The study of eschatology, in other words, should lead people toward a real and vibrant personal obedience to Jesus, as well as a love for him. The knowledge of the last things and a vision of the end of the world should make his people want to follow him carefully and listen to his words.

Eschatology, then, while it deals with cosmic and global themes, should always have a very practical application in our lives. Discussions about the final days of this earth and the coming judgment of Jesus should always make us consider carefully the ways that we are living (or not living!) for Jesus right now.

Be ready. John concludes his introduction to the book of Revelation by saying, quite simply, that the time is "near" (Rev. 1:3). This should lead to an important application for our lives as Christians—one that Jesus points to clearly in all that he says in Matthew 24: we must be ready. Jesus pictures it as "staying awake" (v. 42)—anticipating his return to earth and being constantly watchful.

This does not mean, of course, that we stop being responsible or taking care of various parts of our lives. But it does mean that we think often about the return of Jesus and let the reality of the coming day impact our perspective, our words, and our actions toward others. It means, too, that we should be committed to telling other people about the eternal hope that is found only in Jesus Christ. We should be encouraging other people to be ready for his return as well!

● PRAY!

Humbly ask that God would truly help you make these applications real in your heart and life today as you consider the end of all things, the return of Christ, and the final judgment of the world. Pray that he would keep you "awake" as you get ready for Christ's return.

REVIEW

Hopefully you now know much more than you did about the different perspectives that people have on the millennium and the return of Jesus Christ. Now you're encouraged to move through a time of review, looking back on the main lessons and concepts that you have learned in this chapter. Here are a few key points for you to remember:

Apocalyptic Literature

- In the Bible, apocalyptic literature mainly is found in Revelation and in some parts of Daniel and Zechariah.
- Apocalyptic literature is often future-oriented, but broadly, it has to do with the unveiling or revealing of things that have been hidden.
- Apocalyptic literature contains many symbols, graphic pictures, and metaphorical language, although this does not mean that it never discusses real people or real events.

Key Terms of Eschatology

- "Tribulation" refers to a seven-year period of trial, trouble, violence, and persecution in the last days.
- The "rapture" refers to the "taking up" of Christians into the clouds during the last days.
- The "millennium" is the thousand-year reign of Christ on earth, which is described in Revelation 20.
- The "antichrist" is described in Revelation 13, although different viewpoints have different interpretations about what—or whom—this antichrist is.

Dispensational Premillennialism

- Dispensational premillennialism takes Revelation very literally and understands the millennium as an actual thousand-year earthly reign of Jesus.
- According to this viewpoint, Jesus will rapture Christians before the tribulation, which will be a period of violence, suffering, and judgment on the earth.
- Also according to this viewpoint, there is a distinct role for the literal nation of Israel and people who are ethnically Jewish in God's work of salvation and judgment in the last days.

Historic Premillennialism

- Historic premillennialism has room for more symbolic interpretations of Revelation than does dispensational premillennialism, but it still is a futurist viewpoint—holding that most of the events described in Revelation are still to come.
- According to this viewpoint, believers in Jesus who are on earth during the time of the tribulation will go through it; the rapture of believers and the return of Christ will happen after the tribulation.
- Also according to this viewpoint, there is no special role for ethnic Israelites in the last days because the church of Jesus Christ is the true, "spiritual" Israel of God.

Amillennialism

- Amillennial literally means "no millennium." Proponents of this view read the millennium as a symbolic reign of Christ that began through his death and resurrection.
- According to this viewpoint, Revelation is not describing mainly future events, but symbolically describing deep spiritual realities.
- Also according to this viewpoint, we have already entered the millennium and we await the return of Christ.

Postmillennialism

- Postmillennialism holds that Jesus will return not before but after the millennium, which will be a thousand-year period of Christ's increasing influence on earth.
- Proponents of this position see much of what is described in Revelation as already having occurred during the years following Jesus's ascension.
- This viewpoint sees the world as gradually becoming more and more under the control of Jesus before his return.

THE DOCTRINE OF LAST THINGS

Boundaries of Orthodoxy

- The word *orthodoxy* means "right belief"; we use this term specifically to describe accepted beliefs about the Bible and the gospel by Christians.
- All four major views of eschatology are orthodox views.
- There are some basic beliefs that all biblical Christians should hold about Jesus and the end of the world.

Remember!

Can you say or write your memory verses for this chapter perfectly by memory? Do so right now. As you do, consider the amazing future hope of Christians who have been saved by the blood of Jesus Christ and whose names are written in the book of life.

PRAY!

As you close this chapter, talk to God in the following ways:

- *Ask him for diligence to study his word carefully and to form thoughtful conclusions about eschatology in the future.*
- *Pray that he would give you great hope in the return of Christ Jesus, and that he would give you strength to follow him now as your Savior and Lord.*

THE DOCTRINE OF THE HOLY SPIRIT

If you are like most Christians, you probably do not think very often—or very clearly—about the work of the Holy Spirit. You probably know much more about God the Father and God the Son (Jesus) than you do about God the Holy Spirit. Therefore, in this chapter, our goal is to examine what the Bible has to teach us about the third person of the Trinity.

This will be the final chapter in our study of systematic theology. Having engaged with some of the major categories of biblical doctrine, hopefully you have come to see how helpful these categories can be for theological study, but also how every part of the study of systematic theology must return to the ultimate foundation of God's word—the Bible! That is what we will continue to seek to do as we take up the doctrine of the Holy Spirit.

We will begin our study of this doctrine by looking at its importance for the lives of Christians today. There are some wrong ideas about the Holy Spirit floating around the Christian world today, and we need to make sure that we understand the Bible's teaching on this subject.

Some churches hardly ever mention the Holy Spirit at all. In fact, many Christians go through life rarely thinking—or talking—about the Spirit. This has led some people to call God's church to return to a focus on the Holy Spirit, since he has been so "forgotten."

In one sense, this is good and right: Christians do need to remember that the God who reveals himself to us in Scripture is one God in three persons, and that each person of the Trinity is distinct and fully God in himself. Yet it is also true that the Holy Spirit nowhere demands a sole focus on himself. His role, as we will see, actually has to do with enabling the worship of the Father and the Son.

Other Christians today are very focused on the work of the Spirit. They make his work a focal point in their churches, and they ask him to reveal himself and work in powerful ways in the lives of Christians. While it is good that such churches are so concerned with seeing God work and move actively today, the danger is that the work of the Holy Spirit can be confused. Sometimes a focus on spiritual gifts and new "prophecies" that are attributed to the Holy Spirit can take a wrongly central place in church life. We will discuss this more thoroughly later in the chapter.

As you can tell, there is a great need to understand clearly what the Bible has to teach us about the Spirit. After all, he is God, and we worship him along with the Father and the Son. As we move on in this chapter, then, our goal is to answer the following questions:

- Who is the Holy Spirit and what is his role within the eternal Trinity?
- What does the Holy Spirit do today in the church of Jesus Christ and in the lives and hearts of individual believers?
- What is the connection of the Holy Spirit to spiritual gifts, and how should we think biblically about this controversial issue?

Get ready to dig into God's word as we learn even more about the God we praise, worship, and seek to obey.

Remember!

Your suggested memory verses for this chapter come from the Gospel of John—some of the words of Jesus to his disciples as he prepared to go to the cross, die for sins, and then rise again and return to heaven. With these words, Jesus was telling them about the work of the Holy Spirit, whom he said that he would send to them after he left the earth. Read through these verses several times slowly and thoughtfully, considering all that they say about the Holy Spirit.

When the Spirit of truth comes, he will guide you into all the truth, for he will not speak on his own authority, but whatever he hears he will speak, and he will declare to you the things that are to come. He will glorify me, for he will take what is mine and declare it to you. All that the Father has is mine; therefore I said that he will take what is mine and declare it to you. (John 16:13–15)

PRAY!

Ask God to give you wisdom as you study more about him in this chapter. Pray that he would help you understand him better—the God who reveals himself to us as one God in three persons. Pray that this chapter would help you know and worship him even more!

THE IDENTITY OF THE HOLY SPIRIT

The first part of our examination of God the Holy Spirit is to explore what the Bible teaches about his identity. Our goal is to discover who the Holy Spirit is and so be ready to move into a closer investigation of what he does in the world and the church today.

READ!

Read Genesis 1:26–27—the account of God's creation of human beings. Take special note of the way that God speaks in the plural in verse 26: "Let us . . ." Think about what this means for our understanding of God and for the way that we think about the Holy Spirit.

In this first part of our discussion about the Holy Spirit, we will simply ask three basic questions about his identity, seeking answers from Scripture.

Who *is the Holy Spirit?* First, it is clear from Scripture—and necessary to affirm—that the Holy Spirit is the third person of the Trinity, the one God who is revealed to us in Scripture as existing in three persons. Each of these persons, as we learned in an earlier chapter, is fully God in himself; each person is distinct, and yet God is ultimately one. We have to acknowledge that the Trinity is a mystery that we do not fully grasp or understand, but it is very true to say that the Holy Spirit is fully God.

In many places in the New Testament (such as the introduction to 1 Peter), the Holy Spirit is named with God the Father and God the Son as God. So while the term *Trinity* is never used in the Bible, the concept is certainly there.

We saw, based on the use of "us" in Genesis 1, that God—in three persons—created the earth and made human beings in his image. This means that God the Father, God the Son, and God the Holy Spirit were active in creation, so we also can very truly talk about the Holy Spirit's role in the creation of the world.

What *is the Holy Spirit?* Second, Jesus—God the Son—at one point took on a physical human body. Jesus now lives and reigns in a resurrected and glorified body; he will keep that body forever and will reign in this visible and physical way over his people in the new heaven and new earth.

The Holy Spirit, unlike Jesus, does not have a physical body. It is best to understand him as an invisible spirit, yet with all the power and identity of God himself. To go much further down this road, in terms of the essence of the Holy Spirit, is to say more than what the Bible tells us.

Why *does this matter?* Finally, this discussion matters greatly because Christians need to understand the God whom they worship! He reveals himself to us as the Trinity—one God in three persons. We need to work hard to take seriously what God's word tells us about him.

This subject also is important because while there is unity in the Trinity, there are also very distinct roles for the Father, the Son, and the Holy Spirit, roles that are revealed to us in Scripture. While it is right to say, for example, that the Holy Spirit is God, it is *not* right to say that the Holy Spirit died on the cross. The act of redemption was a distinct role that Jesus Christ—God the Son—performed for God's people.

In the coming pages, then, we will seek to examine the distinct roles of God the Holy Spirit as we understand them from Scripture.

▲ PRAY!

Spend time praising God—one God in three persons. Praise him for the eternal mystery of who he is as the Father, the Son, and the Holy Spirit. Admit to him that you do not fully understand him, but ask him to help you worship and obey him more fully, according to his word.

THE HOLY SPIRIT'S ROLES

The Holy Spirit has a number of roles that are distinct from, and yet connected to, the roles of God the Father and God the Son. Before we begin looking at those roles of the Spirit, it will be helpful to summarize the roles of the Father and the Son. From what we see from the Bible, here is what we can say generally:

- God the Father is fully God! He is the person of the Trinity who is presented to us as holding the sovereign plan for creation, salvation, and judgment. His will accomplishes all his purposes in the universe; the Son is pictured as fully submitting to—and carrying out—the sovereign will of the Father through his life, death, resurrection, and ascension to heaven.
- God the Son is fully God! He is the person of the Trinity who is presented to us as the Savior—the one who took on flesh, is called Jesus, and died and rose again to actually accomplish salvation for God's people. He is fully God, yet he submitted to the will of God the Father to do the work of redemption. He now reigns forever as the great King and Judge.

With that background in place, we can now turn to a consideration of the distinct roles of God the Holy Spirit. The first key area where we see the Spirit working is in the process of regeneration. He also plays important roles in sanctification and worship.

The Holy Spirit's Role in Regeneration

Regeneration, as you learned earlier, refers to the miraculous work of God to make sinners "come alive," repent of sin, and trust Christ as Savior and Lord. What is the Spirit's role in this work?

READ!

Read John 3:1–21—the passage that records Jesus's nighttime conversation with a Pharisee named Nicodemus. In this conversation, Jesus referenced prophecies from the book of Ezekiel, which point to the need for God's people to be "spiritually" reborn. Consider the implications of what Jesus said to Nicodemus. Think about how the work of the Holy Spirit must be involved in the kind of saving work that Jesus described to him.

We know, from Ephesians 2:1–3, that apart from Christ, all human beings are not just bad; they are actually "dead" in sins (v. 1) and servants

THE DOCTRINE OF THE HOLY SPIRIT

of Satan (v. 2). Romans 1–2 makes clear that all people are under God's wrath because of sin and unrighteousness. Biblical passages such as these lead us to the doctrine of total depravity, which means (among other things) that sinful human beings could never actually decide to trust God by their own power and strength.

So there needs to be a miraculous work of God on the human heart. He has to "regenerate" sinners' hearts and enable them to turn to him in faith. This act of regeneration is pictured as coming from the Holy Spirit of God.

The passage you read just above—John 3:1–21—can be a bit difficult to understand. Jesus was explaining to Nicodemus the miracle of regeneration. He was telling this Pharisee that the prophet Ezekiel—in his vision of the "valley of dry bones" (37:1–14)—was picturing the process of miraculous faith—spiritual resurrection—that would come as the Holy Spirit worked miraculously on human hearts to enable them to believe. Wind is a common picture for the Holy Spirit in the Old Testament. So Jesus was telling Nicodemus about the need to be "born again"—to be regenerated by the Holy Spirit toward conversion (repentance of sin and faith in him as the Savior of the world).

So we can say that the Bible teaches that God the Holy Spirit has the primary role in the regeneration of sinners, making them able to turn from sin and choose to put their faith in Jesus Christ. This miraculous work in human hearts actually comes *before* repentance and faith.

▲ PRAY!

Thank God for giving salvation to sinful human beings who could never hope to save themselves by their own choices or actions. Thank him that, by the work of the Holy Spirit, sinners can be regenerated—made alive—so that they can repent of sins and believe the gospel. Are you confident that this has happened in your own heart and life? If not, talk to God about it right now and invite him to do this work in you.

The Holy Spirit's Role in Sanctification

Regeneration, as you learned above, is a work of the Holy Spirit that happens before conversion. Now we are going to discuss another of the Spirit's roles, one that happens not before conversion but after it: sanctification. We studied sanctification in chapter 7, so you should be able to explain this concept clearly. Now we want to focus in on the part that the Holy Spirit plays in this process in the lives of believers in Jesus Christ.

READ!

Read Romans 8:1–17—a powerful passage from the apostle Paul about the reality of life "in the Spirit" for all who follow Jesus Christ by faith. As you read, think about the power for holiness and obedience that Paul describes. Consider where this power comes from. Think about the significance that he attaches to the fact that God's people are truly led by his Holy Spirit and what that means for you today, if you belong to Christ Jesus.

Sanctification literally refers to the process of being "set apart" in holiness, in connection with the worship of God. In the Old Testament context, to "sanctify" something referred to the way the priests would set it apart for holy purposes—usually in the context of the worship of God according to his law.

For believers in Jesus Christ to be sanctified, then, means that they become more and more holy—more and more set apart in their thoughts, actions, and words for the worship of Jesus Christ in obedience to his word.

It is important to differentiate, again, between justification and sanctification. Justification is the once-for-all declaration from God, on the basis of the finished work of Jesus Christ on the cross, that a sinner is forgiven and righteous before him. This happens when a believer repents and puts his or her faith in Jesus as Savior and Lord; it takes effect in an instant. Sanctification, though, is a lifelong process of becoming more like Jesus and growing in holiness. It will not be fully completed until Christians are resurrected and made perfect in Jesus's presence.

The Bible makes clear that the Holy Spirit has a unique and distinct role in the sanctification of believers in Jesus Christ. We see this truth emerge from these basic teachings of the Bible:

- The Holy Spirit indwells individual believers through faith in Jesus. The New Testament teaches that Christians are temples—dwelling places—for the Spirit (1 Cor. 6:19). God the Holy Spirit literally dwells within Christians by faith.
- The Holy Spirit leads believers. This is Paul's teaching in the passage from Romans 8 that you read above (see v. 14). Those who are apart from Christ are led by the flesh; they are slaves to sin. But Christians, who trust and follow Christ Jesus as Savior and Lord, are led by the Spirit, who dwells in them. The Holy Spirit helps instruct them in God's word and helps them say no to sin.

The Holy Spirit helps believers in prayer. Later on in the same passage from Romans 8 that you read above, Paul talks about the Holy Spirit helping Christians pray to God—even when they do not know what to pray (v. 26). In many ways, then, the Holy Spirit is the personal means by which we connect with God the Father and God the Son as we live on this earth. We will learn below about how the Holy Spirit helps us in worship and in growing in God's word.

We should end this discussion by making one clarifying point: the work of sanctification, while it is a work of the Holy Spirit, still involves effort from human beings. The Holy Spirit is active in making Christians more like Jesus, but real effort should go into pursuing Christ and obeying God's word. This kind of active commitment is the right response to God's grace.

▲ PRAY!

Take a long, hard look at your heart and life. Is there evidence of the work of the Holy Spirit in your thoughts, words, and actions? Can you actually say that you are being led by the Spirit in your life? Talk to God about this, very honestly, in a few minutes of prayer. If you want to talk about following Jesus personally, find someone you know who knows him, and talk to that person.

The Holy Spirit's Role in Worship

We will conclude our discussion of the Holy Spirit's roles by considering his work in the context of the worship of God's people. This is a topic about which there is much confusion and disagreement in the church today; there is therefore a need to clarify what exactly the Holy Spirit aims to do as God's people gather to worship. In this section, we will focus specifically on the role of the Holy Spirit with the ministry of the word and the glorification of Jesus Christ.

READ!

Read 2 Peter 1:16–21—a passage in which the apostle Peter looks back to the climactic moment of his experience on the Mount of Transfiguration with Jesus. Take special note of what he says about the word of God and the role of the Holy Spirit in the words and writings of prophecy. Consider what this might mean for the Holy Spirit's role with the written word of God—then and now.

In the global church today, there are many viewpoints on the work of the Holy Spirit in the lives of believers and in the corporate worship of the church. In some contexts, the work of the Spirit in the church can become almost *separate* from the normal work of the teaching of the Bible and the proclamation of the gospel. People begin focusing almost exclusively on the Holy Spirit, inviting him to do "new things" and speak in "new ways" to God's people through miraculous signs and new "words" of prophecy. We will discuss this tendency further in the coming pages as we learn about the concept of the "gifts" of the Holy Spirit.

First, though, we will focus on the central role of the Holy Spirit in the worship of God's people. How should we expect the Holy Spirit to act in the church? What is his role as God's people worship him? Here are two absolutely central points about the Holy Spirit that we should not forget; these should be prominent and prioritized when we consider the work of God the Holy Spirit with his people today:

The Holy Spirit applies God's word powerfully to God's people. In the passage you have been memorizing from the Gospel of John, you have seen how Jesus referred to the Holy Spirit as the "Spirit of truth" (John 16:13). He made it clear to his disciples that the Holy Spirit would come to make the truths that Jesus had taught them even more clear—to both them and to the world. In other words, the Holy Spirit's work is to "illuminate" the truth of Jesus Christ about salvation in his name; it is to bring more clarity to what *God has already spoken.*

The passage from 2 Peter that you read just above also reminds us that the work of the Holy Spirit was prominent and powerful in the prophecies that God gave to his people; this was also true in the actual writing of the books of the Bible, as human beings were "inspired" by the Spirit. Because of this truth, it makes sense that a central concern of the Holy Spirit today is making clear to God's people the word that he inspired and gave to them to be authoritative and truthful.

As we think about the work of the Holy Spirit in the church and in worship, then, we should not think about him as having a separate focus—a role apart from the application and illumination of God's word and truth to God's people. As we study God's word and seek to obey, worship, and follow Jesus, the Holy Spirit will be doing his work—the work that he delights to do in the lives of God's people!

The Holy Spirit glorifies Jesus Christ. There is another tendency in the church today to give special emphasis to the Holy Spirit in worship and prayer. The thought is that we are in danger of neglecting the Holy

Spirit, so we have to seek to give added focus to him as we pray. This is certainly not all wrong, as God reveals himself as one God in three persons; this is the God we are called to worship!

But the passage from John that you are memorizing reminds us of another very central point about the work of the Holy Spirit: he aims to *glorify Jesus* (John 16:14). The work of the Holy Spirit is not to bring glory to himself—even though he is a distinct person of the Trinity—but to illuminate the work of God's word and lift up Jesus to people as beautiful, glorious, powerful, and gracious. So when we worship Jesus Christ as Savior and Lord, we are honoring the Holy Spirit; this is what he wants us—and helps us—to do.

▲ PRAY!

Ask God to help you worship and glorify his Holy Spirit by doing the things that the Spirit wants you to do: obey his word and glorify Jesus. Pray that God would help you be open to the work of the Holy Spirit even as you study his word.

THE HOLY SPIRIT AND SPIRITUAL GIFTS

We're going to turn now to a very difficult—but important—topic with regard to the work of the Holy Spirit: speaking in "tongues" (and other miraculous gifts of the Holy Spirit). In this discussion, we will focus first on what that work looked like in the early days of the New Testament church. Then, in the following pages, we will focus on some conclusions that we can draw about the presence of these miraculous gifts in the church today.

Spiritual Gifts in the Early Church

It is clear from the Bible that miraculous gifts of the Holy Spirit had a major role in the life of the early church and in the initial explosive expansion of the gospel from Jerusalem outward. Thankfully, as we read the New Testament, we can make some basic conclusions about these gifts. That is our goal in this section.

📖 READ!

Take some time to read all of Acts 2:1–41 carefully and thoughtfully. This long passage records the coming of the Holy Spirit at Pentecost, shortly after Jesus had ascended to heaven. Take note of the appearance of tongues in this situation and the results of this miraculous work of the Holy Spirit.

Here are some of the things we can learn from the New Testament about tongues and other spiritual gifts:

Tongues and other New Testament gifts are from the Holy Spirit. There is no doubt that what happened in Acts 2 was the direct result of the working of the Holy Spirit. In fact, Jesus had promised his disciples that this would happen; he had told them that after they waited awhile in Jerusalem, the Holy Spirit would descend on them in power and they would proclaim the gospel to all nations (Acts 1:1–8). This promise was completely fulfilled at Pentecost and in the days and years that followed.

Tongues, at Pentecost, enabled the explosive spread of the gospel. The specific purpose of tongues in that original context seems to have been to facilitate the initial gospel explosion that started at Pentecost. As your reading from Acts 2 ended, you saw that three thousand people put their faith in Jesus Christ after Peter's first great sermon about the Savior. We will talk more below about the continuing influence of tongues (and other gifts) in the New Testament churches, but there is no doubt that the specific purpose of this spiritual gift—at that time— was for the hearing and understanding of the gospel of Jesus Christ by people from many different nations and languages.

Tongues and other gifts were sometimes manifested as the church grew in its early years. It is true that, as the church grew and spread, miraculous signs (gifts of the Holy Spirit) sometimes accompanied the preaching of the gospel. We know that the apostle Paul spoke in tongues and that the apostles healed people and cast out demons in various

places. As these faithful men obeyed Jesus and proclaimed his gospel
to the world, God the Holy Spirit saw fit to accompany their message
with these miraculous signs—markers that what they proclaimed to
the world about Jesus Christ was true.

However, even though these signs were prevalent in the early
days of the church, there is no indication anywhere in Scripture
that the miraculous gifts of the Holy Spirit were intended to be
"normative" (normal or required) for *every* believer who would ever
follow Jesus Christ. We will discuss this below as we examine a right
biblical understanding of the miraculous gifts of the Holy Spirit in
the church today.

PRAY!

*Pause and give praise to God for causing his gospel to go forth in the world
during the early days of the church by the power of his Holy Spirit. You
are hearing about Jesus Christ today because of the work of the Spirit to
enable the proclamation of the gospel to people of all languages!*

Spiritual Gifts in the Church Today

After taking a careful look at the role of spiritual gifts as the church of
Jesus Christ began its explosive expansion during the early days after
Jesus's ascension, we can now apply some of what the Bible teaches
to a carefully formed approach to tongues and other spiritual gifts in
the church today. We will look at Paul's instructions about speaking
in tongues and think broadly about the main focus of the church and
Christian worship. Hopefully this discussion will help you to think
through these issues carefully and biblically in the future.

READ!

*Read 1 Corinthians 14, which is probably the best and fullest New Tes-
tament teaching about the use and place of the spiritual gift of tongues*

in the church today. Consider Paul's words, especially the limits that he places on the use of tongues. Think also about his big-picture concern for the focus of every activity in the church of Jesus Christ.

The topic of the gifts of the Holy Spirit, particularly speaking in tongues, is very contentious today. Entire churches and denominations have split over this issue. It is extremely important, then, that we figure out what the Bible teaches on this subject and seek to apply it well to the way we engage in worship with God's people. Here are just a few general principles that should guide our approach to understanding the miraculous gifts of the Spirit:

We should not limit God. First, we must be very careful not to limit God by saying that he "cannot" or "will not" work in a certain way. Even people who insist that the miraculous gifts of the Holy Spirit were primarily for a certain time in the history of the church should not put themselves above God by saying that he "could not," for instance, choose to heal someone miraculously today in answer to the prayers of his people.

We should not see tongues as normal or required. While we should not limit God, we also should not see tongues (or other miraculous gifts) as normal parts of the Christian life or as aspects that are to be expected or required from Christians who are really "filled" with the Holy Spirit. Such thinking is dangerous and unbiblical, and must be rejected.

There are groups of people—even denominations—that insist there is a "second baptism of the Holy Spirit," separate from conversion, that people should expect and pray for. This "filling," they think, is accompanied by signs such as speaking in tongues. The Bible nowhere teaches that something like this is normal or required for believers. The only filling of the Holy Spirit for Christians—and the only filling that they need—happens at conversion, when Christians are indwelt by the Holy Spirit through faith in Jesus Christ. Christians should never insist that speaking in tongues or other miraculous signs are somehow evidence of a more mature or more real faith in Jesus.

We should obey Paul's instructions regarding tongues. Christians who do believe that the gift of tongues, in particular, is still applicable today should follow the careful instructions of the apostle Paul, which you read about in 1 Corinthians 14. There should always be an interpreter for tongues when this gift is practiced in the context of the church. There should be order rather than many people speaking at once. Everything should be measured against the revealed truth of God's word, the Bible. Finally, the goal should be the "building up" of the church; that is Paul's ultimate concern in everything!

We should remain focused on the gospel. Finally, no matter what one believes about the applicability of spiritual gifts today, the main focus for every Christian should not be on gifts but on the gospel of Jesus Christ. That was Paul's focus; it was why he could say that he would rather speak just a few intelligible words about Jesus than many in tongues if no one could understand them (1 Cor. 14:19). The main focus in the church today must be on Jesus—his identity as the Son of God, his death for sins on the cross, and his resurrection from the dead and eternal reign as the King and Savior of the world.

▲ PRAY!

Ask God to continue to give you wisdom and instruction from his word as you wrestle with the issue of spiritual gifts in the church today. Pray that he would help you stay completely focused on doing all things to build up the body of Christ, of which you are a part.

THE CHRISTIAN RESPONSE TO THE HOLY SPIRIT

As we come to the end of this chapter on the doctrine of the Holy Spirit, you will be focusing especially on the right response to the Spirit—the application for Christians of all that we have been learning and discussing. This is, again, an extremely important step for Christians in all systematic theology study. Our goal is not simply to attain more knowledge about God; it is to worship him more fully, know him better, and love him more deeply!

READ!

Read Romans 6:1–14. Although this passage is not specifically about the Holy Spirit, it describes the attitude that Christians are to have toward sin if they truly belong to Jesus Christ through faith. Consider these verses today in light of the pursuit of sanctification, for which the Holy Spirit gives power and strength.

Since the Holy Spirit is God, the ultimate response that humans must have to him is one of worship. So how do we rightly worship the Holy Spirit, given all that we have learned in this chapter?

Consider the Trinity. First, we worship the Holy Spirit by considering the Trinity. In other words, we think about God rightly and understand him as he truly is (as much as we are able to do this). God clearly presents himself to us in Scripture as one God in three persons, and we should think of him in this way. We should recognize that God is active in the world today—and always has been—and that his actions and works manifest themselves in distinct ways. Thinking rightly about God is pleasing to him, and we should always seek to have our view of him be shaped by his word.

Study God's word. Second, we should worship the Holy Spirit by studying God's word carefully. Your suggested memory verses for this chapter remind you that the Holy Spirit is the Spirit of truth; he was active in the inspiration of Scripture, and he is active now in powerfully interpreting and applying the word to people's lives and hearts. When you work hard to understand the Bible, praying for God's help to do it well, you are honoring God the Holy Spirit and inviting him to do his work in your life and heart in the way that he intends.

Glorify Jesus. Third, we have seen—from John 16:13–15, among other passages—that the goal of the Holy Spirit is to lift up Jesus Christ. So one way that we worship the Holy Spirit and honor his work in our hearts and lives is to glorify Jesus and lift him up in praise and worship. The Holy Spirit intends to make the world more aware of Jesus—his death on the cross, his resurrection, and his eternal glorious reign as the great Judge and King. So when you worship Jesus and give him glory, you are doing exactly what the Holy Spirit wants you to do; you are honoring him!

Pursue sanctification. Finally, we should worship the Holy Spirit and honor his work in our lives and hearts by pursuing sanctification—the process of becoming more and more holy and like Jesus. We can do this, first, by inviting the Holy Spirit to accomplish this work in us. It is by his power alone that this work happens at all; he is the one who dwells within Christians and makes them able to say no to sin and yes to obedience. But we can also strive, with all of the power God gives us, to fight sin and to choose obedience. Those who have the Holy Spirit in them are capable of doing this—of applying their strength along with the work of the Holy Spirit to pursue sanctification. This is pleasing and worshipful to God the Holy Spirit.

● PRAY!

Ask God to help you worship him as he truly is—one God in three persons. Pray that he would help you respond to his Holy Spirit by studying his word and seeking to obey it, by always aiming to glorify Jesus and give him praise as Savior and Lord, and by seeking to grow in holiness.

REVIEW

We will take time now to review the central concepts and lessons that you've been learning about the Holy Spirit in this chapter. Here are a few key points for you to remember:

The Identity of the Holy Spirit

- The Holy Spirit is God—a distinct person of the Trinity, who is one God in three persons.
- While the Trinity has perfect unity in purpose and plan, each of the three persons is described in Scripture as having distinct and unique roles.
- God the Father is presented to us as possessing and carrying out the sovereign plan for judgment and salvation, and God the Son is presented to us as the one who took on human flesh, died, and rose again to accomplish salvation for God's people.
- The Holy Spirit also has distinct roles, playing key parts in regeneration, sanctification, and the worship of God's people.

The Spirit's Role in Regeneration

- The Holy Spirit performs the miracle of regeneration—that act of God that makes sinners "come alive" spiritually to repentance of sin and faith in Jesus Christ.
- The doctrine of total depravity reminds us of the need for regeneration, since humans are naturally dead in their sins and completely unable to choose God on their own.
- Jesus pointed to the reality of regeneration as he talked with Nicodemus about the prophecy of Ezekiel in John 3.

The Spirit's Role in Sanctification

- Sanctification is the process of becoming more and more holy—more set apart for God's holy purposes in Jesus Christ.
- The Holy Spirit is active in the process of sanctification; he literally indwells believers in Jesus Christ and strengthens them to say no to sin and yes to obedience to God's word.

- While the Holy Spirit gives the power for sanctification, believers in Jesus are also called to give effort toward obedience and holiness.

The Spirit's Role in Worship

- According to Jesus, the Holy Spirit is the "Spirit of truth"— he seeks to make God's truth known to human beings through revealing and applying the word of God to human hearts.
- The role of the Holy Spirit, according to John 16, is to glorify Jesus as the Son of God and the Savior of the world.
- These two commitments of the Holy Spirit remind us that he does not have a separate agenda from Scripture and from the work of Christ.

Spiritual Gifts in the Early Church

- In the days of Acts, tongues and other spiritual gifts were manifested in the ministry of the apostles as the gospel began to spread across the world.
- During this time, God seemed to use these miraculous gifts of the Holy Spirit as signs of the power of the true gospel.
- Even during those early days, miraculous gifts of the Holy Spirit were not normative for every Christian.

Spiritual Gifts in the Church Today

- In the church today, there are some who present speaking in tongues (and other spiritual gifts) as signs of a "second baptism" of the Holy Spirit; this is an idea that is not found anywhere in Scripture.
- While we should not limit God's ability to continue to act in miraculous ways in the world today, we should never see tongues and other miraculous gifts of the Spirit as normative for every Christian.
- Paul, in 1 Corinthians 14, gives important guidelines for how tongues should be practiced in the church, when they are to be practiced, and their right place in the order of worship.

Remember!

Can you say or write your memory verses for this chapter perfectly? Do so right now. As you do, consider one more time all that these verses teach us and show us about the work of the Holy Spirit in this world.

⬤ PRAY!

As you close this chapter with prayer, take time to ask God to continue to help you understand him more and more fully through his word. Pray that he would help you, by the power of his Holy Spirit, to apply his word well to your life and to glorify Jesus in your words, your thoughts, and your actions.

CONCLUSION

As we conclude our study of systematic theology, we will look back briefly on the lessons that we have learned about the value of this discipline and the call to Christians that comes from this discipline. Hopefully this introduction to systematic theology has been for you just the beginning of a life given over to learning more and more about the great God of the universe!

READ!

Take a few minutes to read Paul's beautiful prayer for the believers in the ancient church at Ephesus, recorded for us in Ephesians 1:15–23. Take note of how Paul prays for these believers. Consider what he asks God for on their behalf. Think about the way that you pray for people you know and the way that you pray for your own heart and mind.

THE VALUE OF SYSTEMATIC THEOLOGY

First, let's think together about the value of systematic theology that we have discovered together in this book. We know, of course, that Bible study is crucial to the lives of Christians. It is good to study passages of Scripture in a "biblical theological" way from Genesis to Revelation. Yet we have also seen how systematic theology is incredibly valuable for Christians in the following ways:

- It can help Christians organize their thoughts around various subjects and categories. It is helpful, for example, to take the doctrine of the church and to seek to gather together all the clear teachings from the Bible about it in order to inform our thinking. This organization can be very helpful because the Bible does not present theology to us in this systematized way.
- It can help Christians use their minds to grow in an understanding of their Creator and Savior. Systematic theology, as you have hopefully noticed, takes some difficult mental work. It is not easy to think through concepts such as propitiation, total depravity, and historic premillennialism! This is a good discipline for "thinking Christians," who are concerned with using their God-given minds to study Scripture and come to a right understanding of all that is taught there.

THE CALL OF SYSTEMATIC THEOLOGY

Next, though, we should consider a couple of ways that the discipline of systematic theology calls to us as Christians. In other words, we need to think about where we should go from here after being introduced to this study. Here are just two calls as you come to the end of this "God talk" book:

- Keep learning. This is certainly one big takeaway from our study in systematic theology. We have spent twelve chapters studying concepts such as the Trinity, the atonement, and the rapture—and we have barely scratched the surface of all that could be studied about these amazing biblical truths! Hopefully you have discovered that there is much more to learn about the amazing God who created you and acted to save you through the death of his Son on a cross. As you move on from this book's introductory study in systematic theology, do so with the attitude of a learner. Move on with an understanding that you are a finite creature who can still learn very much about the infinite Savior and King of the universe. Do not stop learning about our great God.

- Keep your heart engaged. This has been a common refrain along our way! Our goal, even in the "academic" study of God and his truth, has been to worship the God we are studying and to seek to know him personally. At the end of your life, all the knowledge you have gathered about God will not mean anything if you do not know him personally—through faith in his Son, Jesus Christ. So as you seek to learn more *about* him, remember that you must be seeking *him* personally. He wants to be known by human beings; this is why he sent his own Son into the world to be the Savior.

● PRAY!

As you end this book now, give praise to God for the wonderful truths about him that he has revealed to us in his word. Thank him that he is a God who speaks—a God who has chosen to make himself known to human beings. Finally, ask him to help you do everything that you can to know him better and trust him more.

GENERAL INDEX

Abel, 105
Abraham, 28, 147, 154
accusation, 230
active obedience, of Christ, 125
Adam, 28, 32, 58, 72, 96, 98–99, 100,
    105, 116, 146, 229
adoptionism, 128
amillennialism, 247, 251–53, 262
angels
    category of, 16–17
    Christian response to, 224–26, 237
    creation of, 21–22, 64
    definition of, 220–22
    purpose of, 222–24, 236
    and spiritual realm, 215–17
animals, in heaven, 182
announcement, 223
anthropology, 9–10, 71
antichrist, 18, 245–46
apocalyptic literature, 242–43, 249,
    251, 261
apostles, 198–99, 211
Arianism, 127–28
aseity, 56, 69, 174
atonement, 144, 159–61, 166
attack, 230, 232–33
authorities, 216
awe, 137

baptism, 15, 203–5
Bible
    as "The God Book," 48

as word of God, 28
biblical anthropology, 71
biblical theology, 6, 7, 42, 288
biblical truths, 240
boastfulness, 104
body
    glorification of, 158
    physical nature of, 82–83
    resurrection of, 172, 178
    and soul, 80
boredom, 172
born again, 271
Buddhism, 120

Cain, 105
Christian orthodoxy, 257
Christology, 11–12, 119, 123, 127
Christus Victor theory, 160–61, 166
church
    definition of, 15–16, 21, 193–95,
      212
    doctrine of, 210–12
    leadership in, 205–7
    marks of, 192, 207–9, 214
    primacy of, 211–12
    spiritual gifts in, 278–80, 284
    as universal and local, 195–200
church discipline, 209, 214
church government, 192, 205–7,
    213–14
church leadership, 213–14
circumcision, 203

saving power of, 38–39
and systematic theology, 42–43, 45
second chance, 173
Sermon on the Mount, 32
servants, 221, 225–26
service, 161
shame, 99, 130
sin
and Christians, 111–13, 117
definition of, 95, 116
effects of, 100–113
freedom from, 158
and heaven, 183
and man, 9–10
as opposite of God, 95–96
origin of, 97–100
pleasure of, 112–13
power of, 112
punishment for, 58, 112, 131
requiring blood, 147
seriousness of, 186
ultimate defeat of, 113–15, 117
sinful natures, 104–6, 116
singing, 209
soteriology, 11–12, 143
soul, 80, 81, 83, 178
sovereignty, of God, 61–63, 69–70,
219
special revelation, 26
spiritual beings, 81, 227
spiritual death, 102
spiritual gifts, 266, 276–80
spiritual growth, 156
spiritual Israel, 249, 251
spiritual perfection, 158
spiritual realm, 16–17, 215–20, 236
submission, 31–33, 41
substitution theory, of atonement,
147, 161, 163, 166
suffering servant, 147
symbolism, 239, 243

synagogues, 194
systematic theology
call of, 288–89
categories of, 7–20
discipline of, 6–7
Scripture in, 42–43
as truths of God, xi–xii
value of, 287–88

theology
as boring, xi
definition of, 1–2, 20
as doxology, xii
as practical, 3–4
theology proper, 11, 21, 48, 50
tongues, 277–80
total depravity, 10, 106–8, 110, 117,
271
Tozer, A. W., 47
tribulation, 244–45, 248, 250–51, 253
Trinity, 6, 9, 12, 51, 52–54, 56, 68–69,
120, 204, 266, 268, 269–70, 281
trustworthiness, 37
truth, 36–37, 41, 74, 103, 259, 275, 288

union with Christ, 183
universal church, 192, 196–97, 211,
212–13

victory, 135, 160–61
visible church, 199

Westminster Shorter Catechism, 51,
90
wisdom, 85
women, 206
word of God, 28, 29, 41
world, 4–5
worship, 67, 138, 182, 201, 223, 225,
274–76, 284
wrath, of God, 102–4, 110, 111,
176–77, 185, 186

SCRIPTURE INDEX

More *Knowing God's Truth* Resources

The ***Knowing God's Truth Workbook*** walks through the book's 12 chapters, providing further interaction with the text, Scripture passages, and discussion questions to help readers further understand the basics of systematic theology.

In the ***Knowing God's Truth Video Study***, Jon Nielson uses 10–12 minute videos to explore each chapter of the book, summarize the main points, and give biblical application. Ideally used alongside the *Knowing God's Truth* book and companion workbook, this study is great for both small groups and individuals.

For more information, visit **crossway.org**.